Growing Up in Foster Care

Published by
British Agencies for Adoption & Fostering
(BAAF)
Skyline House
200 Union Street
London SE1 0LX

Charity registration 275689

© Gillian Schofield 2000

British Library Cataloguing in Publication Data
A catalogue record for this book is available
from the British Library

ISBN 1 873868 93 6

Project management by Shaila Shah, Head of
Communications, BAAF
Cover Photograph by APM Studios
Photograph on jigsaw puzzle by
www.JohnBirdsall.co.uk
Designed by Andrew Haig & Associates
Typeset by Avon Dataset Ltd, Bidford on Avon
Printed by Russell Press Ltd. (TU)
Nottingham

Growing Up in Foster Care

by Gillian Schofield, Mary Beek
and Kay Sargent
with June Thoburn

B r i t i s h
A g e n c i e s
f o r **A** d o p t i o n
a n d **F** o s t e r i n g

Notes about the authors

Gillian Schofield is a Senior Lecturer in Psychosocial Studies and Deputy Director of the Centre for Research on the Child and Family at the University of East Anglia. She is also an experienced social worker and guardian *ad litem*. Her research interests are in attachment theory, the impact of maltreatment on children's development and the role of long-term foster care. Her most recent book is *Attachment Theory, Child Maltreatment and Family Support* (Macmillan, 1999 with David Howe, Marian Brandon and Diana Hinings).

Mary Beek is a part-time Senior Research Associate at the University of East Anglia and part-time social worker with Norfolk County Council Adoption and Family Finding Unit. Her practice interests include post adoption support and the placement of older children. She has conducted research into contact after adoption and adult reflections on the experience of being adopted. She is currently involved in a UEA study of contact after divorce (funded by the Rowntree Foundation) in which she has a specialist role as children's interviewer.

Kay Sargent was an experienced social worker and manager before becoming a Lecturer in Social Work. She joined the faculty at the University of East Anglia in 1997. Her research interests include social work practice with birth families, psychiatric services to children and children's emotional development and adjustment to new families. She is currently a Lecturer in Social Work at the School for Policy Studies at Bristol University.

June Thoburn is Dean of the School of Social Work and Psychosocial Studies and Director of the Centre for Research on the Child and Family at the University of East Anglia. She is a qualified social worker who has written and researched in most aspects of child welfare over the last 20 years. Her text book, *Child Placement: Principles and Practice* (Arena, 1994), is widely used in training. Her most recent book is *Permanent Family Placement for Children of Minority Ethnic Origin* (Jessica Kingsley, 2000).

Acknowledgements

Long-term foster care is not a fashionable subject for research. This is not surprising since it is hard to define and reflects such diversity of placements and circumstances. However, for a group of vulnerable children, long-term foster care is the framework in which they live their lives and it holds the key to their future well-being and happiness. Without the thoughtful and often moving accounts of those children, their foster and birth families and their social workers, we would not have been able to begin to make sense of the challenges that creating new families for looked after children currently present. We are very grateful to them all for giving their time to be part of this project and we have tried to do justice to their views and to reflect their stories as faithfully as we can.

The intellectual heart of the project owes a debt to two remarkable and distinguished thinkers, writers and researchers in the field of family placement: Professor June Thoburn, whose commitment to the use of research in permanent family placement is only matched by her warmth, humanity and concern for the children and families involved, and Professor David Howe, whose ability to make sense of the mass of complex ideas in developmental attachment theory and translate it into practice, has produced some of the most significant and original writing and teaching to have informed child and family social work in recent years. We are very fortunate to have June and David as colleagues at the University of East Anglia (UEA) and have valued their support throughout the project.

The research team has also benefited from ideas and guidance from the Nuffield Project Advisory Group: Professor David Berridge, University of Luton; Helen Jones, Department of Health; Dr. Michael Little, Dartington Social Research Unit; Kate Wilson, University of York; Sharon Witherspoon, Assistant Director (Social Research and Innovation) Nuffield Foundation. Additionally, we thank Professor David Berridge for his kind Foreword to the book and Professor John Triseliotis for making valuable comments on the script.

The secretarial work for the project from Heather Cutting and for the book from Anne Borrett has been very much appreciated.

Finally, we must acknowledge a debt of gratitude to our funders, The Nuffield Foundation, and in particular for the kind support and encouragement of Sharon Witherspoon.

Gillian Schofield
August 2000

BAAF is very grateful for the funding made available by The Nuffield Foundation which has enabled us to publish this study.

Shaila Shah
Head of Communications
BAAF

Contents

Foreword

Foster care must be one of the most difficult areas of child welfare practice yet, curiously, it has also been one of the most neglected. There are signs that this is now being rectified and this welcome book by Gillian Schofield, Mary Beek, Kay Sargent and June Thoburn adds to a growing research literature.

Within this field, *long-term* foster care is of particular interest – 'living with a paradox', to use the authors' apt phrase. It has grown unpopular in recent years, in the USA as well as Britain, with little explicit discussion of its merits and deficiencies. Adoption of children is being increasingly advocated, yet there are concerns that its complexities are insufficiently appreciated – certainly by politicians. Some commentators mistakenly see adoption as a panacea for the ills of the child care system and a means to bring a significant area of public expenditure in check. We must ensure that children's individual interests remain paramount. Other approaches to permanence need to be fully explored and so this scrutiny of children growing up in foster care is especially timely. Indeed, this topic has not been examined in detail for the best part of 20 years and, given all the changes in the interim, it is long overdue.

The book has particular authority as it emanates from the Centre for Research on the Child and Family team at the University of East Anglia. Its intensive findings are rich in detail and show detailed insight into social work as well as sensitivity to its dilemmas. Links are made with attachment theory; while it is also a useful study of "middle childhood", so often ignored by researchers more interested in toddlers or teenagers. It is a laudable skill of researchers, such as these, to write academically sound material in an accessible style.

The book raises questions about certain approaches to foster care, such as the boundaries between short- and long-term care, and whether it was wise generally to abandon the term "foster parenting" in favour of "foster care". We are also presented with new conceptual categories which help us to understand problems and characteristics, such as "open book" children or "children on the edge". This aids the inexact science of matching children and carers.

It is an important publication relevant to all interested in the practice and study of child welfare.

David Berridge
Professor of Child and Family Welfare
University of Luton

1 Setting the scene
An introduction to the research

The *Growing up in Foster Care* project is an in-depth study of a group of children under the age of 12 recently placed in long-term foster placements. The book describes the first phase of this longitudinal study. It gives a detailed account of the children and their histories, the birth families, the foster families and the social work practice and planning that led to this placement. It describes the work in the professional systems that plan and support placements, while also exploring the interpersonal, the relationships between the people involved. The aim at this stage is to offer an insight into the events, meaning and experience of long-term foster care for the participants. Attachment theory is used to explain the children's behaviour and to explore how children in middle childhood are building relationships with their foster carers.

Long-term foster care is one of the best kept secrets of the child care system. It is not known how many children are in planned long-term foster care across the country, since care plans are not aggregated by local authorities. In the current debate about the need to secure the future of looked after children, long-term foster care is rarely mentioned alongside adoption as a possible or positive choice for children. This research project came about because of our concerns that there was a group of vulnerable looked after children for whom foster care was the only available chance of a secure, family life, and yet these children were almost invisible; unrecognised by legislation, guidance or, in many agencies, procedures or practice.

In spite of the negative press that the care system receives and the push towards task centred and short-term foster care, we were aware that there were foster carers who continue to give very troubled and challenging children committed care and a permanent place in their families. A recommendation for a permanent or long-term substitute family placement with foster carers does feature in local authority care plans and can be accepted by courts, in spite of its lack of official status. Through this research, we wanted to acknowledge the presence of these children and their carers and to know more about what happened to them. We wanted to know whether there were current models of good social work and foster care practice which could be identified and disseminated. We believed that it was necessary to check the prevailing view that the three options available for looked after children were return home, adoption or drift in care.

From the outset, the intention was to obtain information which would be useful to practitioners; social workers primarily but also the range of psychologists, psychiatrists and lawyers who are involved in decision making about children. Our experience as consultants for and teachers of those involved in child protection, family justice and family placement showed that for practitioners, empirical research was felt to be very helpful in alerting them to important outcome trends but had certain limitations. Research findings, such as those summarised by Thoburn (1994), which suggested that children can benefit from a sense of permanence or that contact might actually help placement security for some children have revolutionised policy and practice. But for practitioners, the inevitable and very appropriate questions still arise: what about *this* child? And the contact with *this* birth parent? How would I know if *this* placement was secure? What are *these* carers currently offering and should I protect and support the placement or move the child on? How can I predict the future for *this* child, given what I know?

Making and defending decisions in individual cases can and should draw on evidence from research but such a defence is significantly more persuasive if it also draws on evidence informed by theory. Making sense of what social workers know from the mass of available information on any individual child, their family and their current placement, requires an understanding based on a theoretical framework. For children growing up in foster care, that theoretical model must inevitably be developmental. In order to understand children who have come from situations of family adversity, much of which is psychological in its long-term impact, who have then experienced separation and loss and who are now expected to be helped by the quality of caregiving in a foster family, it seemed appropriate to use attachment theory (Bowlby, 1969; Howe *et al*, 1999). Attachment theory has thus been woven through the research and through this book in a way which we hope will be of interest and of use to practitioners.

A summary of the historical and research context

Historically, long-term foster care was the model with which the foster care service originated and developed. A belief in rescuing children from "contaminating" families and giving them a fresh start in a new family rather than condemning them to institutional care was the basis of foster care from the second half of the 19th century right up until the 1948 Children Act. This post-war legislation favoured foster care over residential care, but also required local authorities to consider returning children to their birth families (George, 1970). Ambiguities about what foster care should and could offer continued, however, since although foster care was seen officially as a temporary measure it could last for some years. Specific concerns about drift in care were identified during the 1970s (Rowe and Lambert, 1973), as children were seen to be moving between placements without firm plans for their future. Finally, and very powerfully, evidence that children were leaving the care system poorly equipped to cope in the adult world (Stein and Carey, 1986) added to the concerns about what was happening for children during their stay in care. As Thoburn (1999) put it, 'the cracks in the foster care service began to appear and permanence policies emerged'. Given the increasingly negative and impermanent image of the care system in the research and in public perception, permanent substitute family care became generally equated with adoption.

With the emphasis on foster carers working towards returning children to birth families or preparing them for adoption, there was a backlash against the idea of long-term foster care as a placement of choice. Instead, during the 1980s, there was a drive towards recruiting and training short-term foster carers and steering them away from the idea of keeping children as part of their families. This has persisted to the present day. The change of terminology from "foster parents" to "foster carers" reinforced this particular shift. Foster carers started to feel guilty for loving and wanting to protect their foster children, in case they were said to be "claiming" them or excluding birth families. They might be

3

deemed to be failing in their task. For the government and for local authorities, foster care has come almost invariably to mean short-term and task-centred. The development of positive and purposeful practice in relation to long-term fostered children, as advocated 20 years ago by Triseliotis (1980), has been overlooked in favour of the apparently more acceptable practice priorities around moving children back to home or on to adoption.

As Berridge (1997) pointed out, the field of foster care generally has not been well-researched. Some studies have focused on long-term foster care specifically (Rowe et al, 1984; Aldgate et al, 1992; Kelly, 1995). Others have included long-term foster care as part of the range of fostering (Berridge and Cleaver, 1987) or placement options (Rowe et al, 1989; Roy et al, 2000). Particularly relevant, in the current climate of debate over adoption, is the literature on permanent family placements, where long-term fostering is considered alongside adoption (e.g. Fratter et al, 1991; Thoburn et al, 2000). In one of the most recent studies (Quinton et al, 1998), only eight of the 61 children in the sample were placed for long-term foster care. In that study, what was striking were the high levels of emotional and behavioural problems of children in middle childhood placed from care for adoption, a characteristic shared by the children in this study (see below).

Rowe et al (1984) conducted the largest and most detailed study in the UK specifically of long-term foster care. Although the study was of "successful" placements that had lasted at least three years, it raised a number of significant concerns. These revolved particularly around the extent to which placements were too often unplanned and uncertain. The authors were also concerned about the impact of the stress and insecurity of long-term foster care on children's self-esteem and identity. As they acknowledged, such concerns confirmed those raised by Triseliotis (1983) and Fanshel and Shinn (1978). Rowe et al concluded that, even where placements were successful, it was often 'in spite of rather than because of the system'.

Other research from a very different perspective has come up with a rather different picture. Retrospective research, for example, in the UK has suggested that fostering can offer a positive and long-lasting experience of family life. Triseliotis (1980) found that 60 per cent of a group of previously fostered adults enjoyed their fostering experience and were doing well when interviewed in their early 20s. Research was undertaken in the late 1990s by one of the authors (Schofield, in preparation) with a group of 40 young adults who grew up in foster families. Although such research cannot claim to be representative, it nevertheless produced some remarkable stories. In adult life, former foster children often saw themselves as very much part of their foster families. Mothers and fathers in their mid to late 20s regularly drew on the support of their foster carers as grandparents to their children. These local authority foster families had become "real" families and remained sources of care and security for adults who, as young children, had experienced abuse, neglect and separation. Many of these children had found rewarding and stable relationships with foster carers, in spite of the uncertainties of the care system.

Not surprisingly in a complex field with many different variables, the picture that emerges is mixed in terms of outcomes. For older children placed from care, Sellick and Thoburn (1996, p. 68) have offered a summary of the research on breakdown rates:

> Rowe and her colleagues (1989), Berridge and Cleaver (1987), Aldgate (1990) and Kelly (1995) all found that when age at placement was held constant, breakdown rates were not dissimilar between children placed in adoptive families or with foster families who were intended to be permanent substitute parents from the start of the placement.

Although this final sentence might raise questions about long-term foster families that evolve, research supports the idea that, where the placement was originally planned to be short-term but it was then decided that the family could offer a permanent substitute home, the breakdown rate could actually be lower (Borland et al, 1991; Festinger, 1986; Barth and Berry, 1988). However, there remain some particular concerns about the stability of placements for children in middle-childhood, the age of the children in this study. Berridge and Cleaver (1987) found that these had the highest breakdown rate – 46 per cent for children aged 6–11.

In spite of the rather gloomy conclusions of Rowe et al (1984) and the continuing concerns about uncertainty in the care system, long-term foster care persists as a placement plan. Rowe *et al* (1989) commented on how, in spite of the powerful pressure towards permanence through adoption in the 1980s, there were still large numbers of children in long-term foster care. As Kelly (2000, p. 31) has put it, 'it simply didn't go away despite the apparent strength of the arguments ranged against it'. But there is no denying that the research picture is of a high risk population of children placed in a legally insecure system with mixed outcomes. The fact that we know that long-term foster care works for some children in some placements simply means that we need to know more about *which* children in *which* placements – and what can be done to make it work more consistently, given that children's future health and happiness depends on it.

Legal and policy context

It is important to remember that the larger studies that evaluated long-term foster care (Rowe, 1984; Fratter *et al*, 1991) were conducted prior to the implementation of the Children Act 1989. A number of factors and principles in the legislation and guidance have affected practice and planning for looked after children. Partnership with parents, the promotion of contact, the "no order" principle, parents retaining parental responsibility when children are looked after, the role of accommodation as a form of family support – all have a part to play. We do not yet know the impact of such changes, or indeed the introduction of the Looking After Children (LAC) framework, on long-term foster care specifically, but concerns about what is happening for looked after children remain.

Foster care is widely seen as in crisis with a choice of placement being a luxury and placement stability not being achieved (NFCA, 1997; Waterhouse, 1997). Quality Protects (DoH, 1999a), the Government initiative to raise standards in local authority child care, has therefore focused in part on the question of placement stability. Under the first objective, for example, 'to ensure that children are securely attached to carers capable of providing safe and effective care for the duration of childhood', local authorities are to be measured against performance indicators such as the number of children experiencing more than three placement moves in one year. The performance indicator which relates most closely to long-term foster care is, 'the proportion of children who have been looked after continuously for more than four years, who have been in their foster placement for at least two years.' On 31 March 1999, of the 15,600 children looked after for four years, 46 per cent had been in the same foster placement for at least two years. Because the statistics do not record care plans, this figure does not tell us whether those foster homes were *planned* to provide a long-term family, the focus of this study. They might, for example, have been short-term placements where children were waiting for a long-term or adoptive placement.

One further relevant expectation under the same Quality Protects objective regarding secure attachment is that local authorities will promote the use of adoption of children from care. It is not yet clear whether this emphasis on adoption will appropriately reduce the numbers of children waiting for adoption placements or whether it might incidentally lead to a reluctance on the part of local authorities to establish systems to support long-term foster care as a positive care plan option. Will a long-term foster care plan be disregarded, seen as a failure to achieve adoption? If so, then there is a risk that children and carers in those placements will also be disregarded and feel a failure.

Local authority foster care services are therefore having to meet the very long-standing challenge, identified by generations of family placement researchers, of providing secure substitute families within a bureaucratic system, while also having to respond to new demands and pressures.

Attachment theory: secure and insecure attachment patterns

From the point of view of this study, the emphasis on secure attachment as an objective of Quality Protects offers a useful platform for a link to be made between practice developments and the theoretical framework of attachment. This objective cannot be achieved unless we have a good understanding of what "securely attached" means. Attachment theory has for so long been associated with attachment formation in infancy that it is not always easy to translate it into an understanding of the formation of attachment relationships in older children, the challenge facing long-term foster care. This is one of the areas that this study addresses, but first it is necessary to understand some of the key concepts in attachment theory (for a fuller exposition see Howe *et al*, 1999).

When a new born infant arrives and starts to form attachment relationships with caregivers, the infant is in a state of total dependency and has a biological drive for proximity (Bowlby, 1969), a need for care and protection, which makes the infant alert and open to the care on offer, and for security which a concerned and preoccupied parent, to use Winnicott's expression (1965), will be highly motivated to provide. If the caregiver is sensitive, accepting, co-operative and accessible (Ainsworth *et al*, 1978) this enables the infant to develop a *secure* attachment. The infant can readily achieve proximity, learns to manage anxiety when separated, to explore and to use the parent as a secure base.

If, however, the available caregiver is not sensitive and is not able to offer a secure base in this way, then the child is likely to develop an insecure attachment. This takes different forms in response to different caregiving behaviours. Where the primary caregiver is insensitive, inconsistent and unpredictable, the infant needs to maximise displays of attachment behaviour, shows of feeling, in an attempt to attract the caregiver's attention and to achieve some form of proximity. Over time the unpredictability of the caregiver makes the child feel increasingly angry and the needy appeals for love and affection can switch into angry, threatening, coercive behaviours to enforce the caregiver's attention. This is known as an *ambivalent/coercive* attachment pattern (Ainsworth *et al*, 1978; Howe *et al*, 1999). If, however, the primary caregiver is indifferent, psychologically unavailable or actively rejecting and cannot cope with normal infantile demands, then the infant will start to suppress feelings in order to achieve proximity, developing what is known as an *avoidant* attachment. Here the child learns that displays of need are not effective and may provoke further rejection, so that it is safer to shut down on feelings. Over time, the child tends to become self-reliant and compliant. The driving force in both patterns is the infant's anxiety about the availability of others and the need to *adapt* to insensitive or hostile caregiving in order to be, or at least to feel, safe.

These two patterns of insecure attachment described by Ainsworth *et al* (1978) were later extended to include a further category – *disorganised* attachment (Main and Solomon, 1986). This third insecure attachment pattern appears to be most common among infants who have experienced situations in which the caregiver was at times a source of fear, such as when abusive or intoxicated, or appeared frightened themselves, such as when remembering unresolved trauma from childhood or experiencing mental health problems or domestic violence. This pattern is characteristic of at least 80 per cent of maltreated children. Here the infant faces a serious dilemma. Anxiety or fear would usually lead to increased attachment behaviour in the infant, calling for proximity and reassurance from the caregiver. But where the attachment figure is the source of the fear, there is no behavioural strategy which can resolve the dilemma. Infants and young children may appear helpless, freeze or may demonstrate conflicting behaviours, such as crying for comfort but turning away (Main and Solomon, 1986). As children get older, they will develop certain strategies for dealing with their anxiety. They might attempt to achieve some kind of predictability by becoming controlling, through aggression or manipulation, or show bizarre behaviours, such as head-banging or self-harm. They may attempt to resolve the situation through inhibition, leading to compulsive compliance or compulsive caregiving/role-reversal.

Relevance of attachment theory for long-term foster care

Let us consider how this model might be relevant for understanding children entering foster care. When an older child arrives in a foster family, like the infant she or he will still have a need for – even the biological drive for – proximity, care and protection. But for older children, this will now have been affected by a complex history of experiences in caregiving relationships, experiences which will have led to a particular set of mental representations, beliefs and ideas about self and others, what Bowlby (1969) called the *internal working model*. For the secure child, that model will be positive about self, others and relationships. The secure child greets new situations confident in their abilities, with raised self-esteem and self-efficacy, expecting that others will be available and protective.

But where children have experienced poor parenting or been mal-treated, the experience of most although not all long-term fostered children, and have an insecure attachment pattern, their internal working model is more likely to be anxious and negative about the worth of the

9

self, the availability of others and the reliable safety and protectiveness of relationships. These insecurely attached children will have developed behavioural strategies which enabled them to survive, to feel safe, to cope emotionally and psychologically with the experience of unpredictability, neglect, rejection, hostility or fear – or in some cases a combination of these kinds of caregiving – in the birth family. The behaviour patterns were adaptive in that context, but may lead to problems in social relationships and longer term developmental difficulties which will affect the foster placement. Maltreated children with *disorganised* attachment patterns, for example, may be controlling and see the self as powerful, invulnerable and punitive in order to keep dangerous forces at bay. Such children may resort to lies, stealing and other strategies which have the effect of protecting the self and controlling others. These strategies in relationships may be accompanied by a number of more disturbing symptoms which reveal particular difficulties in coping with fear and distress. There are some children who self-harm, for example, or maim and kill animals. Many maltreated children put on false selves, which conceal their disturbance but make them hard to reach.

Separation and loss
When children come into foster care, they will experience separation and loss of parents, siblings, friends and familiar surroundings. This is well known in social work practice and the process of grieving such losses is well documented. But from an attachment theory perspective, what must be remembered is that the need for proximity to the caregiver and the fear of separation are the major sources of anxiety which drive the development of attachment to the caregiver and provoke the set of adaptive strategies which children have adopted in the birth family. When a child experiences the significant separation which is involved when coming into foster care or moving placement, their normal coping strategies may be intensified. The *avoidant* child who normally achieves safe proximity to the rejecting caregiver by shutting down on feelings, may shut down completely and may become simply but coolly compliant. The *ambivalent/coercive* child who normally gets a reaction from underinvolved, inconsistent parents by constant demands, a mix of coy and coercive behaviours, may be very affectionate towards the

carer to begin with but may then turn to anger, rage and disappointment when told no. Finally, the *disorganised* child, who is likely to have experienced fear with his/her birth parent caregiver, may read the situation as requiring compliance to avoid retribution and may put on a false self that talks appealingly to carers but conceals fearfulness – and will only start to show some of the symptoms of their distress by soiling or stealing.

In such cases, there may be no explicit grief reaction as such and it may be thought that the child is not reacting to the separation or even that the child does not have an "attachment" to the birth parent because they are not reacting as common sense would predict by, for example, crying for their parents. So these very different behaviours will be intruding in the process of forming new relationships and may also be confusing the assessment process which social workers will be engaged in.

Recreating previous experiences of caregiving

Attachment theory suggests that children will persist in behaviours which may have been adaptive or protective in the birth family but which risk recreating in the foster family some of the experiences in the birth family. The internal working model becomes a filter through which experiences pass and are given meaning according to the specific attachment pattern. The internal working model can be affected by experience but is likely to organise new experiences into the pattern with which the individual is familiar. The kind action of the foster carer can be experienced by the child as kind or viewed with a mixture of hope and suspicion, as likely to be unreliable, viewed with anxiety, as a prelude to rejection, or viewed with fear, as preceding physical or sexual hurt. For these children and their carers, the carrying over into the foster home of patterns of behaviour which may even have been intensified by the experience of separation, can result in the confirmation of the child's insecure internal working model. It is hard for foster carers to continue to care and to feel valued as a parent by a child who looks at you with suspicion, will not let you comfort her when she cries or is physically hurt, and is aggressive towards other children. The foster carers feel hurt and even angry and may well communicate this to the child, in spite of their best intentions. And of course for many children this adult reaction is in a sense expected and perversely reassuring: 'I knew that foster mother didn't really love me.' They have created their own dysfunctional kind of predictability.

Caregiving and long-term foster carers

So what then might be learned from attachment theory about the caregiving tasks of the long-term foster carers? Children with insecure attachment patterns need to have experiences and relationships with carers which promote secure attachment patterns and disconfirm their internal working model. If children are more likely to cope with the stresses and challenges of everyday life during childhood and into adult life in the context of a secure pattern internal working model, then they need experiences in foster care which enable them to feel and be safe, experiences which alter their negative view of self, others and relationships. If children are to be freed up to think and reflect, to explore and learn, including at school, to make choices in their lives as they get older, then they need to be given the experience of available, sensitive carers, who enable the child to experience themselves as lovable and adults as available. They need to develop a wider repertoire of behaviours, not giving up their present strategies immediately but knowing, for example, when it is best to shut down on feelings and when it is best to allow other people in. This will contribute to a flexible approach to new situations, raised self-esteem and increased self-efficacy, all factors in the development of resilience, a key concept for thinking about the ways in which sensitive caregiving enables children to cope with stress in the present and in later life (Rutter, 1985, 1999; Gilligan, 1997, forthcoming 2000).

These caregiving experiences have to be offered in a way which takes into account *the age, developmental stage and adaptive strategy of the child*. Although what is being offered to the child may in essence be significantly similar to what parents offer infants to promote secure attachment, older children will neither communicate their needs as readily nor respond as readily to signs of affection and concern. This behaviour will always be a mix of the existing insecure patterns and the age and stage of the child. The 11-year-old who never tells you anything about what he did at school may well be avoidant but that particular piece of behaviour, which shuts off routes to closeness for the carer, will not be unusual for a child of that age. The work of Barbara Dockar-Drysdale (1959) has a great deal to offer in her accounts of the way in which the process of nurturing often needs to be symbolic for older children, the touch on the shoulder rather than the sit on a lap; the giving and accepting of small gifts. But such basic points of contact as food and bedtimes continue to be very significant, even for older children. Practical aspects of parenting are at least as important as more obviously emotional exchanges with older children. As with infants, such care communicates concern, sensitivity, availability and the capacity to be in tune with the child. But in formulating hypotheses about caregiving in foster families, we have to take into account also the consequences of what carers bring from their own experiences in relationships, as children, as partners and as parents – their internal working model, which will affect their capacity to provide a secure base.

The *context* of the bringing together of this child and this parent into a relationship – which we can think of as the professional and legal structures that surround family placements – will also play a part in defining the history of each partner in the relationship and in providing a framework for its future development. If we are to understand how that process can best be facilitated to ensure the well-being of the child into adult life, we need to understand what is going on for the older child and the foster carer an attachment relationship is developing, and we need to pay some attention to the context which a range of professionals, but most specifically social workers, will provide.

The research project

The Growing up in Foster Care project is a study of 58 children under the age of 12 placed in long-term foster families in eight local authorities. The research objectives were to:
- explore how the needs of looked after children can be identified and met in long-term foster families provided by the local authority;
- explore the nature of parenting which appears to be associated with more successful outcomes for children in long-term foster care;
- understand the role of birth families when children are in long-term foster care;

- define what forms of assistance and support from local authority social workers are needed by children, long-term foster carers and birth families, in order to sustain a successful long-term foster placement.

These objectives relate to outcomes and cannot be achieved fully until later stages of this longitudinal project. To that extent, the first phase reported on here is broadly speaking descriptive and does not claim to define what makes long-term foster care more or less successful. That question must be left for the next and subsequent phases as we follow up these children into adult life. However, for this first phase it was possible to collect baseline quantitative and qualitative data about each placement – the child, birth family, foster family and social service planning and support – in a way that provides a vivid and detailed account of long-term foster care experience and practice.

Defining long-term foster care

We chose the term "long-term" rather than "permanent" fostering, since we were keen to pick up in the sample cases which may not have been to a permanence panel but were nevertheless clearcut plans for this child to remain in this foster family until adulthood. Even so, one of the many challenges of the study was to define long-term foster care in a way which was specific enough to enable us to look at comparable cases while broad enough to include a range of what might be called long-term fostering. Definitions of long-term foster care used in other research appear to vary from two years (McAuley, 1996) to three years (Rowe *et al*, 1989) through to permanent fostering models closer to adoption (Thoburn, 1991a). For this study, we wanted to focus on those children for whom the plan was that they would be expected to remain *in foster care and in this foster family throughout their childhood*. This allowed us to concentrate on the children for whom the basic need for a stable and secure family life must be met by foster carers, in spite of the lack of the legal security of adoption. The plan had to have been confirmed between September 1997 and August 1998. Some children were in placements which evolved from short-term into long-term while others were matched prior to placement (see subsequent chapters for details). This meant that some children had been with their carers for some time while others had moved to these families a matter of weeks prior to our interviews. This reflects the reality of long-term foster care practice, but does mean that the subsequent analysis of outcomes at later stages in this project will need to take such differences into account. Cases referred to the project therefore had to meet all of the following criteria:

* a long-term placement with foster carers where it is not anticipated that the child will return to the birth family;
* a placement which is planned to be a long-term foster placement, not one which is planned to lead to adoption;
* a placement with a foster family where it is anticipated that the child will remain throughout childhood;
* a placement which is with foster carers who are not relatives.

Although we acknowledge the increasingly important role of relative carers, we were particularly interested in the specific question of whether stranger foster carers, provided as part of a bureaucratic and regulated system, could become "real families" for children. Similarly, although there are important comparisons to be made between adoption and fostering, it was decided, as a modest sized project, to concentrate on establishing a study of placements where the plan was specifically intended to be long-term foster care.

Identifying cases

Identifying cases for the study was far from straightforward because, as mentioned above, local authorities are not required to aggregate data for their looked after children according to different care plans. As a result, it is not possible to arrive at figures that would show how many or which children within or across agencies were the focus of a long-term foster care plan. It was therefore necessary to rely on direct referrals from child care and family placement teams. Visits were made and seminars held in each agency. In spite of a great deal of effort to obtain the referrals, by repeated leaflets and phone calls to every team in every agency, they were often slow in coming. In particular, two agencies (a major city authority and one London borough) selected because of their ethnically diverse populations, failed to provide a single referral. This was a matter of great regret for the project team and reduced the proportion of children of minority ethnic origin in the study sample. Because of the slow rate of referrals it was decided at an early stage to include all members of sibling groups in the sample rather than selecting one. This has some disadvantages in terms of the analysis of quantitative data, but proved a fortunate decision in many respects, in that it has been important to make sense of differences and similarities between siblings with similar histories.

There were significant variations between authorities in terms of the number of referrals relative to the overall size of their looked after populations. This left doubts as to whether the referral rate did in fact reflect different use of long-term foster care as an option, or whether it simply reflected different attitudes to research or different degrees of being overwhelmed by pressure of work. It seemed likely that the children referred were by no means a complete sample for most local authorities.

Social work practice varied at least as much within agencies as between agencies. One team's social workers visited frequently, while a neighbouring team had decided not to allocate long-term care cases. One social work team funded birth relatives' travel to contact by taxi, whereas a few miles away another team did not even pay bus fares. Patterns of practice by individual social workers and teams could be identified more easily than a clear sense of different practice between local authorities. For these reasons, analysis of the findings by authority was not felt to be useful.

Research methods used

- *Questionnaires* were completed by social workers (identifying the child's history, number of placement moves, contact arrangements, reasons for the long-term foster care plan, current well-being on the Looking After Children dimensions) and by foster carers (giving the family composition and fostering history).
- *Goodman's Strengths and Difficulties Questionnaires* were completed by the foster carers.
- *Interviews* were conducted with child care social workers, foster carers, family placement social workers and birth parents/relatives.

These covered the major areas of social work practice and planning, the children's behaviours, the nature of the relationship between the children and the foster carers, the role of birth families and the impact of contact.

• *Interviews* were conducted with children, using adapted ecomaps, puppets, pictures and story stem completions. These enabled children to share information about themselves, their lives in the foster families, their experience of school, memories of birth family life and contact. The story stems gave insights into their mental representations of family life and attachment figures (see below).

Data collection

There were 58 children referred, 26 (45 per cent) boys and 32 (55 per cent) girls. (Details of the sample are covered in the next chapter.) Social worker and foster carer questionnaires were available for all 58 cases. Interviews were conducted in almost all cases (53 out of 58). Cases were proceeded with as part of the interview sample if the social worker and foster carer were both willing to be interviewed. Interviews were conducted with the 43 foster carers, social workers and family placement workers, bearing in mind that we had included sibling groups.

Interviews were also conducted with 37 of the 53 children in the interview sample, with four further children who had severe disabilities being observed in interaction with their carers. Where children (12 in all) were not interviewed, this was for a range of reasons. Four children said no when offered the information leaflets and consent forms by foster carers. The other eight children had carers or social workers who felt that it was not appropriate to ask the children because of their young age (four to five), or because they had been repeatedly interviewed for care or criminal court proceedings. Although very detailed information was available from carers about all the children, the lack of the meeting with these children was a major gap when it came to synthesising the information for each case. This was partly because of the missing interview data but at least as much because spending time with each child on the various activities gave the researchers a much stronger sense of them as people and how they related to others.

Interviewing birth parents or other relatives proved difficult to set up during the main data collection phase. We received additional funding from the Nuffield Foundation during the project, to find the extra research time that it took to seek out more birth relatives. Interviews with them provided invaluable additional information. Seven of the children had no available family because parents had died or disappeared. For nine children, it was decided that contacting parents would not be appropriate for reasons ranging from illness to risk of violence or fragile placements. The remaining 35 children's parents were contacted. Eventually 25 relatives of 20 children were interviewed.

Data analysis

We used SPSS (a software package used for statistical analysis) to analyse the quantitative data from the questionnaires. A sample of 58 is small for statistical analysis, particularly given the very important differences between cases at the outset, such as between cases where children were matched prior to placement and where the placement was previously short-term or between cases where children were accommodated and those where local authorities had parental responsibility. So where statistics are given in subsequent chapters, they are most usefully seen as a description of our sample rather than a reflection of long-term foster placements nationally. However, many figures, such as those relating to high rates of maltreatment and legal status, are comparable with larger samples of children in foster care (for example, Sinclair *et al*, 2000).

We transcribed all interviews and analysed them qualitatively. This was a lengthy process but necessary given our need for detail, particularly about caregiving and children's behaviours and relationships, and because of the longitudinal nature of the study. It is not possible to know at this stage what will prove significant in relation to outcomes and to be able to return later to detailed interviews from early in the placements will, we hope, allow us greater insights into the dynamics of relationships and practice over time.

Applying attachment theory

We wanted to generate information which would test out whether attachment theory would help to make sense of behaviours in the children and relationship building with the foster carers. Each part of the methodology was adapted for this purpose. On the questionnaire, we asked for information about placement moves and changes of caregiver. Social workers and foster carers were asked for a pen picture of the child, which was often a remarkably quick route to an initial hypothesis about the child's attachment pattern. Social workers were also asked to define the child's experience of caregiving in the birth family, according to caregiving characteristics which relate to the four secure and insecure attachment patterns. In some cases information was obtained about caregiving styles in previous foster placements. With the carers, we asked questions that tapped into the way in which the children were showing their feelings. Information about current caregiving styles in the foster home came from our interviews with the carers, but also from descriptions given by children and social workers.

Key for the project though, in the application of attachment theory, were the interviews with the children themselves, all of which took place in the foster home. When thinking of interviewing strategies for the children, we were very much aware of the wide age range of the sample, from 4 to 12 at the time of interview. A range of approaches were used in response to each child's willingness to become involved more with one activity than another. We began with a warm up exercise of compiling a "poster" about themselves, engaging children in discussion about their likes and dislikes, what they liked to eat, what they liked or didn't like about school and so on. Although talking about their favourite kind of school dinner, for example, acted as an unthreatening warm up exercise, it often gave us immediate access to a sense of the child, what was important to her or him, their sense of self-efficacy and self-esteem. The first thing that children chose to tell us was often significant. Some children immediately mentioned a particular child in the foster family or a particular birth relative. One child in describing himself mentioned that he was the only child who had the same colour eyes as his "real" dad. Some children were full of information about likes and dislikes, others seemed unable to express preferences.

During this exercise the children enacted with us behaviours, patterns of relating, which were themselves very revealing. Children might run round the room grabbing foster family photos to show us, or want to take the pen and do all the writing or be reluctant to sit even in the vicinity of the paper on which we were working. As later chapters will show, these encounters were a very important contribution to our understanding of the legacy in attachment terms from their birth families and the present functioning in the foster family. As with much of social work practice, how the children reacted to us was itself a useful piece of the picture.

Using ecomap-style drawings, we then explored fairly gently their relationships with the significant people that they named, birth family members, foster families, peers and social workers. We used puppets, a Wise Hedgehog who could be told about worries and things that were a bit of a muddle for the child and a Hopeful Beaver, with whom children were invited to share hopes and wishes for the future. These puppets were presented as just very good listeners and some children, even older children, confided to the puppets their thoughts and fears, not otherwise in evidence in the session, such as from one five-year-old, 'I'm worried that mummy might die,' or from a nine-year-old, 'I'm worried about what will happen to my children'. It seemed that these simple tools could sometimes 'surprise the unconscious', rather as the adult attachment interview (Main and Goldwyn, 1984) can do for adults. Children in care often have a rather superficial, "pat" account of their childhood, which can be produced when asked by social workers, guardians *ad litem* or child psychiatrists. Interview strategies therefore need to include subtle ways of helping children show us some of their real concerns, without challenging defences.

Story stem completion tests also work well in this respect, by using hypothetical situations. They involve presenting toy family figures and the beginnings of stories, which provoke certain kinds of attachment related anxiety. Then the researcher asks, can you show me or tell me what happens next? They are most commonly used to classify the attachment pattern of younger children aged 4–7 (Steele *et al*, 1999). Given the 4–12 age range of the children, we used them simply to elicit relevant material about the child's understanding and expectations of family relationships. As with the puppets, some children of all ages revealed deep-seated fears and worries in their stories that were not evident from their behaviour and verbal communications. We used four stories, adapted to the children we were interviewing. We chose, for example, not to use the story about a monster in the bedroom, given that so many of the children had been sexually abused, and decided to focus on ordinary domestic scenes – a child at a birthday party, a child who spills a drink, a child who hurts their knee when out in the park, a child who gets lost when out shopping and a reunion scene with the mother (Bretherton *et al*, 1990).

Finally, we used some photographs, partly to capture the interest of the older children, to whom we thought puppets and dolls might appear rather young. These photographs depicted ordinary family scenes that might spark off reactions and could lead to discussions with the children about relationships and expressions of emotion. We had a scene, for example, of an older child watching a mother feeding a baby and an untidy bedroom with an angry parent and child. As with the puppets, some children were dismissive of such scenes when asked about the feelings of the people in the pictures and what might happen next, which may itself be useful information. Others reacted with more heartfelt comments, such as one who said, 'I think the little girl might throw the baby out the window next'. Our concerns about older children finding the puppets and the story stems rather beneath them were mostly unfounded, with several children taking the opportunity to tell us elaborate stories about family life using the figures. Even the puppets appealed to several older children, with one ten-year-old saying to his younger brother after his session: did you talk to the Wise Hedgehog?

Outline of the book

The book is divided into three sections. **Part I** covers the characteristics and histories of the children; the social work practice and planning and the routes to this placement; the foster carers' motivations, family patterns and support networks; and the birth relatives' accounts of their family circumstances and the events that led to the child becoming fostered long-term. **Part II** describes the behaviour and relationship patterns of the children in placement and the caregiving offered by the foster carers. **Part III** considers the social work support to the placements, the perspectives of birth families and the important question of contact. Finally, the concluding chapter sums up key themes from the research which have implications for our understanding of long-term foster care.

Use of case material

This project has relied on the experiences of all the participants for its insights into long-term foster care. In order to reflect that rich material, the book draws heavily on their stories and on their interviews. In order to protect as far as possible the identities of the children, the families and the professionals, all names have been anonymised and individuals are known by different names within chapters and in different parts of the book. Names have been used to bring the stories to life, but they are used randomly. Details of the stories have been changed slightly, where this helps anonymity without affecting accuracy. This has meant that in particular the more distressing but identifiable material has not been used, although it will continue to be part of our overall analysis.

It is inevitable that those involved in the research will recognise themselves and their words. We have done our very best to treat all contributions with respect in the way in which we report them and comment on them.

PART I

The background to the long-term foster care placements

2   What did the children bring to the long-term foster placements?

What experiences and needs do these children bring to their long-term foster placements? They are an extremely diverse group in terms of their family histories. By definition, however, they are all children who are experiencing developmental pathways affected by adversity and for whom the first choice for any child of being brought up by their parents in their own family has been lost to them.

This chapter provides an analysis of the data about the children and their birth families. The emphasis in the first part of the chapter is on key facts about the children, as individuals and as a group. The second part of this chapter offers a focus on the available information about the quality of caregiving experienced by these children in their birth and previous foster families.

This sets the scene for one of the key themes in the study, the impact of previous caregiving on the children's behaviour and capacity to make new secure attachment relationships in the long-term foster family.

Characteristics of the sample children

Age, gender and ethnicity

The age range of the 58 children in the study was 4–12, with 13 (22 per cent) aged 4–6, 17 (30 per cent) aged 7–9 and 28 children, nearly half (48 per cent), aged 10–12. The older children ranged from those who had come into care for the first time at this age to children who had come into care at the age of three or four, but who had experienced placement breakdowns or had waited in vain to be adopted and were now starting a new long-term foster placement at the age of 10 or 11.

The sample, therefore, was weighted towards the older end of the age range. It was hoped that even these children would build new attachment relationships, in which they could put right past emotional and psychological damage, at an age when many children are starting to become more autonomous and focus on life outside the family. It was also an age and stage when children were facing the transition to secondary schools, where more would be expected of them and where disruptive early experiences might be found to make the difference between coping and not coping.

Age was also significant for carers in the sense that there was real anxiety that children might have problems in their teenage years or that they might simply decide to vote with their feet and go back to their birth families. These concerns hovered for carers even at the point where they were making a procedural and emotional commitment to the child.

As mentioned above, Berridge and Cleaver (1987) demonstrated that middle childhood is a high risk for breakdowns (46 per cent among the 6–10 year olds in their sample). The 17 children aged 7–9 had often had chequered careers, with a small but significant minority having multiple placements in early childhood, leaving a legacy of significant behaviour difficulties that included major problems with school (see below).

For the 13 youngest children aged 4–6 (22 per cent), the dilemmas often revolved around the question of whether their placements should be with their older siblings or, if this was not an issue, whether they should be placed for adoption rather than long-term foster care – questions addressed in more detail in the next chapter.

The children were almost evenly divided between boys and girls, with 26 (45 per cent) boys and 32 (55 per cent) girls. The significance of gender was not always clear in placements and certainly when the children were grouped according to social work plans or behavioural characteristics, no clear pattern emerges. This is not to say that gender is not an issue. Certain coping mechanisms, such as the ability to play football with your mates, did appear to be facilitating a useful combination of independence and peer relationship building for boys in ways which were not so apparent for girls. Similarly, cultural expectations about gender and the showing of emotion may have been contributing to the fact that there appeared to be a particular group of bubbly, demonstrative girls and another group of rather reserved boys.

There was only a very small group of three children (5 per cent) of minority ethnic origin.* Even these few cases highlighted issues for

---

* The low numbers here reflect a lack of referrals from two agencies serving ethnically diverse populations, as mentioned above.

local authorities, shire counties in these cases, in dealing with questions of ethnicity. Leroy was a very troubled boy of mixed parentage who was reporting that he suffered from racism at school and was said by the white carers to be blaming all his troubles on his ethnicity. An assessment by an independent black worker was said to have concluded that 'the least of his needs presently was to be placed with a black family'. Leroy did have significant behavioural problems which were seen as a priority, but his legitimate concerns about racism did need to be properly recognised by the foster carer and the social worker needed to continue to have an active role as an advocate for Leroy at school.

Lewis (10), also of mixed parentage, had been drifting in a combination of residential school and respite care placements until a new social worker set about making proper plans. The question of racial matching was discussed but not seen as an option by the social worker: 'matching is a luxury'. However, some life story work had been undertaken by a black worker, and the foster carer and social worker were making efforts to introduce him to his black heritage. Lewis was unsure about these attempts to make links with a father of whom he had frightening memories. In the child's interview, he chose to use the white rather than the black doll figures. As with Leroy, ethnicity was being taken into account but his racial identity needed to be actively addressed with, for example, positive black role models being made available.

In another case, a child from a traveller background was rejected by his mother from infancy. The decision not to place him for adoption as a three-year-old was very much influenced by the idea of close family ties and a cultural heritage only available to him through birth relatives.

There is no question that for practitioners there were competing social work principles around ethnicity and permanent placement alongside concerns about emotional well-being and the urgent need for a family (for the most up-to-date research study on ethnicity and permanent placement see Thoburn et al, 2000).

Legal status

Of the children, 39 (67 per cent) were on Care Orders s.31, and 19 (33 per cent) were accommodated (Children Act 1989, s.20). Shared parental responsibility between local authority and birth parents for children on

Care Orders had to be carefully managed and raised issues about the fact that those who had day-to-day care of the children – the carers – had responsibilities only delegated to them. As subsequent chapters will show, the quality of these relationships varied depending on the carers, the agencies and the birth families.

Where children were accommodated there were some very constructive and positive relationships between careers and birth parents, particularly where children had disabilities. This is very much as intended in the Children Act 1989 (Packman and Hall, 1998). However, there were several cases where social workers or foster carers expressed concern about the fact that the child was accommodated, usually where there were specific issues such as unsettling contact or simply because of the continuing potential for a parent to reappear at any time to "claim" their child.

The fact that children were accommodated did not necessarily mean that there was a harmonious or constructive partnership between the birth parents and the local authority or that the children were less harmed by birth family experiences. Most obvious would be the examples of the children singled out for rejection, discussed in more detail below. Here children were effectively abandoned to care, parents were unenthusiastic even about contact and yet there was a clear sense from the social workers that the parents remained very much in the driving seat.

Where there were serious concerns about placement stability or contact arrangements arising from the children's accommodated status, social workers said that even if they wanted to take the case back to court there would be uncertainty about passing the threshold criteria for significant harm. Some children had been in foster care for some time so that evidence of harm was rather distant and some parents were caring satisfactorily for subsequent children. Court proceedings were in any event seen as extremely disruptive to placements, since they could last up to 18 months. Concerns were primarily about the children. Applications to court mean the involvement of guardians *ad litem* and expert witnesses who have to look at the situation afresh and take into account the child's expressed wishes and feelings. This is a necessary part of court proceedings but may cause confusion all round. To ask a child who is settled in a foster placement whether they would wish to return home, when it is clear to all parties that the child could not and should not return home, is bound to be unsatisfactory. In addition, statements in evidence by social workers and foster carers could threaten the delicate relationships being built with birth parents. It is perhaps not surprising that social workers would prefer to cope with complicated informal negotiations rather than risk this level of upset. It will be important as the children's future careers are tracked to assess the impact of this early decision. But a situation, for example, in which accommodated children were not allowed a holiday with their grandmother because their mother was opposed to it, raised questions about how decisions are managed when children are accommodated but parents are hostile to the local authority and unable to take the welfare of the children into account.

Disabilities
Learning disabilities

Social workers reported that 15 (25 per cent) of the children had a learning disability, of which four (7 per cent) had severe learning disabilities. Only a minority, five (9 per cent) of the children identified by social workers as having a learning disability, were in any kind of special school or special class. This may have been because of their young age in some cases and the difficulty in ascertaining the relative impact of cognitive and emotional/behavioural problems on school performance. The nature of the mild learning disabilities was often unmeasured in any formal sense. There were a number of children for whom it appeared that learning problems at school were put down by foster carers entirely to behaviour or attitude when it seemed possible that the children had a degree of inherited learning difficulties. Given the fact that 31 per cent of the children had mothers with learning disabilities (see below) this would not be unlikely. Experience of mal-treatment would also have affected the children's capacity to function intellectually.

Research has rightly raised many concerns about foster children under-performing at school. As Aldgate et al (1992) pointed out, these children have many special needs which need to be addressed if children are to achieve their potential. Some additional concerns emerged in this study about the cases where unrealistic expectations might be placed on children and/or blame attached to children for not working hard enough, when it seemed entirely possible that even to survive in mainstream school would be an achievement. These uncertainties cannot be addressed without more active involvement of educational psychologists in assessing foster children's potential so that both underachieving and unrealistic expectations can be avoided. This observation from the cases in this study may be one way of explaining the finding of Sinclair *et al* (2000) that the intervention of educational psychologists was a protective factor in placement stability. Such questions need to be addressed urgently given the Quality Protects targets for educational achievement (DoH, 1999a).

Disability and assessment

In some serious cases, the combination of disability and abuse profoundly affected a child's history prior to this placement and the assessment for intervention was straightforward. Gareth would have had significant problems even with adequate care but very neglectful caregiving caused serious damage across a range of developmental areas: physical, emotional, social and intellectual.

Gareth had severe disabilities. These were apparent from an early stage and his mother was unable to provide the care he needed. She is a drug user and was physically and emotionally neglectful. Gareth was exceptionally deprived when he entered the care system, at about six years. He was apparently "locked" in a foetal position, was filthy and made only "animal" like noises.

In other cases, disability or significant medical needs led to complex assessments. Workers had to take into account the question: is this mother neglectful and rejecting or is she struggling with a child who is hard to care for?

Dustin (5) had a potentially life-threatening congenital condition and he was in hospital for the first months of his life. He was in foster care, then at home and then back into foster care [to the same carer] *by the age of three, by which time he was a very disturbed little boy.*

It seems likely from the evidence that this mother would have struggled to parent any child but the child had very particular physical, and after ten months in hospital, emotional needs. Similar questions were raised in another case where the difficulty was around a poorly managed health condition and the child herself was aware of trying to get herself into hospital in order to get her mother's attention. In that case, the condition became the focus of a difficult parent–child relationship, but if there hadn't been life-threatening risks the child might have remained at home. Such factors increase risk but can also delay interventions in ways which may be unavoidable but certainly have an impact on the timing and age of the child when substitute care is seen as necessary.

Severe disabilities

There were other children where it was much clearer that, had there not been such a severe disability, the birth parents would have been able to provide good care. Louise and Nina, for example, both have severe physical and learning disabilities. They had parents who attempted to care for them and simply found that they could not cope.

Louise has severe learning disabilities, combined with severe epilepsy, which has been partially controlled by surgery. She has no language, other than a small number of words and sounds. Her behaviour is volatile. She can be calm and compliant, but frequently has phases where she will bite, kick, scream and be completely un-manageable. These can happen several times a day and are usually connected to a minor change in her routine or an event that she has not been able to predict (e.g. the car stopping at lights). Louise becomes caught in loops of repetitive behaviour or noises which she must repeat dozens of times. At her best, Louise is affectionate and loving towards her carers and known adults. She loves freedom and open spaces and will run around, sing and show obvious delight in the absence of restriction.

Nina suffers from a degenerative condition, leading to profound learning and physical disabilities. Her birth mother was unable to care for her after the birth of her second child. Nina is able to stand, supported by a frame, and walk a few steps. She can no longer crawl. She has no language and no signs but is responsive to known adults.

Her developmental stage is approximately that of a six-month-old baby.

These children bring rewards but also challenges to their carers in terms of their behaviours and physical needs. In all such cases there is anticipatory anxiety about what will happen as children get older; issues around greater dependency, deteriorating medical conditions or the task of providing personal care for older children and teenagers. For these two accommodated children, the long-term foster family had previously provided respite care and the change to a long-term plan signalled a reversal of roles with the birth family continuing to have contact while the foster family took on the full-time parenting role.

Parents' difficulties

Information on the birth families of the 58 children was often complex, but the information that was particularly relevant, given the focus on attachment theory, was the background of primary caregivers. The children's mothers had a strikingly high level of difficulties with 44 (76 per cent) having two or more as the tables (2.1, 2.2) indicate. These figures for maternal difficulties are likely to be an underestimate, since under these categories in up to 29 per cent of cases social workers had put "not known" as the answer. Such levels and combinations of maternal difficulty are likely to have contributed to caregiving problems and need to be taken into account in considering the management of the continuing involvement of the mothers through contact. But also, as Roy *et al* (2000) have suggested, when considering outcomes for children from different kinds of substitute care, their genetic inheritance is relevant and may have added to vulnerabilities in the birth family and in the substitute placement.

Table 2.1
Birth mother difficulties

	N = 58	%	% not known
Abuse in childhood	33	57	24
Mental health problems	32	55	21
Learning disability	18	31	16
Criminal convictions	18	31	21
Serious health problems	12	20	16
Drug misuse	11	19	28
Alcohol misuse	10	17	22
Had been in local authority care	9	15	16
Physical disability	1	2	12
HIV/AIDS	0	0	29

Table 2.2
Numbers of maternal difficulties

	N = 58	%
0	5	9
1	9	15
2	16	28
3	13	22
4	11	19
5	4	7

Information regarding fathers was less available, either because they were unknown or because records were incomplete. In some cases information was not recorded even though the child was having contact. For nearly half the children, social workers did not know if their fathers had mental health problems or a learning disability. Information like this would normally be available for adoptive parents, but where possible it should also be available for foster carers and for children as they grow up (Masson *et al*, 1997).

The children came predominantly from poor families where mothers were unemployed 39 (67 per cent) and about half the fathers (47 per cent) for whom information was available were also unemployed. Other factors affected employment patterns and the socio-economic circumstances of the family. Single mothers, large families including young children, partners in prison and, inevitably, the levels of learning disability, mental and physical health problems described above, all influenced the likely availability of resources in the birth family homes.

Siblings

Almost all of the children – 52 (92 per cent) – had birth siblings, but the combination of full, half and step siblings created a complex picture. Most children came from large families, with 39 (67 per cent) having three or more siblings. A significant group of 34 (59 per cent) had siblings who were being cared for in the birth family.

These sibling networks create extremely complicated stories for children to explain to themselves and to tell to others. Most children had developed or been helped to develop an explanation that went something like, 'My mum loved me but couldn't look after me'. But some had the experience of physical abuse or emotional rejection from mothers who continued to care for other, usually younger, siblings. Such factors meant that the question of sibling relationships for these children was closely related to complex feelings about just why it was that their mother had chosen or not been able to keep them.

Because of continuing contact arrangements, a number of children had experienced their mother going through pregnancy and giving birth to a new baby. Given how powerful an experience it is for any child to see their mother's changing shape and to know that a baby is coming, the feelings of these children who have been permanently separated must inevitably be hard to manage. In so far as it was possible to get some impression of the impact of this event, reactions of the children seemed to vary from veiled jealousy of the new infant through to a fantasy that their foster mother might step in and look after the baby.

Just as complicated is the experience of children who have been fostered where other siblings have been adopted. In Sian's case, she was the only one of a sibling group not to be adopted. Sian was the only child to have contact with her mother and therefore had to carry her mother's distress, anger and hopes of fulfilling her parenting role. For Sian, the question must arise: is it favoured or wanted children who get adopted or less favoured and unwanted children? Does it raise self-esteem to be the one chosen to maintain a relationship with the mother or does it lower self-esteem not to be found an adoptive family? What story can Sian tell about herself?

Placement moves

Although all the children referred were in placements newly confirmed as long-term, the length of stay in this foster placement varied (see Table 2.3).

Table 2.3
Length of stay in this placement

0–1 year	1–2 years	2–3 years	3–4 years	4–5 years
28 (48%)	25 (43%)	4 (7%)	0	1 (2%)

Almost all the children had been in this placement for less than two years. The exceptional case where the child had been in placement for over four years was one where the local authority had a panel system for confirming long-term placements and although the decision had been taken at a review 2–3 years ago, delays and changes of social worker meant that the Form E and Form F were just now being completed to go to panel (see next chapter for discussion of this issue).

The questionnaire data from social workers painted a complex picture of moves and separations for the children prior to these placements but there were only a small minority of "yo-yo" children, who had come into care and returned home on a number of occasions (see Table 2.4).

Table 2.4
Number of care episodes

1	2	3	4+
33 (57%)	14 (24%)	5 (9%)	6 (10%)

Of the 58 children, 47 (81 per cent) had two or fewer care episodes including the present one, of which 33 (57 per cent) had only the one care episode, coming into care on this occasion and remaining on a long-term plan. The reasons for this single but permanent move into care included cases of proven physical or sexual abuse, where intervention was through the courts, and cases of rejection by parents, where children were accommodated and parents rapidly decided that a return home was not possible.

For this sample as a whole, suggestions that social workers might be repeatedly returning children home in attempts at rehabilitation were not borne out. However, for those children who had experienced multiple early placements, the stories were very worrying. For example, Megan's mother had mental health, drug and alcohol problems. From age one to seven, Megan was in care on 12 separate occasions, with nine different foster carers, and each time she was returned home. There was then a final attempt at rehabilitation when the case came to court. Another child had experienced eight different foster carers by the age of four. In such damaging individual cases, it might be helpful for local authorities to examine the planning and practice and learn from them as they would from a section 8 inquiry into a child death or serious injury.

As these cases suggest, one "care episode" could mean staying in one placement or having several changes. From the children's movement charts provided on the questionnaires it was established how many different foster carers each child had been in placement with at some time in their childhood (see Table 2.5).

Table 2.5
Number of different foster carers

1	2	3	4	5+
13 (22%)	20 (35%)	8 (14%)	10 (17%)	7 (12%)

This picture does not reflect multiple foster placements for the majority of the children. It would be expected, for example, for a child coming into care following a serious injury or for respite (where parents then rejected the child), to have one emergency or respite placement, followed by a short-term or bridging placement while rehabilitation was considered and/or permanent placement plans were followed through and then the third placement would be the long-term foster family. The limited number of moves and foster carers in this study were at least in part because so many of the long-term placements were with carers who had previously cared for the child or were a short-term placement that had become long-term. This is not to deny, of course, the fact that for a young child any move is a major stress and to have lived with a birth family and even one foster family is likely to cause cognitive and emotional confusion and insecurity, which need to be addressed.

Although most children may not have had multiple care episodes or multiple carers, one group about whom there must be some concern were those who had experienced extended previous placements and then moved into the present placement. This could have been because of the breakdown of a long-term placement (five children) or because children had spent up to four years in a short-term placement while rehabilitation was attempted and/or when there was a delay in identifying an adoptive or long-term foster family. Here the children were dealing with the loss of two significant families – one birth, one foster. Feelings about these previous placements could vary from children who grieved very much for the good relationships in a previous foster home, to children who had experienced poor emotional care and appeared relieved to be in the current placement. One boy was said to rubbish his previous placements as soon as he had left them, although at the time saying, 'Can I stay if I'm good?'

As with every aspect of this study, there are no simple answers, no easy ways of measuring levels of emotional benefit or damage from the various patterns within a child's care history. There were undoubtedly cases where there was evidence that the decision to move a child from one foster home to another was in their best interests but other cases where issues were less clear. Some moves were beyond the social workers' control, sometimes caused by carers asking for children to be moved, either in a planned way or instantly. The social worker for one five-year-old in an adoptive placement was telephoned to go to the home and found the child with his bag packed at the door, to be removed at once. For such children it is not just the loss but the manner of it which is distressing.

Abuse/neglect

Since the behaviour of these children in placement and the quality of the relationships which they subsequently form is likely to be affected by early experiences of abuse and neglect (Howe *et al*, 1999; Gibbons *et al*, 1995) and since such experiences are also linked with risk of placement breakdown (Thoburn, 1991a), it was particularly important to get a picture of such factors in these children's life histories. Overall the social worker questionnaires revealed high levels of abuse and neglect (see Tables 2.6, 2.7) with 47 (81 per cent) experiencing three or more different categories. Only six (10 per cent) had not experienced abuse or neglect. Erickson *et al* (1989) have shown how serious developmental consequences can occur, not only where there is physical and sexual abuse but also where there is neglectful and psychologically unavailable parenting. As the case histories of these children unfold through the book it can be seen that the majority of the children had experienced forms of maltreatment that had significant legacies in terms of their behaviour and relationships.

Table 2.6
Children's experience of abuse and neglect

	N = 58	%
Physical neglect	43	74
Emotional neglect	39	67
Emotional abuse	24	41
Minor physical abuse	20	35
Sexual abuse (sexual contact)	17	29
Sexual abuse (exposed to acts/materials)	14	24
Physical abuse (moderate/severe)	10	17

Table 2.7
Children's experience of multiple kinds of abuse/neglect

	N = 58	%
0	6	10
1	1	2
2	4	7
3	7	12
4	10	17
5	19	33
6	6	10
7	5	9

Children's behaviour

The important question of the children's behaviour and development at the point of the long-term plan in this placement was addressed in a number of ways. Foster carers were asked to complete the Goodman's Strengths and Difficulties Questionnaire, a standardised behavioural checklist (Goodman, 1997) and social workers were asked on the questionnaire to answer questions about aspects of development under the "Looking after Children" dimensions. More detailed qualitative accounts of the children's behaviour in the placement were obtained through the interviews and the detail of that material is reflected in the second part of the book, Chapters 6–9.

At the point where the Goodman's Questionnaire was being completed for this study, all children had been looked after for at least one year. Even though carers and social workers reported in interviews on the many ways in which the children had made progress since being away from their birth families, the data from the Goodman's reflected a group of children who still had significant behavioural problems. The results show 25 (48 per cent) of the children scored in the "abnormal" range for *total difficulties* and a further nine (17 per cent) scored as borderline. (These figures compare with 10 per cent abnormal and 10 per cent borderline in the community.) *Conduct* was the major problem area, with 30 (58 per cent) of the children scored in the "abnormal" range and a further four (8 per cent) scored as borderline. There was no association between behaviour difficulties and gender, with girls matching and even exceeding boys on the conduct dimension (60 per cent girls with "abnormal" scores compared to 55 per cent boys, not statistically significant).

Difficulties were said by carers to be affecting home life for 35 (67 per cent) and school for 38 (73 per cent) of the children. Interviews with foster carers gave a detailed picture of the serious educational problems facing some of the children, with school exclusion and threats of exclusion featuring in a number of cases, in spite of foster carers' interventions.

The "Looking after Children" questions on the Questionnaire (based on the summary questions in the Assessment and Action records) reflected a mixed picture in the different aspects of children's lives. In the area of education, social workers rated 35 (60 per cent) of the children as having school attainment that matched their ability and 49 (84 per cent) of the children as always or usually happy at school. There appeared to be some discrepancy with the level of school difficulties identified by carers, which was only partly explained by the different wording of these measures and may reflect an underestimate by social workers of the children's educational difficulties.

What emerged from these answers and was confirmed by the interviews was that children had acquired quite a few social and presentational skills, with 34 (59 per cent) rated as average or above average in these areas. This was in contrast to questions around emotional and behavioural development, which suggested that 54 (93 per cent) had emotional and behavioural problems of some kind and 35 (60 per cent) had problems which needed action from foster carers or from professional agencies. It may be that children at first meeting, perhaps with experts for court or potential new carers, look as if they are coping better than they are because they acquire the social skills of politeness and manners from their carers. It may also be that abused and neglected children become skilled in concealing true feelings behind compliant behaviour.

It is important to note that neither the Goodman's nor the Looking after Children questions included in the questionnaires tell the whole story in terms of the degree of difficulty of some of the children. One of the striking features of the study were those cases where children as young as five were self-harming, had suicidal ideas and were injuring family pets; children as old as 11 were soiling and enuretic; and a small number of children of all ages were exhibiting violent and/or sexualised behaviour. Checklists developed for the project which listed behaviours associated with different insecure attachment patterns helped to highlight some of these more disturbed behaviours. It was not possible to establish which children had had therapeutic help at some time, but at the time of the interviews it appeared that very few children, less than ten, were having or were considered to be in need of therapy.

Having emphasised the difficulties presented by the majority of the children, it is important to mention the group of ten children (19 per cent) from across the age range who, from the total data collected including the qualitative interviews, appeared to be functioning well in peer groups and at school and were felt to be rewarding and well-behaved within the foster home. It will be as necessary to examine the outcomes for these apparently resilient children (Rutter, 1985) as it is to trace the outcomes for the more troubled children.

Patterns of caregiving in the birth family

Although there was information from the questionnaires that reflected both the parental difficulties and the types of abuse to which children had been exposed, it was important, in applying an attachment theory per-spective, to understand more specifically the nature of the caregiving experienced in the birth families. Abuse and neglect categories as reflected in *Working Together* (DoH, 1999b) are limited in this respect. From the children's histories there seemed to be a number of different caregiving patterns operating within the traditional maltreatment categories and these patterns were more useful in explaining the different relationship contexts. Emotional abuse, for example, included consistently rejecting, hostile caregiving and entangled, preoccupied and unpredictable caregiving. It was also necessary to have a framework for thinking about caregiving which included the minority of cases where children had not experienced maltreatment, particularly some of the children with disabilities but also some children who had been cared for by grandparents.

Social workers were asked to categorise as far as possible the child's history of caregiving in the birth family and were given categories to choose from that matched the kinds of caregiving associated with different attachment patterns i.e. secure base (secure); rejecting and hostile (avoidant); unpredictable and uncertain (ambivalent/coercive); frightening and out of control (disorganised).

Secure base

It might not be expected that children needing long-term foster care would have experienced secure attachments with previous caregivers and yet some children had had some good experiences of care which need to be taken into account. Miranda had been cared for up to the age of three by her mother who suffered from a physical illness. Although the social worker suggested that the standard of care had not been high physically, there had been no concerns about the child being neglected emotionally or maltreated. Valerie had not been well cared for by her drug using parents but from the age of three to eight had been cared for and loved by her grandmother. Wayne had been abandoned by his mother at an early age but had formed a very close and rewarding relationship with his step-mother. In each case, the relationship may well have given the child some security and the message that they were lovable and that some adults could be trusted to love them.

However, in each of these cases other factors must also be taken into account. Miranda, now six, had lived with the deterioration of her mother's health and perhaps the fear of her death since she first came into care. She had also experienced the inexplicable breakdown of her foster placement prior to this placement. Valerie, now 11, had had a poor early start with her parents, perpetuated by unpredictable contact. She lived with her grandmother while she was dying of cancer for two years and the bereavement was followed by rejection from other birth relatives and unsatisfactory attempts to find her a long-term foster family. Wayne, now 10, did love his step-mother but feared his father, who was violent towards both of them. Such combinations of love and uncertainty may still leave the child with a belief in the possibility of good relationships, but it is not easy to continue to draw on that emotional nourishment when so much else that has gone on is anxiety provoking.

Some children were described as having had secure base parenting from previous carers, often reducing difficult behaviours prior to this new placement. The children had been moved to the current placement, either because the previous carers had ruled themselves out, been ruled out as permanent carers, or because children were moved in order to be placed with siblings. In two of these latter cases, the youngest child in a sibling group had been settled in a previous foster family which offered the first stable and secure care they had received. They were then moved to be with older siblings who displayed more disturbed behaviours. Such decisions raise questions about this group of young children who might otherwise have been placed for adoption. These questions about the relative importance of sibling relationships can only be addressed when the placements are examined at a later phase of this study.

Hostile and rejecting caregiving

Hostile and rejecting parents leave children with major questions about their own worth. Some children were said to have had mothers who did not find them lovable from birth. One mother described a difficult birth and testing early months as symptomatic of her daughter, whom she found hard to love. The child had come into care and been ready to be placed for adoption at three but was reunited with her drug using mother when a second child was born. Now back in the care system as a nine-year-old, she was withdrawn and confused, having lost this early chance of a new start.

One social worker described how mothers sometimes tried to persuade agencies of their lack of feeling for their babies.

Social worker: *There's history from when he was born of his mother saying, I want help, I want him adopted – and unfortunately she was ignored. She wanted him adopted and we were saying, do you want a child minder one day a week?*

Researcher: *Do you know why she wanted him adopted?*

Social worker: *No – because nobody explored this. So many people come in and say, 'I'm fed up with my kids and I want them adopted,' and we pat them on the back and say, 'Never mind we all go through this,' but in reality maybe we're missing the ones who are genuine. Maybe she realised she couldn't love him.*

This boy was physically abused by his mother during his early years and then seriously injured at the age of four.

There were striking cases where children in early or middle childhood had been singled out of sibling groups for rejection (as noted also by Quinton *et al*, 1998). Some abused children who came into care through the courts had been emotionally rejected in their families but others came into the system by parental request. These latter children may often have had no previous contact with social services and yet were arriving in foster families in a highly disturbed state at any age from two to eleven. The move out of the birth family could be very abrupt. One mother requested a month's respite care for two of her six children, aged seven and ten. After one week she rang to ask for them to be adopted. Another mother asked for two weeks respite care for her sons, aged two and four, while she went on holiday and when she returned said she did not want them back.

These children's experiences of rejection were accompanied in all cases by the knowledge that their mother, either in her preferential treatment of other siblings who also came into care or by continuing to care for other children, had found them to be unworthy or unlovable.

Social worker: *From birth, Dean was a small, sickly and difficult to feed child – and mum has always said that she never really liked him, even from a tiny baby. The records state the extent to which she favoured Louis over Dean. I've seen myself the way in which she has almost set out to ensure that Dean fails at a situation and that Louis succeeds. So Dean's feelings for his mother have always been very complicated and lead to disturbed behaviours.*

This rejection of one child in favour of the other could be extreme, with hostility and rejection becoming associated with unpredictable behaviours and fear.

Researcher: *How would you describe the style of caregiving from Adele and Linda's mother: "secure base", "hostile and rejecting", "unpredictable" or "out of control and frightening"?*

Social worker: *The last three all apply – rejecting certainly, hostile certainly, unpredictable certainly – not out of control, except for sometimes, but certainly frightening. I have seen Adele frightened by some of her responses. Linda was the cherished and worshipped child. She was constantly held up as an example of being brighter, taller, more able to read, more able to play, even down to minor things like her ability to whistle. I've observed her responses at contact. Lots of physical affection towards Linda and almost repulsion towards Adele. And consequently, contact with mum was something Linda really looked forward to and enjoyed but Adele got upset.*

Although not all social workers used strong words such as "repulsion", it was clear from some of the accounts given of caregiving by mothers that this was not an exaggeration. The maternal feeling had not simply been one of preferring another child or disliking certain characteristics of this child but was deep-rooted and pathological. The levels of ill-treatment which accompanied those feelings suggested that for the caregiver, this child was no longer the little three- or four-year-old that others might see but had become, in their fantasy, powerful and persecutory, a source of fear, rage, distress. In turn the children experienced treatment that was rejecting and frightening. This was the early childhood of one six-year-old.

At one end of the scale you could call it inappropriate discipline – cold showers when he wet himself, left outside in the rain. Every time he was naughty, he was never forgiven and allowed to start again; the punishment would last for a long time and a four-year-old has no concept of time . . . He was never put to bed properly, had to go into his room when he got home from school, wasn't allowed to eat with his brothers and sisters. He was given certain food which he hated, more or less every day . . . There was no attempt to understand him. He was never read to, never had a cuddle or a kiss good night or was read a story to . . . They felt that the child was being controlling, manipulative, which he may have been but not deliberately because he was so young and was reacting to negative vibes.

This child was placed in a respite family in the week of his sixth birthday and some weeks later as Christmas approached he said to his foster carer, 'Daddy isn't going to come to get me, is he?'

A number of these children were put out of the way in the birth families, *isolated* not only as a punishment but as way of controlling the child and perhaps protecting the caregiver from their own powerful feelings. For the four-year-old in the locked room, shut away from the family and access to possible sources of care and concern which were available for siblings, with all of their own feelings of loneliness and being unloved and unlovable, anxiety is overwhelming. Strategies for achieving proximity to caregivers are not available. The child must try to turn inward for comfort and yet that is an inadequate resource. Such rejection and isolation inevitably lead to confusion, distress and distorted thought patterns. How is a child to make sense of what does not make sense? Why am I locked in my room while my sister watches television, has tea with our parents? When professionals are given accounts of children being disciplined by being isolated in their bedrooms, it may sound like "time out", an often recommended form of behaviour management. However, as these children's stories illustrate, isolation accompanying emotional rejection and ill-treatment destroys a child's self-esteem and also any sense of self-efficacy – how can needs be met, relationships be negotiated, from behind locked doors?

For these children, in contrast to what might be expected, long periods of stability in the birth family without social services involvement appeared to be a recipe for extended exposure to rejecting parenting and emotional distress. Whether or not there was literally a locked door between them and their families, there was certainly an emotional locked door and the messages that came through the door on the occasions when it was opened were that the child was unlovable and worthless and, what is more, was spoiling the lives of caring parents and other innocent children in the family. The target children were powerless but had destructive powers and malicious motives attributed to them. Even if they tried to adopt avoidant defences and shut down on feelings or tried to be good and compliant, this did not make any difference to how they were treated. Over time, some children did inevitably rage and show their distress and try to do whatever they could to assert their sense of personhood in the family. These efforts, which might have been in the form of angry, aggressive behaviour, smearing faeces or in the form of manipulative attempts to retrieve something for themselves, were seen as confirmation of the intrinsic badness and deceitfulness in the child, from which the parents and siblings needed to be protected. This need for the parents to protect themselves from the child, and perhaps the child from them, appeared to lead to the parent's request for the child to be accommodated.

In some cases it seemed hard for social workers to believe that children could be so disturbed and separations could be so abrupt and so final, families even cutting off contact in some cases, when there was no previous history of professional concerns. Reasons for a lack of previous reporting of concerns by schools and other agencies could be associated with assumptions about class. Where rejecting parents were respectable and middle class, their children's behaviour problems were not attributed to their parenting. In complete contrast, one child from a large family came from an impoverished background with a mother with mental health problems, where stealing food from dustbins and urinating out of bedroom windows seems to have been seen by the school as just part of the chaotic family culture. It was therefore only when parents themselves took steps to place children in care that the situation was revealed.

These were not easy cases to manage or plan for and this was compounded by the fact that certainly in some cases, children were left with fantasies of returning home. Kylie, for example, blamed the rejection by her mother on her mother's current partner and had a dream that her birth parents would get back together and all would be well. She even proudly showed the researcher her birth parents' wedding photograph. In the meantime, her behaviour could be very difficult and she was self-harming.

Unpredictable and uncertain

When caregiving is unpredictable and uncertain and parents are under-involved and neglectful, children learn to doubt their parents' availability and their own lovability (Howe *et al*, 1999). Children become emotionally very demanding of parents, raising affect to provoke parental availability. These parents also have exaggerated expectations of the children, reflecting a similar demand for unconditional love from them. Both experience disappointment and anger. Parents and children may talk lovingly and sentimentally about each other at times, while being entangled in an intense, distrustful relationship which both are reluctant to give up.

A number of the children, including some of the most disturbed, were described as being "very close" to a parent, usually the mother. This closeness manifested itself in different ways. Children in one group were described as having been consistently "the favourite" in the birth family, even though aspects of the environment or of the care of the child raised serious concerns. In a second group, children were scapegoated by parents as "the problem" but there still appeared to have been an entangled and preoccupied relationship between parent and child. In these cases, even where parents were rejecting the children in significant ways, social workers were being blamed for the separation by both parents and children, with court cases being fiercely fought by some parents who would not have been able to cope if the child had been returned to them.

One of the questions that arises in relation to the first group is whether it advantages or puts a child more at risk to be the favourite or in a "close" relationship with a mother who is unpredictably available, perhaps because she is mentally ill or misuses drugs. The importance of this question is that it became apparent from interviews with social workers that not only they but also guardians *ad litem* and other professionals had described these relationships as "strong attachments". Once relationships became defined in this way, arguments were then used to suggest that this was a basis for justifying high levels of contact and for choosing foster care over adoption. One example of this would be a case where the new social worker was considering increasing contact, even where it had to be doubly supervised with a senior male manager standing by because of maternal violence. Both the mother and the boy wanted more contact. The concern in these cases must be that the "strong attachment" actually meant a deeply insecure attachment. Mothers and children may talk of missing each other, loving each other and may show significant distress around separations and contact. Yet the same mothers find it difficult to keep the child in mind, giving the child false hopes at contact of magical reunions and then failing to come to the next contact at all. The relationship continues pretty much as it did at home and the child continues to be distressed and to struggle to make sense of it, blaming everybody else, including him or herself, rather than admitting that their mother is unable to sustain that relationship. In these cases, knowledge of the nature of insecure attachments suggests that it is very important to give as much attention to understanding the roots and consequences of "close relationships" as the apparently distant and more obviously rejecting.

Of the "favoured" children there were examples of older children whom mothers had come to rely on. This could be where drug or alcohol misuse meant that older children had to look after themselves and younger siblings. "Older" in this context could be as young as five or six. In several cases where parents had learning disabilities, the child was seen as the "bright one" of the family and favoured for that reason. Such children might end up providing care for their parents and then worrying about them once they were in foster care.

A number of these children were in care as a result of evidence of abuse, including sexual abuse, against older siblings. To an even greater extent than other looked after children, explanations of why they were not with their birth families were difficult for them to understand. The loss of being "favoured" made it more difficult to settle initially in foster care and may have contributed to the fact that some children who did not have major behaviour problems had experienced a breakdown of previous foster placements. Their feelings were muddled – often enjoying many aspects of the care and family life of the foster home while feeling drawn back emotionally to the familiar patterns and relationships in the birth family. This made it harder to prepare children once the decision for long-term fostering was taken. It was common for them to receive explicit or implicit messages at contact that they were in care for no reason, and that their special place in the family was still waiting for them.

Children in the sample who were seen as "the problem" by their birth parents and scapegoated to an extent could nevertheless be having similar difficult issues around closeness to the caregiver. Paula was the least favoured in her sibling group but still shared her older sister's need to parent their mother. In Paula's case, unpredictable caregiving is linked with some frightening experiences.

Foster carer: *Paula is very protective of her mother, protects her from criticism to the point she will say something ridiculous because she thinks we might be criticising mum . . . She tried to play the parent role . . . Her mother gave her very little care. Her older sister Tracey did most of it. Her mother was drinking quite heavily. What she does is, she discusses everything with all the girls including Paula, the youngest. Medical, relationships with partners, her father, social services – everything is related to the children.*

Researcher: *Blurring of boundaries?*

Foster carer: *Yes, definitely.*

Researcher: *Which category of caregiving would you say?*

Foster carer: *Unpredictable and out of control/frightening. When Paula was living at home the out of control/frightening bit was definitely there, certainly, because mother's partner and possibly mother as well were taking drugs and Paula has said she was frightened of him when he was taking drugs. She knew he was taking drugs – you see nothing's hidden from them. And he was strange and frightening. Paula was not protected from anything.*

In this example, the nature of the relationship is a form of role reversal, in which Paula, then aged six, has to care for her mother and her mother burdens her children with her own anxieties. This, for Paula, is in the context of fear, for herself and for her mother, which will threaten her ability to handle all anxieties. The pull of this insecure ambivalent attachment makes it hard for Paula to give up the patterns of her birth family and build relationships in the foster home. Unfortunately, the social work planning and court process, delayed by uncertainty about her mother's ability to stay off drugs, contributed to a long period of emotional tension for Paula and the foster carer.

Social worker: *The whole year and a half it took with Paula's court proceedings – it was supposed to be 3–4 months for*

> *mum to have a detox but basically she left hospital after a week and from there on nobody knew what was going on. It was very hard. Paula wanted answers, she wanted to know. And we didn't have the answers. It took a long time – first for social services to make their mind up and then psychologists and guardians. It was frustrating.*

Researcher: *A long period of uncertainty?*

Social worker: *Especially for Paula – she really wanted to stay with her mum – her mum wanted her to stay and she was really torn apart – still is.*

This one example speaks for a number of cases where the entangled nature of the relationships made it difficult for the child to reach an emotional or psychological resolution. This is then reflected in the professional and legal systems, which also find it hard to reach a resolution, particularly where drugs, alcohol, mental health and learning disability are factors. For these children, the care planning issue might be around whether parents would recover from a particular mental illness or whether one more attempt at a detoxification programme or a parent training class or family support would make the difference. In one case, a child was returned on six occasions. Then once the case comes to court there is a risk that the assessment process starts up again, as if the case is being looked at from scratch rather than in the light of previous assessments. There are no easy answers here but the professional and court systems designed to promote the child's welfare can in practice compound the child's problems and put pressure on the carers and the placement. This was Paula's fourth placement.

Frightening/out of control

Fear featured for many children to some extent, whether it was the fear that a parent would die, fear of a mother or father who was intoxicated, fear of violence directed at the child or fear of abandonment. More than one child had asked to come into care, one even presenting himself at the police station at the age of six saying that his mum was hurting him, another refusing to go home from a school trip. Another child had memories of his mother assaulting him and causing serious head injuries when he was four years old.

In some cases, close involvement of frightening parents, which went beyond even the kind of entangled relationships described above, had confused and distressed children.

Peter's mother had severe personality problems. She had him as a first child in her forties and had kept him very close to her, sleeping with him, keeping him off school to be with her and so on. This was accompanied by significant levels of violence between the parents and threats to Peter of violence and abandonment through maternal suicide. The social work planning was dogged by repeat court applications by his parents for his return, until the court made a s.91 order restricting further applications without leave for a specific period. However, managing the case towards permanence was also affected by the difficulty in handling the fact that Peter was wrapped up in his mother's disturbed thought systems and each contact reinforced this through threats, promises and, on occasion, violent altercations. The frightening aspects of his experience in the birth family were persisting in some forms, with it even becoming necessary for there to be an injunction against the parents approaching the foster home. Whenever asked, he expressed a wish for more contact and to go home. In the research interview, he was largely passive as if waiting for a point in the interview, which came when he was asked if he had any wishes and he said firmly that he wished to go home.

Children who had been sexually abused had all experienced some sense of being intruded on and fear was a feature, either directly relating to violence or indirectly, through threats about what would happen if the child disclosed. Even in these cases there were patterns which reflected differences in caregiving. One pattern was best exemplified by children who had experienced sexual abuse by both parents that was accompanied by sadistic behaviour and violence. The nature of the abuse was associated with such levels of fear and distress that it left the children with a range of aggressive, regressive and complex behaviours; attacking other children or carers, soiling and wetting, being very withdrawn and dependent or being manipulative and hard to trust.

For other children, the sexual abuse was associated with an apparent lack of boundaries. In one case involving parents with learning disabilities, the children did not appear to have experienced the same level of fear, even though the abuse had involved more than one family member. What they were left with, however, was a completely sexualised way of relating to others and showed signs of distress and confusion. Their behaviour was also regressive and aggressive to a degree, but they were more characterised by persistent sexualised behaviours.

Conclusion

What most of these 58 children brought with them into the long-term placement were a range of difficulties and troubling experiences, which left them anxious and struggling to make sense of their situation. They were in almost every respect a high risk group of children coming into care with developmental problems, particularly in social relationships with adults and peers. Unfortunately for this age group of children, there were only a few years available to carers to help build strengths, before adolescence would make fresh demands on children with few cognitive and emotional resources.

Using developmental theory to understand the impact of previous caregiving experiences should assist practitioners in matching children with carers, planning placements, and in determining the kind of therapeutic and educational support which children will need.

Summary

- The age range of the 58 children in the study was 4–12, with 13 (22 per cent) aged 4–6, 17 (30 per cent) aged 7–9 and 28 children, nearly half (48 per cent), aged 10–12. There were 26 (45 per cent) boys and 32 (55 per cent) girls; 39 (67 per cent) on care orders and 19 (33 per cent) accommodated.
- Disability was a factor – 15 (25 per cent) had a learning disability of whom four (7 per cent) had severe learning disabilities.
- Most children had not moved frequently in care or between care and home. A small but significant minority had had multiple care episodes and experienced as many as nine different foster carers.

- Levels of difficulties in the birth mothers were high, with 44 (76 per cent) having two or more of the following: abuse in childhood, mental health problems, serious health problems, learning disabilities, criminal convictions, alcohol or drug misuse, physical illness or a history of being in care themselves.
- Levels of abuse and neglect in the children were high also, with 47 (81 per cent) having experienced three or more different types of abuse or neglect and only six (10 per cent) having experienced none.
- Children's current functioning gave cause for concern with 25 (48 per cent) scoring in the abnormal range and a further nine (17 per cent) in the borderline range for total difficulties on the Goodman's Strengths and Difficulties Questionnaire. Difficulties at school were highlighted by foster carers but not by social workers.
- Patterns of caregiving in the birth family could be understood by applying developmental attachment theory using the following categories: (i) secure base (ii) hostile and rejecting (iii) unpredictable and uncertain or (iv) frightening and out of control.

3   Making the placements
Social work practice and planning

One of the most significant dilemmas facing any social worker of a child who is unable to be cared for within the birth family is how best to identify a substitute family which will meet his or her needs throughout childhood. The choice of options is affected by so many factors: legislative frameworks, practice guidelines, research data on outcomes, rival theoretical definitions of children's needs, the wishes and feelings of children and important adults, and the availability of resources. Nor do these factors stand still; they change constantly. At any one time children are living with the consequences of the combination of factors that influenced the decisions made five, ten, fifteen and more years ago. The careleaver now may still be living with the consequences of decisions made at birth.

Each child's history reflected a number of turning points at which professionals, usually social workers, had to make tough decisions. These decisions could have gone one of a number of ways, if the evidence for making those decisions had been weighed differently, if different resources had been available, or if the climate of opinion around best practice had been tilting one way or another. This was true even in those cases where matters were clear cut in terms of evidence of significant harm, for example, the most serious of the sexual abuse cases where one parent had been convicted and imprisoned. Choices around keeping siblings together, levels of contact with a non-abusing or abusing parent as well as the choice of adoption or fostering had taxed social workers to a significant degree.

The potential risks and benefits attached to such decisions are great and the burden of responsibility for social workers is all the greater for knowing that it is not the many professionals involved with the decision that will live with its consequences in the longer term but the child, the carers and the birth family, who are linked together in a set of bureaucratically created relationships with a great deal of hope invested in them. Collecting data for this study was a reminder of just how complex the issues are and just how troubled social workers had been as they tried to seek out the best possible family placement for individual children. A number of social workers commented, as if embarrassed, on the fact that they had feelings, "a soft spot" as one worker put it, for the children. Many feelings were of anxiety and concern for such vulnerable children.

Colin is the one child I've worked with that I've had sleepless nights over. With Colin especially – lots of sleepless nights. He'd been in foster care a while. He was about five. He didn't know the plan. He knew he wasn't having contact with his mum but he didn't know where his mum was. I took over the case to prepare him for adoption. I just felt so sorry for this little waif. . . I felt he was a child completely lost in the system.

Social workers had often been through so much with the children prior to this placement. One worker had supported two young brothers for five years in a bridge foster family waiting for an adoption or, later, a foster placement. She then had to decide if the foster placement currently on offer was good enough. Another worker had supported a six-year-old child for the previous three years in an apparently very successful long-term foster home only to see the carers decide to "give up fostering". She then had to start all over again in the face of the child's state of shock and distress. With so much at stake, social workers needed to draw on all their professional and personal strengths, hopefully with the help of supervision, to be available to help the children contain their anxiety.

But there were also some very positive and rewarding outcomes which could occur quite unexpectedly. Several workers had placed children for short-term care and began the search for a "forever family" with some trepidation, only to experience the relief of finding that the carers and child have just "clicked". Quite fortuitously, but nevertheless genuinely, some children and carers became increasingly fond of each other and committed to each other to the extent that the search for a new family could stop.

Decision making processes

In all agencies, decisions or recommendations for long-term foster care were made at some stage as part of the statutory review, with carers, parents and sometimes the child present. In some agencies this is where the process stopped, but in others there were additional procedures for assessment/approval/matching, such as a new Form F for carers and a Form E for the child. The final decision in the majority (70 per cent) of cases would then be made by a permanency or fostering panel of some kind.

It was very difficult to evaluate these different systems. First, it should be said that, whatever the level/pattern of decision making, there would be no difference in the legal status of the child. However, the aim was to ensure that certain levels of practice were maintained and that the transition to a long-term foster family was properly assessed and approved. There was also the potential for a ritual transition and celebration, as in adoption. Panels have the advantage of raising the status of long-term foster care and having an overview of the agency's permanency practice.

Feedback from social workers about these systems was mixed. In agencies where the decision was taken to a panel beyond the review, social workers expressed concerns that, when a child had been well settled in a placement for some time, going through the process of completing a Form E and a Form F and taking the case to panel seemed an intrusion in the foster family, an extra distraction for the social worker and a potential source of unnecessary anxiety for the child. Delays in the panel system itself were said by workers to compound the frustration of the seemingly unnecessary paperwork but more importantly to cause a sense of felt insecurity in the placement. In one case where the child had been in placement nearly five years, the decision for long-term foster care in this family had been taken three years previously. Because of court applications by parents, lack of social work continuity and perhaps other factors, the new but temporary social worker was currently working on the Form E to take the case to panel. It is difficult to know what meaning such discussions would have for the child. It must seem as if the question of where he was to live was being revived, in spite of years of reviews and court cases, which had consistently concluded that he should remain in this foster family.

Where these systems were not working particularly well, there could also be different perspectives within the professional network as to the status of the plan; children's social workers and carers were talking to the child about their long-term future together, while the family placement social worker might be stating the official position, which was that the carer was not a long-term carer until this had been approved by the fostering panel. One foster carer had not even been aware of the date when her new approval was going to panel until she received a phone call to apologise that it had been delayed.

It was unclear from the interviews whether the problem was with the panel systems, with delays in panels or with delays by social workers in completing the assessments and paperwork due to pressure of other work. All that can be concluded at this stage is that if cases are going to a further panel, then it has to be done as soon as possible following the review decision. If it takes more than the six months until the next review, the situation for all parties becomes rather unsettling. The plan may be for this to be the child's long-term foster family and yet it is not a "real" plan until it has been approved.

Long-term foster care or adoption?

The choice between long-term foster care and adoption was an important issue for this study. For a minority of children it seems to have been a difficult decision but for others it had been more straightforward, with long-term foster care seen as a positive option. The social work questionnaire responses (see Table 3.1) revealed that the three major factors in favour of long-term foster care relate to whether adoption was seen as appropriate for the child, whether the birth family would object and the child's need for a level of contact not seen as compatible with adoption.

The "adoption not appropriate for this child" category could be linked with a range of factors, with such high proportions of older children who had complex ties to their birth families and whose difficult behaviours would suggest the need for ongoing social work support. Three children had waited several years for adoptive placements that

Table 3.1
Reasons for choosing long-term foster care rather than adoption

	N = 58	%
Adoption is inappropriate for this child	36	62
Child's contact needs not compatible with adoption	34	59
Birth family members opposed to adoption	26	45
No adopters available	11	19
Child opposed to adoption	7	12
Previous adoption placement broken down	2	3
Other reason given: adoption takes too long	1	2

had not materialised. In addition, 19 (33 per cent) of the children were accommodated, making adoption less likely.

Contact is a particularly complicated issue and will be dealt with in more detail in a later chapter. At the planning stage it was felt by some social workers that, even for the few children who were young enough for there to be some possibility of identifying adopters, close relationships and frequency of existing contact with parents or other birth relatives could be seen as important enough to the child to mean that it would override any possible advantages to be gained from adoption or would put such an adoptive placement at risk.

The ties to the birth family

The factor that needs very close examination is the anticipated continuing role of the birth family in what was to be a long-term or permanent placement. The position in relation to valuing birth family ties and the range of other possibly linked factors was put by one social worker, who described why she had advocated long-term foster care for a particularly disturbed young boy.

Long-term foster care was the only way Jake (5) would get a positive image of his background. And he already had formed relationships that were very valuable. I also feel that he needs ongoing contact with his mother because she hasn't been able to work through the past with him. And his siblings – I think it's very important for children to grow up knowing their siblings. He'd been with June [foster carer] a long while and they'd formed a strong attachment and at the time the decision was made, Jake was not an easy child to manage and I felt there was a risk that even if placed with adopters it would break down and he would be further rejected. And I didn't think many adopters would accept the family and the family would certainly not accept the adoption. So that adoption would mean a complete break with his family. Also, I think Jake will eventually go back to his family. He had long enough, even if adopted, he's had long enough that he would want to go back and how could he go back if there was a long period when he hadn't seen these people at all? I think Jake is going to be a difficult adolescent. I think he will be a very difficult adolescent and I think the people who will most accept him and love him are his own family and I'd like to think that they are always going to be there as a safety net for Jake.

This is a complex weighing of risks and benefits, short-term and long-term, in which the links with and views of the birth family are set alongside the strength of this particular placement.

June loves Jake and Jake is able – one of the few areas where he is able to express a view, that is he wants to stay with her and gets very upset at the thought of moving. When he went to contact, he always wanted to be assured that he would be going back . . . And she's known him since he was a tiny baby. She's always been there really. She's as near as he can get to being part of his family.

In this difficult case the mother had only cared for Jake intermittently but his grandmother was significant to him. There were very different perceptions of what long-term foster care meant in this case. The social worker valued the secure attachment which Jake was developing with his foster carer, as did the grandmother. Other members of the extended birth family saw the carer as more like a child-minder, caring for the child until a family member took him home. Contact with the whole family was unsupervised and the social worker felt he had been subject to pressure around going home. As time was going on, the social worker was becoming rather concerned about having to keep re-establishing the plan.

In some cases, the opposition of the birth family and the need to support carers were linked.

Researcher: *Would these carers want to adopt Clive (11)?*

Social worker: *I haven't asked them – I think it would provoke World War III. Mum would go crazy. It is such an emotionally charged case – he is the parents' world. The foster carers are doing brilliantly but they need the support of the Social Services Department.*

In this case there was a risk that the violent, unpredictable parents would continue to intimidate the social workers and the carers, as well as the child.

Adoption had failed before

Adoption was not considered for Jay (7) who had experienced a failed adoption, or Sean (8) because he had already been in a bridge placement, had gone through preparation for adoption, been placed for adoption and then rejected after a few months.

I couldn't have put Sean through trying adoption again. I felt as if we'd blown our chance of that. We'd done all the preparatory work but it hadn't worked. We'd talked about forever families and new mummies and daddies and it hadn't worked. And Sean himself was saying, 'I don't want a new mummy and daddy, I don't want to be adopted'.

It was the combination of the social worker's view *and* the child's wishes and feelings that led to long-term foster care.

A "strong" attachment

Some of the children were subject to care plans which had been made in court and which committed the local authority to foster care rather than adoption. In particular, social workers in some cases noted the key role of the guardian *ad litem* in recommending long-term foster care. In Samantha's case the social worker said that the guardian had emphasised the "attachment" to the birth mother and suggested that she could cope with foster care but not with adopters, who would want to "claim" her. The social worker felt that the outcome had been a good one for this child.

I think we have a permanent foster family who haven't claimed her but she has claimed them. This is what we wanted to happen, the guardian ad litem *had said that this would happen with foster carers but not adopters.*

This idea of a different kind of caring relationship cropped up in relation to another child also. The social worker was asked why she had chosen long-term foster care when adoption had been a real possibility.

. . . Because of Roger's psychological attachment to his family. He knew who his mum was. In the past there was an attachment to his mum and his grandmother and I think if he had a family who wanted to claim him as theirs there might have been some tension. We chose that family because they wanted to make a lifetime commitment – very much so but didn't want another child of their own, to call their own . . . and for that reason they have been more receptive to the level of contact that Roger needed.

These were not the only cases where such a debate had clearly gone on. In relation to the adoption choice, it raises questions about the belief, implicit here, that adoption is not desirable where there are significant relationships with birth relatives, which must be the case with most older looked after children. It also raises questions about the need to consider whether "closeness" and an "attachment" to birth parents is a relationship which needs to be placed at the centre of planning, regardless of whether that relationship is a source of developmental growth and protection for the child, or whether it continues to expose them to insecure and damaging parenting. On the other hand, in relation to beliefs about foster care, the expectation that carers won't "claim" the child needs clarification. Is it that carers who offer a long-term commitment to a child are not expected to experience the same feelings of bonding with the child that other parents, including birth and adoptive parents, feel? Or does the idea of "claiming" suggest that having those feelings is incompatible with accepting and promoting the child's continuing relationship with birth family members? Conflating the carers' or adopters' feelings for the children with their feelings about the birth family risks narrowing the range of both adoption and foster placement options. Carers in either context may be committed to the child and have either positive or negative attitudes to the birth family. As it turned out, in the case of Samantha, the foster carers could not have been more keen to "claim" her as a full member of their family. They said repeatedly how they saw her as their daughter and she called them mum and dad. They were also very concerned about the role that her birth mother continued to play in her life. As they put it:

As far as we're concerned she's ours forever. Her children will be our grandchildren. We would like her to be totally absorbed into our family . . .

The question of blame

One factor affecting planning that was mentioned by one social worker was the idea that, in some circumstances, adoption would not be "fair" to the children or the birth parents.

Right from the start when we realised that there was no way these children could be rehabilitated home, we went for long-term fostering because they already have a Mum and Dad. The fact that the parents are ill is not the children's fault. Who knows, when they are 16 or 18, they may want to go back to Mum and Dad, as most children in the system do go back, and it would be wrong . . . they have an identity with their parents, maybe not a very good one but they have birth parents. It's not as if the parents ever knowingly abused them. The neglect was by omission not commission and we know the neglect was due to the illness. It would be very wrong, in my opinion, to say that purely because parents have a severe mental health problems, their children should be adopted.

Here, adoption was seen as depriving children of their families and as punishing to parents. The comment that 'most children in the system do go back' reflected a kind of fatalism which affected a number of decisions (see also Jake above). This may be due to an unhelpful reading of the research. Statistically most children do go home from care, as Bullock *et al* (1993) demonstrated. But the children in this study were children for whom the birth family had been ruled out as an option, because of evidence of high risk and/or after years of attempts to keep children and families together. They did need a firm plan for their future care throughout childhood.

Post-adoption support

Carers' concerns about the absence of post-adoption support had proved to be decisive in one case. James (4) had been seriously neglected during his first two years. When admitted to care, he had poor muscle tone and was not weight bearing. He was expressionless, did not cry, laugh or smile. He did not react to toys. He screamed for long periods and could not be comforted. He thrived in the placement, as if "waking up". There was no birth family contact, by the birth family's choice, and adoption was the plan, but attempts to find adopters had failed, in spite of his young age. The present carers would have been happy to adopt James but their previous experience of adopting a child with a disability was that there was no subsequent support and they had to struggle for resources, so they decided against it.

Making this placement

It was helpful to distinguish different patterns of planning. The routes to the point of decision making for long-term foster care in this family fall into two broad categories: placements where children and carers were matched on paper and placements where the carers already had the child placed with them short-term or had some knowledge of the child prior to the placement being made.

Matched with foster carers prior to placement

This group of placements was characterised by the following matching process taking place *prior to placement*: the child's need for a long-term foster placement had been agreed; the carers' assessment as long-term carers, sometimes specifically for this child, had occurred; the needs of the child had been matched with what were perceived to be the carers' family situation, skills, resources and general coping capacity; both parties had been informed about each other and a process of introductions had taken place. In summary, a process similar to adoption planning had taken place, although the assessment was generally shorter and was not always subject of a decision by an independent panel. Birth parents would also have been involved in the decision to some extent, unlike most adoption placements. These matched prior to placement cases account for slightly less than half (45 per cent) of the children in the study and include two sibling groups of five and three.

Matched for permanence

In this group were children for whom adoption could have been considered as a possible option by virtue of their age. One child, Jane, aged six, was a little girl with no apparent emotional or behavioural difficulties. She had already experienced the ending of what had appeared to be a successful three year long-term foster placement. Jane had been accommodated as a result of her mother's illness and had contact once a week in the birth family home, an arrangement that had continued throughout the previous placement. The issues were not simple: on the one hand, one long-term foster placement had already failed to last but on the other hand, was adoption appropriate given the mother's situation?

The second child, Hannah (5), had been living with her grandmother and her siblings because her mother, who misused drugs, could not look after them. Her grandmother could no longer cope with all the children and asked for Hannah, then aged three, to be accommodated. Hannah had staying contact with her grandmother and siblings.

Both of these children were placed with carers who had applied to foster in order to offer a child a permanent place in their family. In these cases, the carers' profiles might otherwise have been seen as more characteristic of adopters. One of the couples, for example, had expressed a wish for a young girl with few serious behaviour problems to 'complete their family', but had been told that it might not be possible to match them with such a child. When Jane's previous placement ended suddenly and a new home was being urgently sought, they were available. Jane was exactly the kind of child they had hoped for and the placement was made quite rapidly.

Both placements were seen as highly fortuitous by the relevant social workers. Appropriately in both cases much thought and work were given by social workers to establishing with the carers whether they understood the nature of fostering as opposed to adoption and both carers were adamant that they wanted to foster. Both children had significant links with their birth families, which were taken into account as one of the reasons for foster care, but had obvious implications in terms of the future delicate balance between the role of the new parents and the continuing role of birth relatives.

Other placements also followed the pattern of pre-placement matching, but in circumstances where adoption was not considered to be a serious option. In the main, the children were older and had behaviour problems. They were disturbed children for whom sustaining any family placement might be considered a difficult task. So in this group were children who were needing to be matched carefully because they were known to have very special needs. Kieran (11) had been in residential care for a number of years because of his emotional and behavioural difficulties and had been assessed by an independent adoption agency as unsuitable for family placement. It was only the determination of the social worker and the possibility of a match with an experienced local foster carer which led to this placement. Because of the complex needs of the child and the pessimistic outlook for him, a great deal of thought and assessment work went into this placement. Kieran himself was extremely reluctant to move from the residential home and it was only when he had been in his foster home for a little while that he was able to acknowledge the advantages for him of family care.

Matched with a trial period

Rather different but still within this group were placements which were matched and intended to be long-term but where specific factors led to an initial trial period. There were just two cases from different local authorities in this group and they demonstrate important planning and practice dilemmas. These two sibling groups had experienced sexual abuse, for which in one case a parent had been imprisoned and in the other case both parents were cautioned. One sibling group had been in residential care for a year and the other had been in separate foster homes prior to this placement. So in both cases, coming to this foster family was their first chance at substitute family care as a sibling group.

On the one hand, the clearcut nature of their abusive backgrounds made it easier to plan for the children. Care orders had been made and they were not going home. On the other hand, the combination of disturbed sexualised behaviour and the factor of the sibling group meant that achieving a permanence plan would be difficult. One of the factors that might also have been complicating the planning was that in each family there was a youngest child who appeared relatively unharmed and showed few behavioural problems. In contrast, older siblings were showing a range of sexualised, aggressive and regressive behaviours.

Both foster families were chosen because of their professional caring experience, as well as experience as foster carers. They fell clearly into the "professional" group of carers (see next chapter). In both placements, an arrangement had been reached between the carers and the local authorities whereby the carers were able to commit themselves to a period of time during which it would be possible to ascertain from everyone's point of view if the foster family was viable and would meet the needs of all the children. Both families took on the task knowing that the children needed long-term care and were willing, in principle, to provide it. The idea of what could be called a trial period might seem like a contradiction in permanence planning terms but one of the carers gave us the reasons:

Foster carer: *The court case hadn't happened when they were placed. We're older. Also, we wanted to do it for two years and see how it went. We felt that if possible we would always keep them – we don't want children to have to move on.*

Their argument was that it would be worse to promise the children at the very beginning that they would never have to leave. With such disturbed children there was no way of knowing until they were placed whether the sibling group could be coped with together or even whether it would continue to be in each child's interest to stay together. In both families, it appeared that it was not only the placement but also the package of support that needed to be kept under review. One sibling group was to be reviewed after 6–9 months, but this was at least as much to do with seeing how much support for the carers and therapy for the children was needed as to review the long-term plan.

From the social workers' point of view both were excellent placements. However, one social worker could still imagine the need for moves, if this was seen to be in the interests of the children.

I'm just so impressed with how things are going. But whether in time we might think it would be better to move Marie or place Joanna and Rose separately, I don't know, but at the moment it was felt it is best to keep them together and fortunately we've been able to do that . . . This placement's been like a gift from heaven. Particularly since the carers were only five minutes from the children's home – so it was possible for them to remain in the same schools and maintain the few links that they had.

Care had been taken by the social worker to match these very demanding and needy children with skilled carers who were willing and able to offer a long-term home. But the point of final decision making was to come about as and when it was clear that the relationships were developing and the family was a viable prospect for the longer term. Although this might be said to lead to a degree of uncertainty for the carers and the children or even that the children might feel under some pressure to behave well, it may be that this will prove to have some advantages. The carers give the message to the children: 'we know what it is like to live with you but we care for you and we want you to be part of our family'. It may also take some of the pressure off the children – uncertainty can be a source of anxiety but for these kind of vulnerable children so often is the "blind date" of a permanent placement, with the message on day one, this is your "forever family".

Chemistry: matched with foster carers known to them

Slightly more than half the children (55 per cent) were known to the carers at the time the plan was made. When the histories of these cases were looked at in more detail, they fell into two rather different groups. The first group, the "chose to keep" group, was of children who had been placed in the foster family on a short-term basis, with a minimum of preparation, and stayed on when the "matching" decision was made that their future was to be secured with these foster carers. A second group of children – the "chose to have" group – were matched, in that the child's need for a long-term placement was already decided prior to their arrival on this occasion, but the basis for the placement was the carers' previous knowledge of or relationship with the child. Carers felt that there was a good fit, a good match, between them and this child and that they could commit themselves to offering the child a long-term place in their family.

Chose to keep

Social workers for these 19 children had been in the position of seeing that a short-term, respite, bridge or emergency placement was working well for the child and then either quietly hoped or openly advocated for the placement to become the long-term choice. Carers were willing to make this longer term commitment because they already felt affection or concern for the child, because the child simply fitted in well with their family, or both. Social workers were pleased to see that the placement could succeed and further moves for the child would be avoided. Just as with some of the "matched prior to placement" group, the boundaries and differences between adoption and long-term foster care had been explored, so with this group it was the shift from short to long-term caring roles that needed close scrutiny from social workers. Because this group of placements were not only originally designed to be short-term but were generally with carers who had been recruited and trained for short-term work, social workers spoke of their appropriate levels of concern and consequent assessment/preparation work around this major shift of role. This involved both the child care and the family placement social workers.

Christine (9) came into her placement on a short-term basis. Her family history was of neglect from parents with learning disabilities and there had also been sexual abuse of older siblings. Christine had been in the care of another foster family since the age of four, with her two older sisters. However, she had been the least favoured of the girls and the foster carer asked for her to be moved. Christine arrived in this placement one month after her new carer had been approved as a short-term carer. The new foster mother had to deal with Christine's multiple losses and low self-esteem. As she said:

> Christine understands why she's away from her birth family but she can't understand why she's had to leave her foster family.

In spite of her difficult past experiences, in her birth family and in her previous foster family, Christine fitted in from the beginning with the carer and her teenage daughters. The social worker said that he fairly soon started to think about the possibility of this becoming a long-term placement for Christine. However, the carer was clear that she needed to take her time to make sure that this was the right decision for the child and for her family, because long-term care was not what she had anticipated when she went into fostering.

I can't remember how long she'd been here when it was put to me. I can't remember. They kept putting it to me but I couldn't make that decision at first. It took me a long time to make the decision. We had a lot of discussion with the girls to make sure they were happy. It was always in the back of my mind. I was scared that once I made that decision that the breakdown that happened with the previous foster family could happen with me. I discussed it with my link worker and social worker – they said that if it really came to that we'd have to move her again, which would have been unfair to Christine.

The system in this authority encouraged support and reassessment in the light of a change to a long-term plan, including an updating of the Form F. But the carer herself needed to make sure it was right. From the department's point of view, losing an energetic, newly approved short-term carer was a significant loss. In spite of this, the needs of Christine and the wishes of the carer were given priority.

The initial experience of a short-term placement with carers was perceived as having some psychological advantages in certain situations. In one rather similar placement in a different local authority, the social worker commented that the fact of it being a bridge placement in the early weeks and months took the pressure off the relationship. Ellen (7) had also come from a birth family where parents had learning disabilities and sexual abuse had been the concern. She, too, had moved to this placement from a previous foster placement which had not been very successful and she needed time to get used to this new family. Ellen was described by her social worker as being like a "block" at the beginning of this placement.

Social worker: *We envisaged it as a long bridge placement, taking 18*

<blockquote>

months maybe two years, because she could never give anything to anybody emotionally. If she'd been placed for adoption, it would have been very difficult for new parents, not getting anything back from her.

</blockquote>

Researcher: *Julie* [the foster carer] *didn't have that problem?*

Social worker: *Because it was a bridge placement, she didn't look for anything back. There was no pressure on Julie. She could go at Ellen's speed. Julie was just doing her role. And Ellen just responded marvellously. Now she's just delighted to be in that position where she can stay where she is.*

A number of short-term carers, including Christine's and Ellen's, had developed a close relationship with the children but had clearly seen themselves as part of a plan to move the child on to a permanent family. Since all carers in the agencies in the study were trained as short-term carers, the "letting go" was something they had been taught to expect. What is more, carers who wanted the best for the child had mental images of ideal families who could offer more than they could. It was thus quite often the social workers who had to suggest tentatively that perhaps the carers might consider whether they themselves could offer the child a family home into adulthood. When carers came to realise that they were offering as good a home, and in many respects a better home, than could be located elsewhere, they gave the idea serious consideration. Carers also recognised that, for children who had had several placements already, the advantage of continuity and the risk of another move swung the balance in their favour. So although the initial motivation to foster was more to do with using their parenting skills to help children in difficulty, the carers themselves felt they had something special to offer this particular child and it made sense to offer the child a place in their family long term.

In these cases and others like them, social workers were assessing and monitoring the natural evolution of the carer–child relationship alongside assessments of whether other options or even return home were possible. In most cases it would be fair to say there was significant relief that placements were working so well. But what was most encouraging was that there were no placements in this group where social workers felt that the child was remaining in an unsatisfactory placement. On the contrary, social workers for all 19 children felt some degree of optimism about the placements and saw them as offering a good prospect of meeting the children's future needs.

Chose to have

For this group of 10 children, social workers carried out assessments of the children's needs and matched them with carers who already knew them from previous contacts. This was usually from having the children on a short-term or respite basis on previous occasions but sometimes because of simply knowing the child through other connections. As with the "chose to keep" group, carers, social workers and, to some extent children also, thus made an informed decision. The previous connections with the children were very varied but from a social work practice perspective, it was clear that for children whose futures were in jeopardy, social workers were trying to build on links into families where the carers, and in some cases the children themselves, could have some confidence that the relationships would work in the longer term.

Attempts had been made to place Tony (11) and his older brother for adoption when they were younger but in spite of advertising on two occasions no suitable carers came forward. Then the parents of the short-term foster father, who were regularly seeing the boys and were themselves foster carers for another authority, approached the social worker. This couple had followed the boys' progress over the years and played the role of grandparents. They described the boys' route to placement with them.

Foster carer: *They* [the social services department] *definitely wanted them adopted because they were these two cute handsome children. They were at Mike's* [the short-term foster home] *for a year – then home for a year with every possible help, someone actually living there, then back to Mike's and they were then seven or eight. And then they started making long-term plans.*

Researcher: *And they couldn't find anyone?*

Foster carer: *One family came forward and they were investigated.*

Then there was another family possibly but they had two older girls . . . it all takes a lot of time. Then eventually we said, well they're practically living here anyway . . . and we put it to the social worker, but she already had it in her mind and was quite delighted.

These boys made the move to this foster home when aged 11 and 12 respectively. The delay of six years from initially coming into care was partly attributable to the attempted rehabilitation and then the difficulty in identifying adopters or foster carers. For Tony, the move to this placement was certainly a loss but it offered some significant continuities in terms of relationships, school, geographical area and continuing contact with the previous carers. From the social worker's point of view, it was as good an outcome as she could have hoped for by that stage, and in many respects better.

Carol, also aged 11, had a placement which was similar in certain respects in that her foster carers had previously been more in the role of substitute grandparent than parent. Her birth parents had given up caring for her when she was three years old due to a range of problems including drug abuse. Her paternal grandmother had then cared for her but died when she was eight. Although birth family relatives were tried and then a prolonged short-term foster home, it was a very close friend of the paternal grandmother who stepped in, having maintained a role in Carol's life through week-end stays and so on. Striking in this case was the fact that, although this family friend was not a birth relative of Carol, she had been invited by the social worker to attend all the reviews through this period and was seen as a significant person in Carol's life. This seemed an excellent piece of social work practice and proved to be decisive for this child's future.

Carol's foster family would never have become a foster family if it had not been for this sense of commitment to a specific child and even then, as with a number of the short-term carers, it took a while to make the decision to offer her a long-term family home. When asked about how they came to be foster carers, the female carer said:

In Carol's case it was the only way we could have her, to save complication for her. We had had her to live with us for six months before she went into foster care. We had no intention of having her long-term. She used to stay every fortnight while she was in the foster home – but as time went on she was just going down and down and we just couldn't stand it. It was – silly thing to say – but it was doing me in every time we saw her. The glitter had gone out of her eye. And things were happening that I didn't like – nothing drastic but not right for her. We kept complaining but in the end the only way was – the social worker said – why don't you take her? And I said, no, no, no. My husband's not well and we knew that we wanted to move so we said no. But the more we kept talking about it, it just fell into place. The social worker was a bit pushy, I'd known her for quite a while. The problem Carol had was no-one would take her long term. And we were the only people.

The carers realised that they were Carol's best bet for a stable family life but they did still struggle initially with the sense that they would have liked to continue in the role of "supplementary" parents, perhaps, rather than substitute parents. Interesting in this case was that this was a child who had no behaviour problems, having had significant experiences of love and care from her grandmother, yet she was still found to be "hard to place". For the social worker, it seemed obvious that at 11, Carol could not wait any longer to be settled and here was a family already known and trusted by the child. This placement had all the advantages of a birth relative fostering placement in there being no stigma attached. Although from Carol's point of view, to have gone from parents, to grandmother, to aunt and uncle, to foster family and now her new placement, meant a significant string of losses.

More indirect knowledge of children may also lead to links that change children's and foster families' lives. Alan's current foster family, like Carol's, would not have thought of becoming foster carers if it hadn't been for the fact that they had known of this particular child. They had known of his difficulties in earlier years first in his adoptive family, and then as a highly disturbed child in a short-term foster family. As in cases where short term became long term, the social worker was relieved and pleased for the child that the placement had materialised, even if it was in an unorthodox manner.

Social worker:	*With Alan's presentation recruiting long-term carers would have been problematic – very difficult. They would have been scared off.*
Researcher:	*So going to a family that he knew has helped him?*
Social worker:	*It's been vital.*
Researcher:	*So you haven't had too many decisions to make?*
Social worker:	*No, but being very aware of the support necessary – it's only too easy to forget that. The carers themselves said after they'd been for a break with relatives for a few days, 'Oh gosh, we've just realised the challenge that he is. Not to say we don't want him anymore but to say there's a cost to it.'*

As this social worker points out, the fact that these carers have volunteered for this particular child may make it seem like a more informal arrangement, when in fact such placements still need significant planning and support.

Apart from these rather distinctive cases, "chose to have" carers fell into two groups: those where children had been in and out of care as crises occurred in the life of the family and had passed through this foster family at some stage, and those where there had been planned respite, which eventually led to a permanent family placement. For the first group of children there is the advantage of familiarity with the carers and their children, homes, pets and so on. However, as for some "chose to keep" children, the potential disadvantage here is that the decision for long-term care breaks the previous pattern of returning home in a way that the children might find hard to comprehend. What is more, carers too may feel anxious that, since rehabilitation has been tried before, what is to stop the social services department, either unilaterally or under pressure from courts or parents, giving it one more try? It could be in these cases that permanency panels might have helped to focus everyone's mind on the change of plan.

More straightforward were the cases where respite care for children with disabilities changed into a long-term placement. Here, too, children had to adapt to different patterns but carers could feel more comfortable and secure. The simplest example of this process was the way in which

Sonia (9), a child with severe disabilities who had received regular respite care from the same family for some years, became too difficult for her parents to cope with. The foster family were happy to change role because they felt that, with increasing visits over the years, Sonia was already very much part of the family. From the social worker's point of view, the transition was a smooth one, with the birth family continuing to play an active role.

Each of these cases tells a unique story and yet the thread which links them is not only the relationship chemistry but also the continuity. These carers were familiar with the child and familiar to the child. In most cases the carers knew the child when she or he was little, a priceless piece of the "life story", and had chosen to care for her or him, an equally priceless gift to the child's self-esteem. From the social workers' point of view, the planning and matching were often a mixture of careful assessment and opportunism. It was sometimes a matter of going against conventional or practice wisdom, taking a risk perhaps, and seeing in the relationship the potential for growth and commitment. The social work accounts reflect histories of children who could not wait any longer to be settled, which contributed to the assessment of risks and benefits.

Conclusion

The variety of routes to these long-term placements reflects the variety of the circumstances and histories of the children combined with the differences between agencies in terms of their practice and planning systems. Although models of good practice do need to be identified and systems need to be more consistent, it seems likely that social workers will continue to need to exercise a degree of flexibility based on professional judgement in order to take advantage of placement opportunities that arise. Some of these will be where foster carer–child relationships can be built on rather than replaced.

Summary

- Placing children in middle childhood in long-term foster families is a complex, demanding and stressful task for social workers.
- Planning systems vary between agencies, with some using fostering

panels, some using permanence panels and others relying on the review decision. Whatever the system, there were concerns and frustrations where delay added to insecurity or where the long-term plan was not officially established and acted on.

- The choice of long-term foster care rather than adoption was linked to several factors in most cases. The most common were:
  - age and complex ties to birth families;
  - behaviour problems needing ongoing support;
  - existing relationship with foster carers;
  - adoption not seen as appropriate for this child;
  - birth family objecting to adoption;
  - the child's need for levels of contact seen as incompatible with adoption.
- Three routes to the long-term plan in this placement were identified:
  - matched with carers prior to placement;
  - matched, where short term carers "chose to keep" the child;
  - matched, where carers "chose to have" a child previously known to them.
- These routes reflected the difference in the children's histories, the differences in practice and planning, and the need for flexibility to secure a placement for "hard to place" children.

4   The foster carers

Background information about the foster families was gleaned from questionnaires, with more detailed information coming from in-depth interviews. We aimed to build up a picture of who the carers were in terms of age and life stage, why they had been attracted to fostering and, most importantly, how they had come to make the commitment to the long-term placement of this child. We also hoped to gain understandings of the rewards and frustrations of fostering and of the nature and significance of support networks. In this chapter, we focus on the carers' perceptions of themselves and their fostering roles and responsibilities. Material relating to the building of relationships with the children is covered in Chapter 10.

The carers – age, religion, ethnicity and gender

Just over half of the carers were in their 40s, with the remainder divided equally above and below them in age. This meant that many were older than the birth parents of the sample children, with some approaching the age of their birth grandparents.

All were white and all, except one, were English, living in predominantly white, English communities. Most were practising or nominal Christians, with a small number having no religious affiliation. A significant minority were deeply committed Christians who saw their faith as a source of strength and looked to their church community for support, friendship and comfort.

There were 38 couples and seven single female carers in the sample. Predominantly, it was women who were the primary carers, although there were nine couples where neither partner worked outside the home. Even in this group, however, the women judged themselves to be the person who spent most time caring for the child. Twenty-eight of the mothers did not work outside the home and 11 worked part time. Some saw fostering as "a job from home", most felt that parenting was "what they did best" and had no desire for other employment. At the same time, many recognised that the high levels of need in the children would prevent them from having sufficient time or energy for paid work.

Why foster?

Some of the broader motivations for fostering were shared by most of the carers interviewed. There was a universal love and enjoyment of children.

> *I love children. I love the every day kerfuffle of a big family, the comings and goings, sorting them all out. I find that very fulfilling. I love it . . .*

Alongside was a sense of wanting to do something worthwhile, to make a difference, to offer something to help children in need. Altruistic motivation was complex, however, since personal needs were often being met alongside the needs of the child. As with other forms of parenting, fostering could offer a chance to gain self-esteem, emotional rewards or to heal the wounds of the past. Similarly, motivation for all carers and all parents can operate at both conscious and unconscious levels. Conscious enjoyment of the bustle of a busy family life might be accompanied by an unconscious need for it. This could be sustaining through difficult times, but equally meant that carers were investing a great deal of themselves in the process. The stakes were often quite high for the carers as well as the children.

Researcher: *What do you enjoy about fostering?*

Foster carer: *What you get back from it. All the children keep in touch and it's lovely to see that you've done some good with them. They haven't got a clue what normal life is like really, they've missed out on such a lot, and just the pleasure of being able to see them and give them all that – it's lovely.*

Researcher: *What is the most important thing about parenting Craig?*

Foster carer: *To know that we're totally behind him all the way and that there's nothing we wouldn't do for him and just to know that he's really loved and cared for really. At the end of it, he is a part of the family and because he knows that, that's why he's getting on so well.*

When children become part of the family, but the background circumstances feel unpredictable or unstable, the pleasure of the relationship can be mingled with anxieties about separation and loss, for both the carers and the children. As Craig's carer put it:

> *A couple of times when his mum said about him living back with her,*
> *I went, oh no, because we know it wouldn't work and we're really*
> *attached to him, obviously, and I think we can do so much for him. I*
> *know we shouldn't think this way.*

Becoming long-term foster carers

The meaning and reasoning behind the decision to foster long term were not universal and the carers fell into three broad groupings in this respect:

The *"family builders"* were couples or single carers who were seeking to establish or increase their young families through long-term fostering.

The *"second families"* were couples or individuals who had older birth, adopted or foster children soon to leave home or already established independently. For them, long-term fostering was a chance to rear a second family.

The *"professionals"* were couples or individuals for whom fostering was seen as a form of skilled employment. They were paid salaries or enhanced fostering rates, with the expectation that they were caring for children with high levels of need. These carers still saw the children as part of their families.

Each of these groups had an associated pattern of hopes and expectations of themselves, their relationships with the child, the birth families and the social services department.

The family builders
Family patterns

This group of eight couples and two single carers consisted of people who were seeking to create a new family or extend an existing one through long-term fostering. Most were currently parenting birth or adopted children in middle childhood and, on the whole, they were younger people, in their 30s or early 40s. One couple were fostering a sibling group, the rest, single children. None were fostering children with disabilities or serious health problems. Typical of the "family builders" was the following family.

Barry and Tracey had a nine-year-old birth son, Adrian. They wanted to complete their family by offering a home to a younger girl, who could be a sister for Adrian and a daughter for themselves. They did not feel able to cope with a deeply disturbed child. They had chosen to foster rather than adopt because adoption felt 'so total, so final – for us and for the child'.

Motivation

For the carers in this group, fostering represented an extension of their parenting roles. Often they were mothers who enjoyed being at home and who valued the role of a full-time parent. They did not want to go out to work while their children were young and they saw fostering as doing more of what they were already enjoying. Additionally, in families where there were already single children, fostering was a way of providing companionship for that child if another pregnancy was not possible or desired. For some, the motivation included a sense that caring for a child might fulfil similar goals to those of a career, in terms of using skills and doing something which was intrinsically satisfying.

Caroline's an only child. I'm on my own, and I've always had a houseful of other people's children. Why not do something useful and help some children who actually need it? Also so that Caroline wasn't brought up as an only child.

Motivation for long-term fostering

For the family builders, the motivation to choose long-term fostering varied according to whether they were newly approved or experienced carers.

The new carers were either childless or had secondary infertility. For them, fostering was a way of combining their own needs to parent with the desire to do something worthwhile for a child. Adoption might have been the obvious choice for them, but they shared a view that adoption seemed too final, too permanent, both for themselves and the child. This area of motivation had been an area of much debate during the assessments, with the possibility of adoption being suggested.

*We upset the social workers by sticking with long-term fostering. They
said if you're going to make a long-term commitment, why not adopt?
We went round and round the houses but that's what we felt we could
offer... we thought it would fulfil our needs, which the social
workers didn't believe, but we thought it would be enough – or at least
for now. And we also thought – it sounds do-gooding – but we also
thought it would be helpful, it would be a nice thing to do.*

Short-term fostering had also been suggested to another couple:

*When we said we only wanted long-term, they said we should try
short-term first, but we didn't want children coming in and going out,
we wanted a child to look after, to bring up. It sounds selfish, I know,
but that's what we wanted. They also said, 'you don't know a child is
for a long-term placement until they've been in short-term and sometimes it turns into long-term'. Well, we didn't really want that. We
wanted to know from the start that this child which we would have,
which we would give and do for would be there for good, for as long
as they wanted.*

For the experienced carers in this group, motivation to do long-term
fostering was different. Some had found that the 'coming and going' of
short-term fostering was not compatible with the needs of their own
children. Others had found it hard to part with children they had come to
love. For example, June and David's two daughters had been 'absolutely
distraught' when they had to part with a 10-month-old baby who had
been with them almost from birth. Others had not enjoyed the 'whirlwind'
of new placements which had hardly settled before the child returned
home. Pete and Monica's 10-year-old adopted son had taken short-term
fostering in his stride when younger, but had recently found it unsettling
and asked if he might have a brother 'to keep'.

Matching

Matching issues also varied according to whether the carers were
experienced or newly approved. For experienced carers, if a "short-term"
child fitted well into the existing family and the plan then changed to
"long-term", it was an obvious and natural step to ask if the child could

stay. "Fitting in" might mean that the child accorded with the carers' own values, perhaps a child who was warm and outgoing or showed appreciation of new things or experiences. However, the most significant area of "fit" tended to be compatibility with the existing children in the family. Dwayne, for instance, came as a short-term placement, but immediately hit it off with his new "brothers" – one of whom was adopted, the other long-term fostered. He changed his allegiance to the same football team as them and they 'helped each other' by sharing their experiences of having been born to other families. Christine and Dave felt that it would be unkind to all of them if Dwayne had to move on. They had come to feel 'just like an ordinary family'.

Similarly, Maria's foster mother, Elaine, spoke warmly of the wonderful imaginary games that Maria played with her young daughter and the way in which this child had come to 'love and adore' Maria. This was the deciding factor for Elaine in making a long-term commitment to Maria.

The first time carers were dependent on the social services department for "matching" a child with them, predicting the "fit" on the basis of what was known of both the family and the child. On the whole this worked well, but a lack of mutual understanding at the home study stage could lead to further confusion and a sense of powerlessness when it came to the stage of discussing a possible child:

> *You don't want to say no – you feel you can't say no to any particular child. You feel like you're being tested: are you really committed to long-term fostering, or will you fall at the first hurdle?*

When a match was made, the most important factor for these couples was that the child was compatible with their way of life and their own needs to parent. Pam and Adam, a professional couple, were delighted that Jasmine (5) loved learning and was beginning to share their enjoyment of wildlife. But they were also anxious that she might feel lonely in their isolated and otherwise childless home.

A child who was resistant to being parented could create particular stress for this group of first time carers. For example, Roy was bitterly disappointed to find that Ken's strong sense of loyalty to his birth father made it hard for him to accept Roy as a new father figure.

Support

On the whole, the "family builders" relied on "normal" parenting supports, rather than those provided by the social services department. Primarily, couples looked to each other to discuss problems and issues relating to the children. Parenting was usually shared as much as possible. The next level of support tended to be from extended family, friends and neighbours. Grandparents were used as babysitters whenever possible and neighbours acted as informal childminders for short periods. The carers were usually part of a network of young families with children at the same stages and it was here that they looked for practical and emotional support. Only two carers in this group felt that they related closely to other foster carers. One was a single mother who valued the foster carer support group, another happened to live in a close where there were two other foster carers and so they were neighbours as well and formed a natural alliance.

Working with the child's social worker

In this group of carers, social workers were valued if they were offering a service that acknowledged and respected 'the whole family'. Louise and Jim were pleased that the social worker always included their birth daughter when he took the children out to McDonald's. Mary saw the social worker as there for all of them:

> Our social worker is very good. Sometimes I've got a lot on after school with the other children and I can ring Linda and she will take Andy to contact for me. Anything we need, she'll do it for us. I try to do most things on my own because he's a permanent placement. But it's good to know that Linda's always there for us.

For other carers, the social worker had become a rather distant figure, reducing his or her involvement as the children had settled down in their placements:

> He keeps more in the background, now. We don't see much of him. He lets us get on with it and that's how it should be. He comes to the reviews and looks after the legal side of things.

Most of the carers were happy with this, feeling that the reduced social work role enabled them to 'get on and be a normal family'. However, carers expressed disquiet if social workers were perceived as being 'disinterested' in the child, or as having a stronger allegiance to the birth parents:

> *The last social worker was absolutely appalling. She was far more interested in the mother's welfare than the child's. She put the mother before the child and she wasn't really interested in the child at all.*

Working with the family placement social worker

On the whole, family placement social workers were seen by this group as helpful, supportive and 'there when you need them'. They were valued for being 'on the end of a telephone' if required, rather than as closely involved, proactive working partners.

However, in some cases, the desire to be 'just a normal family' resulted in a sense of distance from the care system and misunderstanding of the roles of the different professionals. For example, when asked about her fostering support, one foster mother replied:

> *I know they have to come round to make sure things are OK but really, the less they come the better. As long as I know they're there if I need them, that's fine. They should trust me to come to them if I need to.*

There was a similar sense of independence regarding financial support, with many of the carers regarding allowances as almost irrelevant:

> *With Andy – he is like one of the family and there isn't anything he needs that he doesn't have. With holidays, sometimes he's so much one of our own that I don't ask. If he needs anything, I get it. I want him to have the best we can afford, like our own do.*

Working with the birth family

The approaches of the family builders towards birth families varied from inclusive through to ambivalent or exclusive (Holman, 1988). Some of the experienced carers had high levels of empathy for the position of the birth parents and had established warm, co-operative relationships with them. Others, however, particularly those who had unfulfilled parenting needs, could find it hard to accept the children's strong feelings for their birth parents. Expressions of these feelings could be experienced as threatening and hurtful.

Sometimes, she will write a list of the three most important people in her life and her Mum will always come first, which, I have to admit, is hurtful. Perhaps not hurtful, that's a funny word to use, but it does upset me and I let her know that I'm upset.

For carers who needed and wanted to be the primary source of care, comfort and protection to the child, it could be hard to encompass the complex feelings and relationships between the child and the birth parents.

Second families
Family patterns
This was the largest group of carers and comprised 21 couples and four single women, for whom long-term fostering was a means of establishing or extending a second family. They tended to be more mature people, usually in their 40s or 50s. Some had fostered large numbers of children in the past – the majority had experienced more than ten placements, one couple boasted 80 and another, over 100. Often, in these families, it was the women who took the driving seat in parenting, with the men being quietly supportive, but more in the background or playing a more traditional role, involving the children in outside activities, taking them to the football and so on. These carers had previously parented children, either through birth, adoption, short or long-term fostering, or often a combination of all four. Whatever the constitution of the "first families", they were now largely grown up, either having left home or being in their late teens and planning to move on in the foreseeable future. The current long-term placement, therefore was a chance to build or extend a second family and the newly placed child often acquired an extended family of adult "brothers and sisters" and their children.

Typical of the "second families" group are Jean and Nigel.

Jean was the mother of three children, adopted in the 1960s. Nigel was her second husband. They had done some short-term fostering together but felt dissatisfied with this. They really wanted to "make a difference" to a child by offering a permanent home. Nigel had recently been made redundant, and they had decided to become full-time long-term carers. They now had three boys, all fostered long-term.

Motivation

When considering their general motivation for fostering, most of this group were looking back many years and yet the reasons were readily accessible and clearly articulated. It seemed that the carers had discussed or reflected on their motivation to foster on many previous occasions.

Initial motivations were varied. The wish to foster children was often linked to direct or indirect experience of sad or even traumatic events in their own lives. Some carers had suffered troubled childhoods, due to parental neglect, physical or mental illness or divorce. Three had lived in children's homes. One had a younger sister who had gone into care. Pauline decided to foster after her life had been 'turned upside down' by a serious illness and a particularly stressful divorce. Some told moving stories of how they had 'by chance' encountered children in the care system. For a few newly approved carers, there had been sad events amongst their friends or family which had led to the placement of a specific child. Other carers, however, recalled happy and secure child-hoods which they felt provided a firm foundation from which to care for children in need.

Even within this group, the carers fell into two very different categories. For many, once the fostering career had become established, caring had become an absorbing way of life, a "habit" that was hard to break. Pat expressed this position clearly:

> Our friends think we're nuts, but now, we couldn't face living in a family home without children. We're just not ready to wind down family life. We still like doing kids' things. We'd have more if we had more room.

These households were distinguished by being extremely busy. Older birth, adopted or fostered children might live nearby and visit frequently. Grandchildren were part of everyday life. Other children might be offered short-term care, respite care or childminding. More often than not, there would be several pets and other "caring" responsibilities to family, neighbours or the community.

Other second families were rather different. Their boundaries were more closed and tightly drawn, more like those of a conventional nuclear family. Carol's carer, who is newly approved, would be more typical of this group.

Jane was a divorced mother of two teenage children. She had cared for her elderly parents until they died. She felt that she had something to offer, some energy to spare now that her children are older and she wanted to offer this to a younger child who needs a family. Her household was very calm and provided a soothing environment for a restless child who came from a chaotic birth family.

Such households contrasted with those where there was a constant hive of activity and an urge to absorb allcomers. Children were thriving in both kinds of families but their experiences were very different.

Motivation for long-term fostering

There was a range of reasons for the decision to create or expand a second family through long-term fostering. Some people had done short-term caring and not enjoyed seeing the children return home:

We never intended that anyone should stay, but after a while, we decided that short-term was not for us. We felt we were almost helping to make things worse because the children would have a different experience, then go back to an unsatisfactory situation and it became increasingly hard to do. We almost gave up fostering. We would probably have been better suited to long-term from the outset, but we didn't feel ready for it then.

Others had become closely attached to children and been deeply affected by the loss of moving them on.

I had a particularly painful year. The children we'd had for nearly three years were moved on and I'd become particularly attached and they to us. And although they've been adopted by a smashing couple, it's been really hard. And I've come to the point where I just can't do it again. That was one of my lows. I felt emotionally drained.

A small number had never wanted "short stays" and had entered fostering with the intention of offering a place in their family for keeps.

However, all of these "second family" carers were driven by a further, very powerful motivating force – that of wanting to heal, restore and make a "real" difference in the life of a child. This, they felt, could not be achieved in short-term placements. Diane and Tony, for instance, had chosen long-term fostering . . .

. . . because you have a child who is usually damaged in some way and you have an opportunity to try and put right some of the things that have gone wrong and give them a home and a base to work from to build their future. With short-term, you don't get that opportunity. We just hope really to undo some of the hurt, to let them see what a happy family is and what belonging to a family means.

Matching

Being matched with the "right child" was not a critical issue for many of these carers. Some had simply taken the next child that came along that needed a long-term family; others had agreed to take on a child with only the briefest information, a one off meeting and very little sense of whether or not there was a "fit" with the existing family.

He came for a morning. A dear little boy with big round eyes and enormous glasses. We took to him straight away. He moved in the next week.

Again, there were differences. For the carers with busy complex households, there was often a sense of "rising to the challenge" of a particularly troubled child. When Gerald was introduced to Thelma and Rod, he made it plain that he did not wish to move in. He said they were too old for him, he didn't like the house, and he wanted to live with his friend's family. Thelma knew that this was not possible and that they might be Gerald's "last chance" to leave residential care and have a family life.

I thought, 'if I go for it and I fail, I've lost nothing, but Gerald's been given the chance to see me as a Mum'. You could tell, somehow, that Gerald wanted an adult to say what should happen in his life. He was having too much say and he was only 11. And I thought he's taking control of his life and the adults should be doing that.

Thelma proceeded with the placement, despite Gerald's continued resistance. Other carers shared this sense that they were the "last hope" that a child had of a stable family life:

> *Lynn had had nine placement breakdowns, bless her, including one for adoption. At the time, it was a feeling that no one else would be able to cope with her and no other placement would survive. Now it's because I love her too much to let her go but I have to admit, that wasn't really the motivation when I first made the offer.*

In general, therefore, there was a sense that these carers could take "allcomers", that, within reason, they could have taken on almost any child that came their way and that they had made themselves "fit the child", rather than the child needing to fit with them.

For other carers there was a more measured assessment of exactly what they could cope with and what sort of child would fit with their family life. This was very much the case for a small sub-group of "second families" who were fostering children already known to them through connection with friends or family. These parents had "stepped in" to situations of family breakdown, motivated by adult loyalties and sympathy for the child who needed a home. In at least two of these cases, the carers would not have taken on this role at all, had it not been for the plight of the particular child and they had thought long and hard before making their commitment.

Support

Most of the carers in this group were strong, confident parents who, first and foremost, looked to their own resources for support:

> *We see the social services as a last resort if issues have not been resolvable within the immediate or extended family. We really feel, we are two grown adults, here 24 hours a day and we really ought to be able to deal with things ourselves.*

However, as experienced carers, most had a strong sense of working in partnership with the social services department and valued the support that was available. Again, the exceptions were the carers approved specifically for a known child. They were not accustomed to the role of social workers in the lives of children and carers and were often unsure about what to expect.

Working with the child's social worker

When social workers had sustained, consistent relationships with the child, the carers saw them as immensely valuable and supportive. In one such case there was a proposal to take the social worker off the case.

Wendy knows Helen inside out – she's got that friendship, she's got that commitment there. I think it would be the worse thing that could happen.

However, external factors meant that social workers could be ever changing and moving on. Five of the carers in this group had children with social workers who were about to leave, had just left, or had no social worker at all. This could be frustrating:

The last one we had was very nice, very polite, but he only stayed a few months. That's the trouble, they're always changing and you have to keep starting all over again. The children think, 'why bother? I probably won't see him or her again'.

Working with the family placement social worker

On the whole, there was a much lower turnover of these workers and their consistency was highly valued by the carers. Sophie and Neil's support worker had done their homestudy many years ago and seen them through many ups and downs:

He is more like a family friend really. He has been helpful to Rosie [birth daughter] *too. We all feel supported by him, we could talk about anything to him. He has always been there and available to us.*

Some of the fostering workers were frequently and proactively involved and this was greatly appreciated by even the most experienced carers. Sheila and Ben had fostered more than 70 children over 18 years:

Foster carer: *Ros comes every three weeks. We put the next visit in the diary each time. It's very valuable.*

Researcher: *You are very experienced carers. Can you say why is it still valuable to have regular support?*

Foster carer: *Well, I think, in a way, because we are so experienced,*
                  we could quite easily be forgotten. But we are here, we
                  sometimes do need a bit of guidance. I often save things
                  up to chat over, knowing that she's coming and that's
                  very useful.

In the few cases where there was not a positive working relationship
with the fostering worker, this was experienced by the carers as a real
gap:
   Ruth – she's new and overloaded. She's only been twice – we're out of
   the area for her, or something. It was strange – I had to fill her in on
   what children we had. I thought they had files on all these things. It's
   a shame it's like that. The last one we had was really good, supportive.

Working with birth parents
Carers in the "second families" group found it easier, generally, to accept
their children's strong feelings for their birth parents:
   He has a very very great love for his father, a very deep love. He's
   aware of what his Dad's done, but he loves him dearly, he really loves
   him.

Regarding decision making, many of the carers had been told that they
could assume responsibility for most of the day-to-day decision making,
and this was welcomed. However, several carers chose to discuss matters
with the birth parents, feeling, paradoxically, that by including and
informing them, they were also showing the parents that the child was a
fully involved member of their family.
   I told him when James was excluded from school for fighting. Of
   course he said it can't have been James's fault. I told him firmly that
   both boys were equally responsible and that was the way we were
   dealing with it. I also rang him and told him we were going up to my
   son's wedding. So that he would know that James is fully involved in
   our family life. I want him to know that James is part of our life but
   that he [Dad] is not excluded from it.

The professionals

This group consisted of seven couples and two single women. They were all receiving additional payments for fostering, with the expectation that they would be caring for the most vulnerable and needy of children. Some of the carers were salaried, some were receiving enhanced allowances and some were attached to specialist schemes, run independently or by the local authority. In all cases, at least one person was a full-time carer, with two couples being both full-time carers and another couple job-sharing a professional role outside the home in order to provide 24-hour cover for their children. The specialist status usually involved additional training, support and respite care.

In total, these carers were looking after 14 of the children in the sample, with two couples having sibling groups of five and three children. Two of the children placed in these families had profound physical and learning disabilities, two had serious medical conditions and one had moderate learning disabilities.

All except one of these carers had previous fostering or adoption experience and most were more mature people for whom professional fostering was a distinct life choice. Fiona and Mike were typical of this group:

Fiona and Mike have an adopted teenage son and have fostered two children from middle childhood into adult life. They are both involved professionally in working with children and wish to use their skills as parents and professionals to foster a sibling group of very needy children. They receive enhanced fostering rates but otherwise work under the same terms and conditions as other foster carers.

Other carers received salaries and one carer was part of an independent fostering agency.

Motivation

As well as their fostering and adoption experience, many of these carers had worked with children or families in need in the past. Two women had been nurses and one a midwife. There was a strong sense, therefore of this being 'a job from home' which would harness existing skills and experiences for the benefit of a child or sibling group.

Natalie had resigned from her career in the health service, feeling that she was in need of 'a life change'. A friend suggested that she might try some respite care and this had led her to Rory, a child with profound disabilities. Natalie had found a compelling combination of 'falling' for Rory alongside the discovery of a new direction in her life and she subsequently applied to become his permanent carer.

Ed had worked as a residential worker and then as a sessional worker for the social services department. Here he had been disturbed by the splitting of siblings and gained a sense that they should be kept together if at all possible:

> I would be picking up siblings from different places – two sisters from here, one brother from there, two from somewhere else. Take them to see Mum and Dad, then, as you drop them off, tears from all of them because they don't want to leave their siblings. It seemed crazy to have them all over the county.

For Ed and his wife, therefore, it made sense to take on the "project" of caring for a large sibling group.

Matching

Three of the carers had come to know their children through initially providing respite care or short-term fostering for them. Close relationships had developed and when the children came to need long-term fostering, it felt 'natural' to make the offer. For the other carers, there had been no previous relationships. They had been 'approached' by the social workers for the children and, after some discussion, had agreed to 'take them on'.

The carers attached to specialist schemes seemed to enjoy the challenge of tackling the most extreme difficulties and felt that they had been selected and equipped to do so.

> We are specialist carers. That means we are more highly trained and prepared to take on the most abused teenagers and the very difficult, hard to place children . . . We felt that this fits in with our maturity and experience. I gave up my work to do it because one of the criteria is that one partner must be available 24 hours a day. Basically, we're here to take anything they throw at us and sometimes, that's literally!!

Support

Generally, this group was distinguished by the much higher level of professional support and lower levels of self-reliance or assistance from friends, family or neighbours. Most of the carers seemed to have developed "individualised" support packages which may or may not involve the social services department. Two carers relied on their own professional skills, not entirely by choice.

For the children with disabilities or health problems, specialised support, tailored to the needs of the child was seen as particularly valuable. Viv and Cliff found that their primary support came from the special nursery at the hospital and another carer ran a group for other carers of children with disabilities. Erica and Ian felt that Lindsey's social worker was a good source of support to them as she came from a specialist team for children with disabilities and 'really knows the issues in caring for these children'.

Respite care

Because the children placed with them had such high levels of need, they could be exceptionally draining, both physically and emotionally. The carers found that it was not usually possible to rely on friends or relatives for babysitting, or childminding and so respite care was often an integral part of the placement.

As a single carer, Frances found the one weekend a month of respite care to be particularly valuable:

That weekend's a godsend. I really do need it. I get to this point in the month when I can tell, I really do need it. Not because I don't love him, but it's good for us to be apart for a couple of days.

Ed and Joanne also valued the respite care that was provided for their sibling group, particularly as it could involve a male and a female carer coming to their home while they went out, thus minimising the disruption to the children. One couple who had taken a sibling group said they would make respite care a condition of the long-term placement arrangements.

Working with social workers: teamwork

Of all the carers, this group had the strongest sense of working as part of a team, in the interests of the child. Correspondingly, there was less emphasis on the value of the child's relationship with the social worker. The "teamwork" aspect was generally seen as positive and enjoyable:

I enjoy working with the adults as much as the child. If I had my own children and I was at home with them all day, it would drive me mad. But you go to meetings and get involved with the plans and decisions and you're always working towards things. It's brilliant.

One of the couples who were caring for a sibling group felt empowered as "co-ordinators" of their team of supporters and this enabled them to feel "in control" as they would with a family born to them:

We are like the co-ordinators of the team. For instance, I had to go and stay with my Mum because my Dad was ill. I rang up the support workers – I didn't have to ask permission from a social worker. I could just ring the worker and say, 'I need you from 4 until 10 on Wednesday. Can you do it?'

This sense of teamwork did not necessarily mean that relationships were always harmonious. These carers felt empowered to 'speak up' for what they felt was best for the child and this could mean a crossing of paths at times:

We fight on the children's side. While they're here, I tell them I will fight their corner as hard if not harder than any natural parent. These kids have been let down all along the line and it's up to us to fight their corner. That may mean disagreements with social workers sometimes, but we get through it.

In one case, unusually in this group, the social worker had been only peripherally involved. In view of the child's exceptional needs, this had left the carers feeling exposed and vulnerable:

I have only seen the social worker once or twice this year [in seven months]. *Given that the SSD is the responsible parent, I don't feel that this provides Marcus with enough protection or support. It makes me both angry and anxious.*

For professional carers, there was the potential for tension around who was "in charge". Whether or not there was intensive support to the placement, there were questions about whether the status of being a professional carer led to more delegation of power or responsibility. Issues had arisen over decision making for two of the children and one couple was at odds with their family placement worker over their wish to take on further placements.

Finances

There was no doubt in these carers' minds that they were doing a complex and demanding job for which they should be adequately paid. Most found that there were many additional expenses and they were able to use their fees or salaries to improve the quality of care for the children. One couple, for example, used some of their fostering fees to employ domestic help and a gardener as this enabled them to spend more time with the children. Frances was pleased that she had been able to buy a specially adapted swing for Marcus to use in the garden as most play areas were unsuitable for him.

For many, fostering was their sole or major source of income. Mandy had started to foster professionally after her divorce:

Researcher: *So, fostering was a career choice for you?*

Foster carer: *Definitely. Because luckily enough, before we split up, they brought the fee in. Which is just enough so I don't have to work. Without the fee, I would not be able to foster – it's as simple as that.*

Catherine and Clive, along with other carers in the same local authority were shocked and outraged at proposals to reduce the payments to carers of children with disabilities. Clive had given up work to help with Moira who was assessed as needing two full-time carers. They had sought legal advice and were heading a campaign of protest.

Professional caring or parenting?

In these "professional" placements, there was an increased potential for tension between the "caring" and "parenting" roles. If the balance tipped towards the professional tasks, the children could have an experience that was closer to residential care than family life. One couple caring for a sibling group tried to clarify the nature of professional, long-term foster caring:

Foster father: *I think personally I see a dual role. There's the professional role, the foster carer bit, but generally there will be the parenting. You've got to get on with it and be with the children, all their foibles and all the things, the fun, all the things that parents do, the interaction between parents and children, can be as best as we can possibly make it. We're not perfect but we'll do our best, caring for them. I think that's a feeling that I have with these children – carrying on, being very positive and so on. But that's the way I see it.*

Foster mother: *One of the best things we can do for these children is offer a stable home. During their childhood and maybe past 18.*

Foster father: *We are childcare professionals but it's funny, there's not much that comes up professionally with the children as far as I'm concerned. I know we have to deal with things, but I look at it from the point of view a⁵ although I'm a professional carer working here, the way I see it, you can't help but just love them, love the children.*

Working with birth parents

For the professional carers, working with birth parents was generally viewed as one of the range of tasks that they undertook. The exceptional needs of some of the children could mean that working with birth parents was seen as a fairly minor issue, compared with that of the day-to-day management of the children. A notable exception to this was the approach of one couple who cared for a child with profound learning disabilities. Part of their motivation to foster children with disabilities was because they saw this as offering a better chance of working in partnership with birth parents:

We wanted to work with the whole family, not just the child. Because that's one of the hardest things about fostering, that hostility with a compulsory Care Order – it's dreadful.

They had, accordingly, worked hard to include both birth parents in decision making and had created an atmosphere in which both families could freely demonstrate their interest and concern for the child.

With these exceptions, however, the professional carers tended to have stronger partnerships with the local authority or with other professionals and there was less of a sense of partnership with birth parents than some though not all of the "second families" group. Dealing with the birth relatives was seen as a necessary "task", with little emotional content and there was a professional distance and detachment that was unique to this group.

Conclusion

In all groups, for all carers, the balance was being negotiated between being a "real" family for the child and being foster carers for the local authorities. Motivation for long-term fostering was a crucial factor in determining the emphasis that different families placed upon these roles. Whatever their motivation, however, the vast majority of the foster carers were expressing a heartfelt commitment to supporting the children throughout childhood and beyond, whatever the future might bring.

Summary

- The motivation to foster long term followed the experience of fostering short term for some but not all, with some carers specifically wanting to foster long term at the outset.
- Three categories of motivation/family patterns could be identified among the long-term foster carers in this study:
  - family builders, who were seeking to establish or increase their young families through long-term fostering;
  - second families, who had older birth, fostered or adopted children soon to leave home or already established independently;
  - professionals, who saw fostering as a form of skilled employment, were paid salaries or enhanced rates and cared for children with the

highest levels of needs, but who still saw the children as members of their families.

- These groups had different expectations of their role as carers/parents, the child's role in their family, the role of the birth family and the role of the child care and family placement social workers. Such differences were recognised by some but not all social workers, even though they were impacting on the placement in significant ways.

5   Birth families' accounts of events leading up to the separation

So far, the children's early experiences, the social work planning of the placements, and the circumstances and motivations of the foster carers have been examined. It was also an important objective of the research to understand the perspective of the children's birth families. Foster care research generally has not always included the voices and opinions of birth relatives (Berridge, 1997). It was vital to do this, even though other research experience has shown that this is not always an easy task. It is often hard for children and social workers to maintain good links with birth family members, although their importance is emphasised in the Children Act 1989, and generally recognised by social workers and families as necessary (Masson *et al*, 1997). It is also hard for birth family members who have had difficult relationships with professional agencies, to contemplate speaking to researchers, strangers from official sounding places, about why they no longer care for their children.

Children looked after inevitably come from families where there is likely to be a higher than average degree of change in family structure and circumstance. Many children have complex family backgrounds with a network of birth and step-parents, full and half-siblings, some of whom are cared for by extended family or adopted or in different foster homes (Fratter *et al*, 1991). This was true for the children in our project. Other research into children who return to their families after a period away has found that they are almost always returning to a differently structured family in terms of both adults and children (Bullock *et al*, 1993). Partnerships between children's original parents are dissolved and new ones begun. There may be other older children who leave or new children born. Families also move house and locality.

Social services departments are also subject to frequent restructuring and change of allocated caseworker, which contributes to the difficulty of knowing the whereabouts of the birth families and keeping in touch with them. In addition to this, as we have seen, many of the key family members have their own difficulties to cope with. It is hard for some of them to manage daily life and maintain contact with their children, let alone consider research studies and whether or not to take part in them. We found that it needed considerable detective work to locate and contact some of the families of the children, to inform them of the research and ask if they would agree to sharing their views. Having done this, those who did agree shared their experiences, opinions and feelings extensively and thoughtfully, and contributed a vital perspective.

Because it had been decided to include sibling groups in the project, the 53 children came from 42 families. In terms of availability to the research the families fell into four groups (see Table 5.1).

Table 5.1
Birth families' availability

Not contacted		Contacted	
Family not available	7	Refused interview	9
Family contact not advised	9	Interviewed	17

With two of these groups, accounting for 16 of the families, we did not make contact with family members. Seven of the children had no available family. This was because birth parents had died, their where-abouts were unknown or they did not want to take any part in the lives of the children, to have any contact with them or with social services. Two of these children had been placed for adoption, but the placements had disrupted. For the other nine families, a decision was taken in discussion with social workers not to request a meeting with family members. Two children's placements were considered too fragile, and two had parents who were too unwell to be interviewed. Social workers considered that the parents of the other five children were too violent and unpredictable to be asked to take part in the research. In all of these five cases, including two where parents had quite seriously assaulted social workers in the past, there was contact with their children.

For the remaining 26 families, at least one family member was located, informed about the research and asked to participate. In nine of these cases there was either no reply or a refusal, two of these parents saying that they would have found this too difficult and painful an experience. Eventually, 25 relatives from 17 families of 20 of the children were interviewed. This 40 per cent of families compares favourably with Rowe *et al* (1984) who interviewed 23 per cent, although her sample children were at least three years into placement and only a minority (21 per cent) had face-to-face contact, reducing the likelihood of continuing involvement.

The largest group interviewed were mothers (13) followed by grand-parents (8). In line with other research into the role of fathers (Bradshaw *et al*, 1999) fathers were the least available group and only two fathers and one step-father were interviewed. One older sibling at home was also interviewed.

Although the birth relatives whose views are reflected here were characterised in the main by having a continuing interest in the children, they covered a wide range: parents of children with severe disabilities; parents who had abused or neglected children; parents who had rejected children; parents with drug and alcohol misuse problems; parents with learning disabilities; grandparents who had not been able to cope with the full responsibility for children with difficult behaviours and some who had perhaps contributed to their grandchildren's difficult behaviours. Although this group of relatives tended to be those who were more co-operative with the social services department, it did include a number who felt angry and negative about their experience. The proportion of interview cases involving children on care orders (65 per cent) and children accommodated (35 per cent) roughly reflected the proportion in the sample as a whole. With the exception of the most violent parents and those who had abandoned the children entirely, it represented a reasonable cross-section of the families.

Birth relatives' responses to separation were extremely varied and not always easy to disentangle. Their responses were always a product not just of current circumstances but also of the difficult family histories that they shared with the children. Those who were interviewed were asked about their lives with the children while they were living in their families, what had happened before and up to the point when the children had left home, their experience of fostering, and their relationship both with foster carers and with social workers (their views on the placement are covered in Chapter 12). They were assured of the researcher's independent status and of confidentiality. They gave a range of accounts and opinions, but all of them, even if expressing anger or distress, seemed to appreciate the opportunity to put their point of view, and have someone listen to their story.

Early years

Families contain and transmit a wealth of information about family members. Many of those interviewed outlined the past family history of the children in a lively and vital way, full of details which were not apparent in interviews with social workers, and were unlikely to be on social services files. It is important that this source of material and information continues to be available to children. Family members could recall and describe in detail the children in infancy and early childhood, their looks and behaviour, and they often brought out photographs as they talked. They also gave clear descriptions of their early relationships, and the children's early years. It was striking how often early memories seemed to be at either end of the spectrum of good or difficult, rather than somewhere in the middle, suggesting a tendency to split children into good and bad rather than seeing them as a normal mix of both. For example:

She was very headstrong, had a rum temper on her. She was, she still is, hard work.

Or:

All he ever wanted to do was eat or sleep, and he never wanted to be cuddled. When he was awake he used to scream.

Compared with:

I was convinced she was an angel, and I know that sounds trite, but I was. She was just beautiful.

On the whole there were more memories of children described as likeable and lovable in very early years than otherwise, and memories of some expression of affection and physical contact. Two of the parents could recall very little of their early time with the children, referring to them as 'just normal really', or 'not a lot to say about her'.

It was clear from some of these accounts of early years that the difficulties which led to the eventual breakdown of care and the need for the children to be looked after were often present from these early times. Those interviewed had experienced a range of problems representative of the whole group of parents, and included those with learning difficulties, with a history of mental health problems, or drug and alcohol abuse, as well as those with past experience themselves of family abuse or breakdown, including periods of local authority care. Coping with these problems had used a lot of their energy and resources. With the exception of two children with severe disabilities, all of their children had experienced periods of deprivation while living at home. Many of their children had also suffered harm through neglect, physical, sexual or emotional abuse. In caring for some of the children there were also factors such as the child's own physical or learning disability which posed additional problems.

The families attributed their difficulties in parenting to a variety of causes. The parents of the two children with severe disabilities had found it impossible to continue to meet their extensive care needs at home, despite tremendous effort. Some of the other families, however, struggled to find reasons to explain their difficulties, coming up with several different explanations of the problems they had had. One mother went through several possible explanations for her difficulties with her daughter, including inherited temperament, or an as yet undiagnosed medical condition, such as Attention Deficit Hyperactivity Disorder (ADHD).

There was a tendency for some to minimise the experience of the children. For example, one mother described her partner as 'a bit heavy handed with the children', when in fact he had received a jail sentence for his assault on one of them. Grandparents were sometimes able to be a little more objective, although a grandparent of two children in care as a result of allegations of sexual abuse said:

We thought we were doing right by them, but the welfare thought different. He was just a bit overweight really.

It was hard for these parents to acknowledge that their own problems could have played a part in their inability to care for their children, and the honesty of this mother who had lived a chaotic life for many years because of her heroin addiction was rare.

Some of the things I done were dreadful. They certainly weren't the way you should look after a child. I think I must have moved house 30 or 40 times before she went where she is now, and I wasn't feeding her properly, just throwing a bag of crisps at her – do you know what I mean?

As they continued to describe their lives with the children, it was possible to see how stability and care could not be maintained. Families gave accounts of incidents of domestic violence, episodes of mental ill health, or periods of alcohol and drug abuse. Families and the children in them suffered the effects of disruption and of poverty. Some of the parents were so caught up in their own problems that they could not possibly have had enough energy to attend to their children's needs, such as this mother with longstanding mental health problems:

She didn't stand a chance really, what with me being ill and not knowing what the matter was, and in and out of hospital right from when she was born.

Others tried hard to keep things going, but found that their relationship with the children were becoming more and more difficult. It was possible to see patterns emerging of a variety of early difficulties, which affected the children in different ways. The description of many of the children showed the beginnings of the attachment problems and behavioural and relationship difficulties which could be traced on through their later histories. One grandmother described her grandson's acute anxiety whenever he was separated from her:

He used to have a feeling that I was going to die and leave him. He used to run out of school just to come and give me a kiss and to see if I was OK.

One mother described her inability to feel close to her daughter:

I just didn't feel motherly towards her, if anything I wanted to pretend she was a friend, my little mate. I used to just lean over her on the bed to feed her, sort of just about give her the breast, but not pick her up and cuddle her.

105

Whatever the origin of these difficulties, parents were describing early relationships which were not able to meet children's needs, and these initial problems in turn led to the beginnings of problematic behaviour in the children. Their reactive emotional and behavioural problems made for increasing levels of difficulty for everyone, both at home and at school, as shown in the following examples.

If you had a toy and gave it him, two minutes, three minutes and that's it. It would be hurled across the room.

She just wasn't mixing in with people like she should have done.

She'd stomp around slamming doors, just doing the opposite of everything we said.

The teacher couldn't handle him. He stuck a fork in one of the other children and then head-butted her.

A few of the parents recalled children showing levels of acute distress, threatening harm both to themselves and others. At the age of eight, Drew got into such extreme tantrums that he ran blindly across dual carriageways and jumped into stairwells, needing sedation to calm him down. Frank threatened to kill his baby brother, and laid traps with belts to trip family members on the stairs. The mothers of both these children described themselves as totally overwhelmed with the problems of trying to manage them safely. In other cases the parents seemed much less aware of the difficulties.

I really don't know why the social workers were making such a fuss. They kept saying he was neglected, but I was looking after them all right. I only ever smacked them lightly.

First experiences of seeking help

As the situation became more difficult, families sought various sources of additional help. Many of the mothers had felt very isolated. As might be expected they first looked for support from their own families and social networks. A few were able to gain some help here, including the parents of a child with severe disabilities who were helped by a large extended family and indeed the whole village community. Often, how-ever, family relationships were complicated and strained, and wider family networks were not available. Two mothers were only 16 when their first children were born. Neither of these had a supportive relation-ship with their own family. Older mothers too felt that there was no one to turn to. Jackie's mother felt trapped within her own family where she had been sexually and physically abused by her father and brother in her own childhood, and now feared for her own children's safety.

In other families it was at this point that some of the grandparents had become more actively involved in direct care of the children. Sometimes this help was seen as positive by birth parents, but at others it might create more problems. Jodie's grandmother and aunt had visited her mother several times, and supplied food parcels, becoming increas-ingly concerned about the care of her four children, without fully realising that there were problems with drug addiction. Finally they visited when there were no adults in the house, and the eldest daughter, aged seven, was caring for her three younger siblings. They took all the children back to the grandmother's home, beginning a period of conflict within the family over who should be the children's main carers.

As other research studies have shown (Quinne and Pahl, 1985), professionals, particularly social workers, are often the last source from which parents in difficulty seek help. The primary care provided by GPs and health visitors might appear more accessible, and this was certainly true for those parents whose children had disabilities, but parents were both bewildered and apprehensive at the thought of turning to social workers for advice.

I looked in the phone book to see what you are supposed to do, and it was like, well social services, and then you get all the different depart-ments and you think, well, what department do I want?

The consequences of seeking help were also unknown.

I was too afraid to ask for help. I needed a push to do anything about it. I was afraid for my other children and well, just afraid.

Some families did not have any choice about social work involvement. Concerns about the children meant that a referral was made from another source, and a social worker made contact anyway. Again, as in other research (Thoburn *et al*, 1995), whether the relationship between social workers and families began as a request for help or an official visit in response to a statutory duty did not always set its subsequent pattern. The reasons that social workers were found to be more or less helpful seem dependent on a range of factors, one of the most important being the worker's personality and approach. Both of these comments refer to social workers who responded to child protection concerns.

Mike was really there. He was friendly, he was warm, he was laughy. He was everything you didn't think a social worker was.

I felt I could build up a relationship with her. I phoned her up and just burst into tears, and she came over within half an hour.

The way in which families viewed the support that they had received at this stage varied. Some expressed regret or anger that, as they saw it, more had not been done to enable them to continue to care for the children.

I didn't feel as if they had helped in any way. They said we would have a family get together with the mediators, but we didn't.

She just kept looking in the cupboards to see what I was feeding them.

The few families who had received respite care felt this had been helpful, and family centres and parenting classes were also both mentioned very positively. Echoing the comments made in Teresa Smith's research (Smith, 1998), these were seen as non judgmental, and offering good practical advice on how to play with children, or manage difficult behaviour. Listening to peers experiencing similar problems was also seen as helpful.

Almost everyone interviewed expressed a need both at this stage and later for someone to support them in their own right. They believed that the social workers were primarily interested in the children, but felt that they too needed someone.

I just really wanted someone to talk to, to listen to me.

The Children Act Guidance does set out a duty of local authorities to see parents as people in their own right and to offer help. Some parents had found social workers helpful but for a few parents this help had been provided from an independent source such as a family centre or counselling service. Most remembered continuing to feel isolated and alone.

You think there is only you, and nothing like this has happened to anyone else, and you don't understand what is happening.

Family breakdown and separation

As described in Chapter 3, the routes by which children in the sample came to long-term foster care were very varied. The length of time they spent with birth parents, the number of early periods spent with other carers, kin, friends, or foster carers, the role of the courts, the age and circumstances at which the final separation to more permanent care happened, all made for a different experience in each family. Whatever the route to this separation, what emerged most clearly from the interviews was the emotional impact on mothers, fathers, grandparents and siblings, of the children moving away from family care. This was most often described in terms of grief and bereavement.

It's like a death, except there isn't a funeral.

It's like a grieving that just goes on and on. I can't believe how long it has been.

Mothers and grandparents who had had constant daily care of the children found the changes brought about by their absence bewildering and painful, and described all of the emotions common to the bereaved: anger, sadness, disbelief and despair.

I felt lost. One day I was the mother of three children, and then a mother with no children. There was nothing to do. I was lost, no children to look after.

I couldn't understand how I could bring someone up for eight years, and then he suddenly disappeared and was taken off. I didn't want him to be taken off.

The mother of two girls described the experience of living in the same house after her children had finally moved into long-term foster care.

I was in the same place for six months after they left. It was like their bedrooms were just as they left them. I didn't change the sheets. Her hairbrush was still in there, with hair in. It was just as if they had died . . . horrible.

One grandmother attributed her husband's heart attack to the loss of his grandchildren, and two of the mothers described feeling suicidal. One of them drove her car off the road 'because I just didn't know where I was at the time'. Another described walking along the canal:

I walked around thinking what am I going to do. I might just as well end it all and throw myself in.

The impact of this loss and attempts at its resolution were a theme which was returned to throughout the interviews. However difficult the relationship had been, whatever problems had been encountered, families, including the two siblings interviewed, expressed a strong sense of the child belonging, of being kin, which had been disrupted. The few family members who did not speak in this way seemed flat and unemotional when talking about other areas of their life also, almost to be denying any emotional connection at all.

The feelings of grief were present, however the separation had happened and whatever the degree of parental responsibilities for the harm suffered by the child. It did not seem to make any difference to their feelings whether the children had been separated by legal process and court orders, or been relinquished by voluntary agreement, although these were of course very different experiences. Court processes are bound to be difficult for families, as other research has shown (Freeman and Hunt, 1998). All those who had been involved in court cases had found them traumatic and anxiety provoking. Some had also borne financial costs. Proceedings had also disrupted relationships with social workers, and those who mentioned the guardian *ad litem* saw them as court officials and part of the establishment, not as a source of support.

She [the guardian *ad litem*] *said she wasn't taking sides, but I felt at the end of it she was. Because I thought, she's part of their system, so she is going to back the authorities all the way.*

There was a general feeling that it would not be possible to win the case:
I did everything they asked. But it seemed like the more I did, the more adamant they became that it wasn't working . . .

and that it was better to accept this than not:
What was the point of me fighting? My solicitor said, 'You aren't going to win against that lot'. I sounded like the mother from Hell. So I gave in and didn't fight.

The one positive result of a court case mentioned was that the decision was taken by a judge, which could then be given as an explanation to the child, and the family relieved of the burden of decision making, and possibly of blame.
I wanted to explain to her that it was the judge who had made the decision, and it didn't mean that we didn't love her or want her.

For others the court decision was the final straw, and they were left feeling angry and bitter, and with continuing resentment against the court and the social workers.
I hate them all, all social workers. They never done anything for me.

When the decision for the child to leave the family had been taken within the family, this had often been a difficult process. Anthony's mother sought help from child and adolescent psychiatrists as well as social services as his behaviour problems escalated to the point that she felt he was only safe when locked in his room. In the end she began to think that he would have to leave the family for the sake of her other children.
It felt like I had to have my arm cut off, but I decided yes, he had to leave the household.

Linda's mother coped with her serious physical and learning difficulties which included major epileptic fits. When she and Linda's father separated, she continued to care for her with respite support. However, with a new partner, and again pregnant, and with her daughter growing in size and strength she realised she could not manage any longer.

The reality really hit me after I had got pregnant. I thought, 'Oh my goodness, what am I going to do?' My husband said I had to make the decision, because he didn't ever want me to say to him that he had made me get rid of my daughter, which I understood. And so I did. I sat there, and then I rang the social worker, and she visited and explained it to me and I said, 'You had better find me a family then'. After she walked out the door I just burst into tears.

Some birth relatives were more able to accept and move on through the grieving process than others. This seemed to be related to the ability to recognise and understand their own feelings, and to order the experience intellectually. The ability to process their experience and move on seemed important in the subsequent relationship between the families and their children, foster carers and social workers. There were a few family members, including both mothers and grandmothers, who did not seem able to do this, but remained preoccupied with their own anger, grief or despair. One grandmother had cared for her grandson from 10 days after his birth, and had a very complicated and entangled relationship with him, which had continued through his separation and fostering. She would ask for extended stay contact, talk to him about how much she loved him, and then ask for him to be taken back within days of his arrival. She cried quietly throughout the interview, so that the messages to the researcher became as powerful and contradictory as they were to the child.

For others, these feelings of guilt and blame needed to be faced and accepted as well as the sadness. It helped if they could feel that they had done their best in their own estimation, whether or not this was understood by others. This mother agreed to a court order being made for her children after a period of separation.

I did give them up in the end, when it went to court. I felt guilty, but the guilt was less because I agreed to it. The social worker said to me that maybe one day I would put the children first, not myself. I was gobsmacked. I thought I was putting them first, letting them be fostered. If I didn't think that, how else could I give them up?

This mother's partner had allegedly physically abused her daughter:

I felt that eventually I had to make a choice between her and my husband, and I chose him. Nobody accepted that at all.

One mother with learning difficulties seemed to have accepted the fact that her children, who had been sexually abused by both parents, should come into care. She had wanted to end the cycle of sexual abuse in her family. She said that she had chosen her husband and didn't regret the decision.

They said we'll take the four kids and you keep your husband or you can have the children on your own. I said no, I don't want to do it that way. Michael's a trouble, Patricia's a trouble, you have the kids . . . I'm not going to break my marriage like that.

This couple were also very positive about the social work support and the contact, seeming to feel that caring for the children had been beyond them and almost relieved to be able to live the quiet life together which they enjoyed while still keeping in touch with the children.

Having someone to talk to during this time this had been appreciated, again the support often coming from a particular close friend or independent counsellor. The passage of time also brought change and acceptance for some, as this account from the mother of a severely disabled child shows.

I didn't understand what was happening to me, until my doctor put me in touch with a counsellor. She was brilliant. She made me understand that I wasn't depressed or mad, just grieving. As time is getting on I am gradually letting go. When she first left I wanted to be there all the time, go to all the doctor's appointments and school meetings, but now, it is OK not to. I have let go. I will sit and look at a picture and think, that is my two girls, my two daughters, but now I have only got one. Even though I go and visit her, that little girl I had is gone now.

If parents and grandparents did not accept this process of letting go it did not seem likely that they would be able to make a relationship with the children's new carers, and eventually to move into a new relationship with their child. They needed to accept that, although they no longer had continuous day-to-day care, they could remain important people in the child's life both practically and psychologically. For some of these families this was not going to be an easy task, and even managing parenting at some remove from the children would pose challenges. For others there seemed more hope that they would be able to achieve this, after the children had settled into their new placements.

All I ever wanted really was for him to be safe, and to know that I could see him sometimes, that he hadn't really left us for ever.

Summary

- Interviews were conducted with 25 birth relatives of 20 children. This group of relatives covered a wide range: parents of children with severe disabilities; parents who had abused or neglected children; parents who had rejected children; parents with drug and alcohol misuse problems; parents with learning disabilities; grandparents who had not been able to cope with the full responsibility for children with difficult behaviours and some who had perhaps contributed to their grandchildren's difficult behaviours.

- Although this group of relatives tended to be those who were more co-operative with the social services department, it did include a number who felt angry and negative about their experience. The proportion of children on care orders and accommodated was roughly the same as the sample as a whole. With the exception of the most violent parents and those who had abandoned the children entirely, it represented a reasonable cross-section of the families.

- The interviews reflected the diversity of family experience leading up to the separation of the children from the birth families and the different routes towards long-term foster care. Some questioned whether the right help had been offered to them once children became difficult but some also acknowledged that they hadn't always been good parents. Feelings of upset about court proceedings in particular lingered.

- There were similarities in terms of the sense of loss and sadness experienced by most birth relatives at the family breakdown. This was true whether children had been removed by court order or accommodated at the relatives' request. Several had the benefit of social networks or independent counsellors who offered support and understanding but some felt isolated and stigmatised.

- Birth family members, like the children, had to reflect on and manage their experience of loss and separation. They had to work towards a point where they could, to some degree, accept the children's move to a new life in a new family and be ready to work with carers and social workers.

Part II

Behaviour patterns and relationship building in the long-term placements

Introduction

At this point in the book, we move to look more closely at what is happening for the children in the long-term foster placements. Here the focus is on what we know about the children and carers, to see if we can make sense of *current* behavioural and relationship patterns. The information on which we based the analysis of the children's behaviour has come from a close reading of all the interviews, including the interviews with the children, the story stems, responses to puppets and so on. The descriptions of behaviour, accounts of specific incidents, the choice of words used to describe the children, how the children made carers and social workers feel, how they made us as researchers feel when we met them – all of this is the evidence on which we drew. For each case, transcripts were read by more than one researcher and classifications were agreed.

Although we are making some inevitable connections with the children's past experiences, the aim is to develop an understanding of the children's current cognitive, emotional and behavioural strategies in relationships. The children were coping with the situation in which they found themselves, separated from birth families and placed in a foster family with a plan for this to become their family for childhood, if not for life. But they were coping in ways which reflected different and distinctive patterns, adaptations which were attempts to survive loss, adversity, abuse or neglect in their birth families but which may prove maladaptive in other social contexts, such as at school, with peers and in the new family.

The theoretical framework used for the analysis of the different patterns is attachment theory. Even without the use of attachment category labels, we believe that the children could have fallen into the four patterns which are reflected in the four chapters that follow. However, since the questions we asked social workers and carers and the interviews with the children were targeted at eliciting attachment relevant information about, for example, how children showed their feelings or cope with stress, attachment theory has been used to understand the pictures that emerged.

Given the age range of the children, 4–12, there were difficulties in using formal attachment measures alongside our more qualitative material, so our classifications must be seen as tentative. We hope to demonstrate, nevertheless, that behaviour patterns can be observed and understood by practitioners utilising a range of fairly easily accessible methods and sources of information. Of the essence here is the need to look for evidence of patterns in order to explain current behaviours and relationships and anticipate future behaviours and relationships. Putting children in categories is less relevant in this sense for practitioners than using categorisations to aid understanding of the motivations and mechanisms that lie behind the individual child's behaviour.

The four categories into which the children's behaviour fell have been called "open book", "closed book", "on the edge" and "rewarding". The four categories, each explained in detail in subsequent chapters, reflect the different ways in which children showed their feelings of happiness, sadness and anger; how they responded to stress and anxiety; and how they responded to their foster carers' attempts to offer care and concern. The three children whom we have left unclassified were two four-year-olds, youngest in sibling groups and about whom the information seemed insufficiently detailed, and one child whose severe disabilities affected her behaviour in ways which made classification difficult. Because of the relatively small sample, the figures for each category (see below) should be seen as descriptive of this sample group, rather than necessarily reflecting proportions in the general population of children in long-term foster care.

Behavioural categories

	N = 53	%
Open book	14	26
Closed book	9	17
On the edge	17	32
Rewarding	10	19
Unclassified	3	5

The chapter on parenting began as an account of a number of parenting strategies which had been identified in the foster carers as they responded to the demanding behaviours of the children. Here again it seemed that using attachment theory, in this case Ainsworth's dimensions of parenting (1971), provided an excellent way of giving shape to the stories that had emerged and analysing the adaptive parenting strategies of the foster carers, as they attempted to remain sensitive and available in the face of almost overwhelming levels of need, confusion and distress.

Some carers showed certain characteristics, for example sensitivity, across a range of situations while others were more successful in some areas than others, for example, carers who were sensitive to the child's current needs but not so sensitive about the past and the birth family. For this reason we have decided not to formally rate carers on each dimension but to try instead to use the theory to analyse how different carers attempted to rise to the challenge of building relationships – providing a secure base in attachment terms – with the children.

6 Open book children

For one group of children, a remarkably similar range of adjectives cropped up in the accounts given by social workers and foster carers. They identified features which as researchers we were sometimes able to see in the children even on first meeting. These children could be bubbly, bouncy, fun children. Even when upset, their emotions were always on the outside. They were said to be an "open book" by their carers and we have adopted that term. Some children put their feelings into words but more often the children displayed their pleasure and anger, their hunger for affection and anxiety about rejection, in their faces and in their behaviour. They were preoccupied with relationships and used feelings to attract and hold on to the attention of others.

The bubbly picture did have a downside, however. That openness in the foster family, that sharing of feelings and looking for affection to carers, was too often accompanied by openness to any passerby, making the children vulnerable and worrying their carers. Within the family, the eagerness to please constantly could for some children become persistently clingy behaviour. That demand for reassurance was a constant reminder of their low self-esteem, and the desperation that lay behind it pointed to a deep well of need. Disappointment followed for the children when carers or peers inevitably could not match up to the hoped for unconditional love and children were said to "turn" – sometimes into "spitfires" who bit and kicked and yelled hurtful abuse.

These children were often very loud – if you took them on holiday or out for a hamburger, everyone would know that they were there. Across crowded swimming pools and supermarkets, these children made their presence felt. They were children who could also use these raised feelings to demand and insist, to persuade charmingly or coerce with threats of even worse, even louder behaviour. They were often very restless and active – having problems with concentration at school and with relaxing in front of the telly at home. Fun to be with perhaps, but enormously wearing. Some carers found the brightness and energy levels engaging and endearing while others, exposed to more of the rage and anger, found them so demanding as to drain their energies, to test their patience, and sometimes their sanity, to the limit.

In attachment theory terms, these were children with a predominantly *ambivalent-coercive* style of attachment. They attempted to achieve proximity by raised attachment behaviour, at times appealing for love directly and vociferously, at others being angry and coercive, when they felt that the unconditional love they craved was not available. These children had experienced unpredictable, under-involved caregiving which led to these persistently high levels of emotional demand. Unpredictable caregiving had also contributed to impaired thought processes. Feelings could be trusted but reason could not. Being safe meant being alert to the possibility of betrayal. Most children had experienced some level of fear in their history, associated with violence, sexual abuse, actual or threatened abandonment, parental drug taking and so on. This fear would have had a disorganising effect on their defensive strategies. They attempted to achieve proximity to caregivers with their coy and coercive behaviours but also to defend against anxiety with their high levels of activity.

So let us look in more detail at how these children fared in their placements. How did the children cope with their relationships in foster families? What were these children like to live with?

Showing feelings

When carers of these children were asked as a part of the interviews how each child showed certain feelings, they invariably began by saying the child was like "an open book". His carer said of Keith (6):

Foster carer: *When he's happy, he's the loveliest boy in the world. Totally enthusiastic, you can read him like an open book. There's no secrets with Keith.*
Researcher: *Would he come up and hug you?*
Foster carer: *No – Keith's never been cuddled. If you attempt to put your arms round him he'd sort of stiffen.*

Significant here in a way which needs to be kept in mind is that the expression of feelings, even the most positive, is generally on the children's terms. There is a recurring theme of displays of feelings used to produce certain reactions in carers. This is perhaps an inevitable consequence of children whose experiences in birth families were of needing to get the best from unpromising parenting and of children who, in some cases, have learned from moves in foster care that displays of feeling can bring about attention from stranger carers. Sometimes displays of even positive feelings can be wearing:

Researcher: *How does Kirsty show that she is pleased and excited?*

Foster carer: *She talks and talks about it – does not hold anything back. She can go really over the top. She's too demonstrative at times – she does everything to excess.*

But displays of negative feelings can overwhelm carers. Kirsty's carers were asked how they would know if she was upset.

Foster carer: *She screams and cries and gets aggressive.*

Researcher: *How does that make you feel?*

Foster carer: *Hurt. She knows it hurts and that's why she does it.*

For Kirsty's carers, the potential rewards of having an open book child were diminished by the sense that she was using her displays of positive feelings in a way that felt false and then used negative feelings to hurt them. They found the sheer strength of her feelings provoked strong feelings of their own of anxiety and hurt.

The fact that strong feelings get expressed can often mean a range of behaviours, of which actually communicating in words might not be the first.

Researcher: *How does Leanne show that she is feeling upset?*

Foster carer: *By being loud, miserable, abusive . . . she can't say, 'I've had a dreadful day' or 'No-one would play with me' . . . but later on if I give her a little bit of extra time at bedtime, it will all come tumbling out. But mostly she takes it out on me first. She speaks to me in such a way that it is so insulting. She is very abusive, verbally, personally. It's not nice but I have to bear it. Sometimes I think she drains me dry.*

Just as feelings may be revealed apparently openly but often strategically, so pieces of information will also spill out rather selectively.

Foster carer: *Susie is sometimes very forthcoming, but sometimes won't let on about something. For example, she tells me about falling in and out with friends but didn't tell me when a little boy put his hand down her knickers.*

For a child who has disclosed sexual abuse from a birth relative, this pattern of selective communication of information is not likely to be random. However, explanations could range from the possibility that for Susie (10), sexual activity is secret and fearful or expected and not worth mentioning.

Often this pattern of displays of feeling but selective disclosure of information was quite clearly revealed in the research interviews with the children. Tracey, aged nine, greeted the researcher with a big smile, warmth and enthusiasm as she hurtled down the stairs carrying her foster carer's baby grandson. She was excited and pleased to start the interview. Within a minute or two she was off to show the researcher her things – piles of photographs of herself in her foster family, video recordings of herself at a ballet school performance with her foster sister. Like a number of other children in this category, she talked a great deal about people she knew, babies she liked and so on, but was not "open" to questions or direction and steered clear of too much talk about her birth mother and the siblings her mother still cared for at home. Explanations for this selectivity could range from the possibility that she is so deeply involved in her foster family's life that they are now more vivid and important to her than her birth family (one hypothesis) through to the likelihood that Tracey keeps a secret part of her mind in which all that sense of hurt, rejection and longing about her birth mother is hidden away. The presentation is thus bright and breezy, if confused and frenetic. Such presentations may offer the social worker false reassurance, although in this case the social worker was well aware of Tracey's troubled thoughts.

Preoccupied with relationships: bubbly and sentimental but angry and coercive

Openness, as in Tracey's case, often seems to be associated with other key adjectives – in particular "bright" and "bubbly". "Bubbly" became such a common description in the research interviews that it almost seemed instantly diagnostic of this particular category. Gavin's social worker's pen picture of him was:

Gavin is bright and bubbly, ready smile, inquisitive, talkative and very busy, flying about . . . He greets me enthusiastically.

His foster carer gave a similar picture:

He's a cheerful, lively, funny, lovely little boy. That's one of the first things you notice about him really, his sense of humour – lovely.

Gavin, aged six, had a history of very poor care when young from his mother. Neglect, emotional abuse and domestic violence were part of his experience from birth until his admission to care at the age of three. So, striking to most observers of these children is not only their "bubbliness" but also the inevitable contrast with histories of abuse and harmful experiences. These are children whose carers and social workers are impressed by how cheerful the children are in spite of their experiences. As a learned behaviour, this bright presentation has clear protective qualities. The experience of having a mother who is only very rarely emotionally available and who has a violent partner who needs to be placated, would make the ready smile and the upbeat approach a necessary strategy for gaining her positive attention and avoiding his anger. The word "bubbly" seems also to be associated with a sense of an ongoing performance, a persistent use of positive affect to increase the likelihood that adults will give them care.

Commonly, though, accounts were given of bubbly children for whom there is a very big *but* – there can be a drastic switch to negative behaviours and attitudes to carers which sometimes makes it hard for them to hang onto the positive feelings that the bubbliness evoked. For these children, the bubbliness at times has something rather false and sentimental about it. Expressions of love for carers can too easily switch to hate and rage. It was common for these children to be preoccupied with relationships – needing to be with others and getting constant feedback from others and yet jealous, resentful and prone to outbursts of rage when other people, particularly carers but also potential friends, were perceived as letting them down.

Emma, nine years old, with a birth family history of scapegoating, rejection, physical assaults and probable sexual abuse, had developed what is in some respects an affectionate relationship with her carer. Emma would say, 'I love my Diane,' to her foster carer but also, 'I hate you, you're a witch. I don't want to live in this stinky house with a stinky lady.' What is more, Emma's carers had doubts about the depth of their relationship, when these switches of mood occurred. This was reinforced by her sense that, even after two years, Emma would still go off with any stranger with a bag of sweets. Although it appeared that Diane was offering Emma commitment and reliable, affectionate care, the anxiety remained that for Emma, relationships were likely to remain shallow in significant ways as she continued to struggle with the demons of past experiences of which she was able to make no sense.

Although there are some boys in this category, there seemed to be a strikingly similar group of girls. For these girls the switch of mood was the biggest challenge for them and their carers. Stephanie's carer said of her:

At her best she is lovely, warm and affectionate. But she can be a regular spitfire with glowering looks to go with it.

She was described by her social worker:

She has a bouncy, generous streak. Would give you anything, full of energy. But she can be unco-operative if you push the wrong button.

Both Emma and Stephanie's carers were extremely fond of them and found that their warmth and energy were appealing enough to enable them to develop a relationship which could just about survive the consequences when the wrong button is pushed. But there were some girls and carers for whom the battles were almost too bitter to allow for recovery and healing.

Anna was a seven-year-old child whose mother had mental health problems. She was placed with her older brother, who was more settled in this placement. Anna was described by her social worker as a 'bubbly little girl' in an excellent placement where the guardian *ad litem* was able to report that she had "blossomed". This may be true but the carers raised some of their own concerns.

Anna is a complicated child. She is small for her age – a non-stop chatterbox. She has two sides – street angel, home devil. At home she is stubborn, has a temper, can be very hurtful. Attention seeking, very jealous. She blows hot and cold and has a short fuse.

The imagery here is very striking and highlights one of the main differences for some of these children which may prove to make or break placements in the longer term. Some children appear to show their best side, both their capacity for warmth and their capacity to live within reasonable boundaries, to their carers. It frustrates their carers that the children are so wild at school but it also gives them some cause for satisfaction. One carer told us with pride that the headteacher had said that he wished they could have a cardboard cut out of her at school since the child's behaviour was so much better whenever she was around. But Anna's carers are faced with the fact that the world sees the bright and bubbly exterior, a gift to strangers, whereas they who care for her every day cope with the rages and the moods. The hurtfulness for the carers is clear and for Anna, the favoured child of her birth mother, the contrast in being the least appealing of her siblings in this family probably adds to the level of her own hurt and sense of loss and fuels the intensity of her rages.

Many of these children used their shows of anger to force concessions from their foster carers. Where children were young or it felt as if the situation remained in the control of the carers, this was not too troublesome.

Foster carer: *There's no malice in it and Greg doesn't mean it but he's very bossy. If I'm hoovering he'll say, 'I can't see the television,' or 'You're making too much noise!' We just take it with a pinch of salt – he's probably got it from his older sisters. But he does like to be leader of the gang.*

Similarly for some carers, children's shows of anger were somehow acceptable. This carer found this six-year-old's anger easier to handle than other emotions:

He gets angry but he's not sad – a lot of children in care have this overwhelming sadness and that's very hard to live with.

For some of the children, the sense of burning anger and resentment was an occasional flash but for others, it seemed never far away and could mean children going "berserk".

Foster carer: *Helen fell off the breakfast bar and she went absolutely mad – the chairs went, the stools went, everything went off the table, kicking the patio doors . . . all this anger.*

In these children's rages, not only toys but furniture went flying, making the children expensive to keep. Dinners got thrown on the floor when homework was mentioned. Some carers experienced direct assaults. When asked what happened when Mary got angry, her carer said:

She will shout. She used to lose it completely, bite, scratch, hit. She doesn't do that now. She will shout, slump down on her bottom, fold her arms, say 'I'm not going to,' then the thumb goes in the mouth. If I can't defuse the situation, then the tears and screaming will start.

Even when carers felt they had made some headway, the possibility of rages was never far away. For some children, these feelings were said to be connected directly with feelings about being fostered. When Sally got jealous, she had threatened her previous foster carers that her mother would come and kill them if she wasn't allowed to do what she wanted. She saw her mother as her protector but also as dangerous and violent. Since she identified so closely with her birth mother, it was not surprising that extreme anger for her meant extreme retribution. Her current carers felt quite upset by her anger and stubbornness:

We send Sally to her room, tell her to calm down. We can hear her shouting and screaming but she stays there. She won't give in, she's very stubborn. She comes downstairs but she hasn't really given in. We've taken away privileges, pocket money. We know when she has got over it – she comes for a cuddle.

A battle like this is exhausting and particularly wearing if at the end of it you feel that you haven't won – and even the cuddle sometimes feels suspiciously like a concession or a placation rather than a relationship. Preoccupation with relationships mixed with the need to be in charge caused havoc with friendships. These children would claim to have hundreds of friends and large numbers might be invited to birthday parties. Often, though, they had no real friends and other children found them difficult to be around, with this "love you one day/hate you the next" approach. Every day was a drama, with children apparently lacking any sense of how to negotiate and co-operate within relationships.

Foster carer: *Neil's got this very loud voice, very loud personality. We thought he was being bullied at this school but when I went into it, he was drawing this attention to himself. He'll call people names and when they retaliate he comes home and says they said this to me. And the school know now that Neil has made himself a target. Not just for his own group but for everybody. And they're all sort of teasing . . . but Neil's bringing it on himself. You try to sit down and explain it to him but . . .*

Researcher: *So it's hard at school?*

Foster carer: *But it can happen anywhere. He can go swimming tonight and he can get into a fight. He'll call someone a name. He doesn't know how to deal with people.*

Unfortunately for Neil (10), accurate though this description may be, the behaviour is beyond his conscious control. He lacks the self-esteem, empathy for others and co-operative strategies which would help him negotiate friendships. Unfortunately, the fact that he is thought to be doing it "deliberately" may cut him off from sympathy and support.

The children's needy but angry preoccupation with relationships included in most cases, inevitably, a preoccupation with birth families. Some of the children had been favoured at home and others had been scapegoated, but whatever the dynamics of the situation, all in this group had been exposed to unpredictable and chaotic parenting, with some children exposed to added ingredients of fear and anxiety about violence, abuse, or threats of separation. Although the children were now settled or beginning to settle in foster families, almost all carers felt that given the choice they would want to be back with their birth families.

Foster carer: *Ideally he'd like to be with his mum, but I think he's happy being here. It's a second choice. I don't think he's thinking about it every day but if you were to sit him down and say who do you want to live with, it would be mum but I think he's very happy here.*

These children, because of their extreme neediness to be in a relationship, were sometimes drawn into close relationships with foster carers and became very preoccupied with them also. But in their minds, reconciling the multiple loyalties, particularly when they have a tendency to split significant others into the good guys and the bad guys, created conflicts that could not easily be resolved. In the foster homes, this contributed to both the sense of falseness at times in the bright facade and the extent of the anger when foster carers slipped into being the bad guys. Some children resisted being drawn into relationships with foster carers at all, preferring to preserve the idealised relationship with the birth parent and cast the foster carer in the role of the enemy or the abductor. Even where close relationships developed, children were left with some very serious questions. Several children constantly wanted to know how it was that they were in foster care because 'mum can't look after me' while their mother looked after younger siblings.

Hungry for love and eager to please

The children's preoccupation with relationships was pretty firmly rooted in a preoccupation with the big questions, 'Am I lovable and will you love me?' alongside the inevitable, 'Why did my mummy and daddy not love me enough to keep me?'

Not surprisingly for needy children with a history of deprivation, food often became a real and symbolic focus of their hunger for love. Carers were aware of these links and Paul's carer's said:

Paul has known what it was virtually to starve. They come from a very deprived background. They lived in a house with no food, they'd be lucky if they had a packet of biscuits between the three children.

It was often useful to ask carers what children were like after school:

> *She loves it, she comes running in and that's always arms round me, love you Pat, so I think she's really pleased to see me. She looks forward to coming home and that's a drink and biscuit then an hour later there's tea . . . and her life revolves around food. She's always, always hungry and when she gets up in the morning, she'll ask what she's having for dinner at night and even Sunday she'll say, 'Is it roast today?' and I say, 'What do we normally have on a Sunday? Roast!'* [laughs].

Feeding oneself, being fed and feeding others all feature food as a key symbol and currency of love. At her interview, Sharon rushed to open the door to the researcher and offered to share her chocolate bar. A number of these children were overweight, though not severely, and a number were teased at school as a result. However, it was not something carers could deal with in too much of a hurry so early in placements and while children were still so young.

A common strategy for winning love and pleasing others was to become a caregiver. Sharon is ten years old and had a history of being the favourite youngest child in a family where older children had disclosed sexual abuse. Her parents had moderate learning disabilities and she had at the very least experienced neglect. Coming into care as a four-year-old she was placed with an older brother. This placement ended after four years in which she had been increasingly seen as the problem child. She was moved at short notice to a newly approved short-term foster carer, with her brother remaining in the previous placement. In her pen picture, her carer described Sharon as:

> *Very caring, very helpful, always there and ready to help. Loving, affectionate but still quite low self-esteem. The more you praise her – she just won't accept it.*

Her social worker described her as:

> *Lively, bubbly, in some senses extroverted, in some sense lacking in self-esteem/self-worth . . . She is adaptable, very caring.*

For Sharon, the best chance, as she clearly saw it, of making herself appealing and avoiding further rejection was to be alert to opportunities to be helpful, an adaptive strategy brought from the birth family but continuing to be useful – even in winning the approval of the social worker.

Being eager to please in this way was appealing to carers even though, as with Sharon's carer, they recognised its origin in low-self esteem. But it also caused some concern if only because it spilled out in the impulsive, undiscriminating way we would expect of these fragile children. This is one foster carer's account of her nine-year-old foster child.

She is quite a sweet girl I must admit. She does come over as a lovable child. She is perhaps too lovable to strangers who knock at the door, especially male . . . always got to stroke. She's crying out for affection. She really wants to be loved. She's ALWAYS saying to me, do you love me? Do you love me? And if she's done something wrong, Don't you love me anymore? I say, Of course I do – just because you've done something wrong doesn't mean I don't love you.

Her social worker said of this child:

She's got very low self-esteem, she's always asking you, 'Have I been a good girl, Janet? Tell [foster mother] I've been a good girl at mummy's.' She has a great fear of failure and of losing the foster carer.

The children's perception of themselves in our interviews often echoed the preoccupation with 'caring' as described by others. This is generally reflected in their rather sentimental accounts of themselves as 'kind' and 'caring'. Anna (8) talks of another child as being 'a really special person'. A friend at school is described as someone who is 'always there for me' and 'looking after me'. She talks of herself as a caring person and most girls and some boys in this group had adopted this as a way of valuing themselves.

Significant in this respect was the way in which a number of these girls were particularly caring about and interested in babies. Ann (9) and Stephanie (10) were intensely interested in the babies which their carers mind or have fostered short-term and their carers' grandchildren. With these babies they demonstrated practically to themselves and others what caring children they were and these infants rewarded them by smiling at them and allowing themselves to be carried about. For Stephanie's carer, who had been tested by the level of her emotional demands, this was reassuring and was testament to the fact that Stephanie could give as well as take. It even made some respite for her. She said, 'Stephanie helps me with them and doesn't mind little ones getting my attention as long as she gets her fair share'.

For boys, the fact that they could be gentle and loving with babies and little children was also special, not only in terms of their sense of themselves but also in what it meant to the carers. Michael, who could be so wearing and impulsive, was devoted to his carer's grandchild and this relationship had become part of the glue that sealed Michael's place in the family circle. Significantly for such a young child, only six years old, he was even able to articulate something of this, saying to his carer about her daughter and granddaughter, 'I'm so lucky that Sue had Janey,' a remark that endeared him to them even more. These children all had younger siblings who were being cared for at home or in other place-ments, so the experience perhaps enhanced their sense of themselves as valued big brothers and sisters. Alternatively, it allowed them to defend themselves against their feelings of envy towards their birth siblings.

Although this interest in babies may seem similar to other children of their age, the meaning of babyhood to these children who had experienced such damaging infancies and lost mothers and fathers as a result, could not be that simple. This was revealed most clearly in the children's own interviews, though often through references to baby animals or other indirect routes. Unconscious preoccupations with mother and babies were often linked to what were probably bigger questions about where babies come from. For children to whom distinc-tions between multiple mothers, only one of whom was a "birth" mother, were confusing, such questions would not be surprising. Michael, who was so fond of his carer's grandchild, talked about Midnight, the family rabbit, who was sitting very still in the garden.

She hasn't got any babies . . . I bet she's 'tending . . . Bet she's thinking she's got some babies . . . but she hasn't.

Tracey talked about all the previous baby boys in the foster home, over and over again, and showed the researcher the photographs, saying 'Ah, isn't he lovely!' Even when she played the video of her ballet performance she said repeatedly, 'Listen, that's Liam crying – you can hear, he's making a noise again!!' She then said, 'You know Stacey? She had her babies but they're stuck in her tummy and they can't get out!'

Tracey's interest in babies, where they come from and how they get out, was accompanied by her frequently expressed wish to have babies herself as soon as she's older – and her preoccupation with boys, kiss chase and so on. Her liveliness is often flirtatious and seductive and her interest in babies betrays her confusion about sexuality and whether she is a mummy or a baby, alongside other issues of life and death. When asked about memories of her childhood, she said that she had been 'as good as gold' when she was a baby but then became naughty, 'a little pain'. She was asked what she did when she was naughty.

I was got all the breakfast down, went to the shop on my own. With my buggy and my baby. My mummy will send me to bed. Boohoo mummy. Just mummy, mummy dead.

Her stream of consciousness speech makes unconscious thoughts and connections more available and gives some indication of the anxious internal world behind the bright exterior.

Restless, loud, impulsive with poor concentration

Very distinctive of these children, and a characteristic that caused them and their carers a great deal of difficulty, was that they were rarely still – they rushed about, flew round, knocked things over and generally caused mayhem. This restlessness and impulsivity created many problems for their functioning at home, at school and with their peer group. This was often part of the major "but" that followed after the description of the child as "bubbly". Lynette's social worker said:

She draws people – she has an attractiveness about her which people respond to but she's a damaged little girl and has very poor concentration, moves from one thing to another. In one way she's a delight – in another way she tests people to the utmost.

The foster carer used another favourite epithet – scatty – which might be thought of as rather a euphemism but captures the attempts carers made to put a positive spin on these difficult behaviours:

She's very scatty. Hyperactive I think she is. Fidgety – can't sit still. Always talking. No concentration. Very loud.

Lynette had been diagnosed as having ADHD and was prescribed ritalin for a period by a psychiatrist. Both the carer and her school teachers felt that this then lost them the "real" Lynette. On ritalin she was quieter but also tearful and sad. 'She was a depressed child. She sat and cried and that wasn't Lynette.' They found the smiley, scatty Lynette easier to relate to, but one might speculate about how ritalin had taken away a major defensive strategy and left her in some real distress.

There was an understanding among some carers that this level of activity was connected to children's experiences of chaotic households in the birth family, with children running about and on the streets uncontrolled and unsafe, but also connected to their current experiences of anxiety. Such anxiety would break through the smiley exterior and need to be fended off. Sue's foster carer said:

Sue's a happy little girl but there's always something lurking under the surface and it doesn't take much for it to bubble up. She is very loud and exuberant. We do a lot of dog walking in wide open spaces, so she can let off steam, shout and scream and really let go. If she's been able to do this, she is generally quieter. If she's high with anxiety she often needs some physical activity to release it.

This alternative use of the bubbly metaphor makes helpful connections between the bubbliness of champagne, perhaps, when these children are at their best and the bubbliness of volcanoes where levels of heat/anger/anxiety build up and have to burst out somewhere, when these children are at their most explosive and challenging.

For some children, these high levels of activity are not only or not necessarily to let off steam but have a range of functions. Again, this was vividly represented in the children's interviews. Children flitted back and forth and effectively avoided difficult issues and in some cases took control. They told us a lot but mainly what they wanted to tell us in between emptying all the videos on the floor or bringing out their own dolls and puppets or going through every school book in their possession.

Some children used a mix of such activities with other kinds of controlling strategies.

Samantha's interview was dominated by a combination of flitting in and out of the room and her use of sweeties. (Note again here the link to food as control and currency in relationships.) She fetched things to show and plied the researcher endlessly with sweets, pictures and presents. The sweets seemed to have various functions: sweeties to placate, sweeties to impress, sweeties to please, sweeties to control. Sweets were given for the researcher to give to other children in the project. Samantha even made the researcher a sweetie holder to take the sweeties home in and instructed her on what she must say to the children. The flow of sweeties into mouths and between child and adult seems to suggest poor boundaries. In feeding the researcher, Samantha was also feeding herself, roles merged and switched between adult and child, mother and baby – reflected in a role play which Samantha spontaneously set up in which the researcher was instructed to play the defiant child to her stern mother. She made links between herself and the researcher's 'other children', at home and in the research. This could be a form of rivalry but seemed also to reflect her chaotic inner world, in which boundaries between people are unclear and her self is merged, unintegrated. In the frenetic activity of the interview, all this span round together, bits flying out as in a centrifuge, with the researcher attempting to locate the stop button. This was also the carer's experience.

For some particularly disturbed children, the activities could take on an obsessive/compulsive aspect. When she was first placed, one child needed to go to the toilet dozens of times before going to bed. She wouldn't settle during this period and whenever the carer said no, she would scream and scream. She could scream abuse for three hours at a time. With this kind of behaviour, the child becomes almost impossible to reach, being lost in her own nightmarish world.

Some children appeared to talk compulsively, as if this was a symptom of their poor impulse control and need for activity and constant stimulation. For Jamie (6), this was felt by the carers to be a major problem. He was said to talk about anything, or nothing – rubbish – over and over. For others, the talk would focus on a particular thing.

When it's Halloween or Christmas, Jamie would go on and on constantly – he gets obsessive and he's talking about it all the time. Over and over.

For all of these children, high levels of activity were associated with poor concentration on the task in hand. At home this might reveal itself in small ways. Jamie would go upstairs to get a jumper and then sit there in his own world, as if in a trance. At school, however, poor concentration was causing serious problems which were often much harder to shift than other behaviours.

Jamie's biggest problem is concentration and I can't really say that's improved a lot. This year, at least, he's sitting down at a table – last school year he was getting up and wondering around – he couldn't sit at a task.

For children like Jamie and most others in this category, the combination of physical restlessness with mental lack of concentration made school life very hard. At the very least school work suffers, but for many of these children they were also seen as having serious behaviour problems and a number of children had either been excluded from school, or were almost constantly under threat of exclusion. Although in some ways easier to cope with than bad behaviour targeted at the carers, it was a situation which was also very hard for carers to manage. Eleven-year-old Neil's carers felt that they were constantly on to him from the time he got in about homework and phone calls received from school. Yet they realised he simply couldn't cope. Even keeping up with the basics defeated him since he moved to secondary school and there would be angry outbursts at teachers.

It's just his temper, exasperation – he can't cope, can't handle it . . . He's got a lot more to contend with now, his schooling. A lot of it is he always loses things, his homework, diary . . . this is all pressure. The teachers give him extra, it's all pressure and it's too much for him.

For a number of these children there were acknowledged learning difficulties and one or two had had IQ tests to measure their intellectual deficits. These children were more likely to be in special units or getting some limited extra help in mainstream school. But for others it seemed to us that there needed to be a more careful assessment of their learning difficulties. Children struggling in mainstream school often gave indications that their thought processes were distorted and they found it hard to make sense of even simple things. Neil (11), for example, had great difficulty remembering significant street routes around the area where he lived. However often they were explained to him, he seemed to be unable to remember even simple directions. For such children, the behavioural factors, such as activity levels and attention problems, may well be compounded by learning difficulties of diverse kinds. It is impossible to know whether these were genetic or environmental but it may well be both. A number of their parents had learning difficulties and early caregiving experiences were of unpredictable, chaotic and often confusing worlds, where two plus two probably did not make four in any predictable way.

Risk-taking behaviour

One of the major concerns arising from children's openness, eagerness to please and impulsiveness was that children would put themselves at risk physically and sexually. Even though attempts were being made in a minority of cases to address this through therapy, it seemed a complex phenomenon. One social worker described the situation for one eight-year-old:

> *She has had play therapy for two years to help her calm down, to understand where she is, to play out what's troubling her, to learn about safe boundaries in her sexual behaviour and physical behaviour. But she is a very boisterous child and puts herself at risk. At therapy she goes up the stairs and sits on the window sill and plays with locks and then she'll jump down half the staircase.*

Although the social worker felt that the carer was providing the necesssary 'vigilant care', there were times when even in the house this was not easy.

> *There's no containing her really. She gets very excited. Like they'll be in the kitchen dancing – she'd fall into the tables or up against the patio doors – she has no sense of danger. She's such a vulnerable child. She'd go off with someone who knocks on the door and offers*

her a bag of sweets. If you'd been here this morning she would have gone with you. She is such a vulnerable child. That's why I can't let her play out. There's so many dangers for her.

Another similarly vulnerable child (8) had shown some quite serious risk-taking behaviour. Apart from approaching strangers without discrimination, she jumped into the deep end of a swimming pool after being told by the carer that it was deep and dangerous. The foster carer said: 'The attendants didn't see her. By the time I reached her she was going under for the third time.' When out in the park the child was warned by her carer not to take her shoes off because of broken glass but she carried on and had to have stitches in her foot.

Not only did the children seem willing to risk danger but sexual abuse had left some of them more sexualised, and emotional damage and low self-esteem had left all of them more likely to be easily led and suggestible.

Fearful fantasies

In spite of the bubbly facade that these children displayed and risk-taking behaviour that suggested they disregarded dangers, for some children there were signs that their internal worlds were rather fearful. Risk-taking can be understood as a defence of invulnerability in the face of fears.

Paul (6) was quite obsessed with violence – police sirens and broken windows, and police cars taking people away. I think he's witnessed people being arrested. This has decreased . . . The obsessions with the dark things have gone.

Although this improvement was apparent in some aspects of the child's interview, these concerns surfaced in one of the story stem completions. When faced with the story of the boy, Jim, who gets lost while out shopping with his mum, Paul described how a stranger came along and put Jim in his house and Jim had to escape. The stranger gets thrown in jail but reappears and starts knocking people down. The stranger is then back in jail but reappears and tricks people by pretending to be shopkeeper. The story does not get properly resolved with all the family going home but then 'falling down', except for dad. Dangerous people who cannot even be held in jail feature, but protective parents do not. Children also revealed preoccupations with supernatural figures such as witches. Such themes may not be necessarily revealed in ways that one would expect. During her interview, the first thing Helen said was:

You know Cliff Richard – we've got his CD. It's got Devil Woman on. You know next door to us, you know Flopsy the rabbit, he went over there yeah, well . . . you know that lady she came out and said get that stupid rabbit out of my house! Out of my garden!

Later in the interview, out of the blue she asked if the researcher liked the Wizard of Oz.

Helen:	*You know that ugly witch, she locks Toto up.*
Researcher:	*What happens to the witch at the end?*
Helen:	*She's dead.*

Later out of a pile of videos she picked one:

The Witches! I hate that! I hate that! When this witch takes off her mask, and she's all lumpy and bumpy and disgusting!

These diverse links, even to the extent of including the Cliff Richard song that does not use the word "witch", and the account of the "witch" next door, was very striking. It gave the impression also of a child whose thoughts run on along their own unconscious tracks, which makes it unsurprising that she finds it so hard to focus on school work.

Helen's story stem narratives dwell on the subject of babies, as she does throughout the interview, but this time the babies are crying and then one baby dies. In her story stem completion for the spilled drink scenario, she said:

Look at me baby [Crying baby noises]. Mummy, baby, baby! All the grown ups come and the baby is fast asleep. Oh my gosh! What's happened to the baby? It's dead because everybody had to crowd round it.

In the lost child story, she switched to her own story.

Pretend the baby's got stuck and it couldn't get down.

Helen with no prompting, in fact with the researcher trying to gently encourage her to complete some of the planned material around family relationships, spilled out her muddled and confusing world of witches and dead babies. She was familiar to social workers and carers as a bubbly child, who could be both hyperactive and coercive. These behaviours are attempts to protect herself from experiencing both her fears and her losses to be able at some level to feel safe.

Another dead baby appeared in Samantha's response to the picture of a child standing next to a mother feeding a baby:

Samantha: *He's sad because his mum loves the baby and not him.*
Researcher: *So what might happen next?*
Samantha: *He will strangle the baby* [said without emotion].

Conclusion

Children who show these patterns of behaviour are vulnerable in a number of significant ways. Their behaviours are challenging and yet they are not children who can learn easily from experience or from instruction. They are driven by feelings – reason is not trusted, only emotion appears to work for them. They need boundaries to keep them safe and to contain anxieties but they will continue to coerce and demand to be loved. Carers often found such children engaging initially, because of their affectionate overtures, and rewarding because of their transparent neediness. Over time, the test will be whether behaviours will settle down or whether what is seen as exuberance with the occasional tantrum will be as acceptable in an older child or teenager.

Summary

Characteristics of open book children
- Showing feelings;
- Preoccupied with relationships: bubbly and sentimental but angry and coercive;
- Hungry for love and eager to please;
- Restless, loud, impulsive and with poor concentration;
- Risk-taking;
- Fearful fantasies.

In attachment theory terms

These children use a predominantly ambivalent/coercive strategy but experiences of fear and abuse mean that they have disorganised features and trauma remains unresolved. In relationships with foster carers they can be rewarding because of their shows of emotion and need for closeness. But they are also very draining, because of the constant switch from needy to coercive and sometimes out of control behaviour.

They may cause concern

- In the foster home, because they can provoke carers or wear them out. Their preoccupation with demanding but unpredictable birth families may also be a source of stress.
- At school, because of their lack of concentration, restlessness, confused thoughts and stormy, love–hate relationships with peers (and teachers).
- In the community, because they are too often risk-taking and needy/angry/indiscriminate in relationships.

7 Closed book children

Some of the foster children appeared to be holding on to their feelings. Reluctant to share happy feelings and even more reluctant to share their worries and fears with carers, they were making it very difficult for carers to get close. These children can be quite compliant and in some situations hold themselves together and act appropriately. Indeed they may be described as really nice, well-behaved children.

But they have to be the best. They find it hard to admit that they need others or need to learn. They like to be in charge. Some will be prone to violent outbursts if it becomes too painfully clear that they may not be best or in charge but are in fact rejected by their birth family and powerless. Feelings of anger or distress might burst out but not in ways which allow them to be soothed or comforted. On the contrary, at times the anger is another way of keeping other people at bay. Some children, however, continue with rather a flat, shut off manner, avoiding the risk of intimacy.

The avoidant/defensive strategies we are describing here break down for a number of the children. Only a few children with such histories of abuse, neglect and repeated separations can, for example, successfully retreat from feelings into mental processes such as achieving success at school. Children who have been physically frightened or emotionally rejected – particularly those singled out for rejection – are likely to find that disorganising experiences of unsafe caregivers have led to confused thought processes. They are also often too anxious to be able to accept the authority of teachers or make friends comfortably.

As Howe *et al* (1999) put it, for these children felt security is achieved by over-reliance on the self and under-reliance on other people. For fragile, powerless children this is hard to sustain. When these children face story stem completion tests they tend to do what they do in life: 'they immobilise the attachment system by systematically scanning, sorting and excluding fear, pain and sadness from conscious awareness' (George, 1996, p. 415). Unfortunately for a number of these children, experience of abuse had left painful memories which intruded. For others, placement moves and contact with parents who continued to reject and hurt them emotionally forced pain and loss past these tentative defences. In attachment terms, therefore, although we have grouped these children as having significant *avoidant* characteristics which impact on the relationship building process in the foster homes, trauma is largely unresolved and they might more accurately be described as disorganised children for whom avoidant is the 'best fit' (Howe *et al*, 1999).

Closed and guarded

Douglas is ten years old and is the oldest of three children. He was sexually abused by both parents and still shows signs of sexualised behaviour, although he has been looked after for two years, 15 months of which is in the current placement. His foster carer observes:

Foster carer: *Douglas wants to keep people at a distance. When he first came he would hide under beds, hide in wardrobes. He still finds it hard to let people get close.*

His social worker also finds it hard to get close and attributes this to the sense of insecurity which placement moves have given him, but also to feelings that were not safe to reveal.

There's just a feeling that there's a lot that he's holding on to. He doesn't want to let anybody know. A lot of feelings that . . . he might feel that he's caused some of the split with the family . . . Also they'd experienced things like people throwing bricks through the window. Violent memories.

Some children, such as Marsha (9), had been told directly by parents not to talk about what was happening in the family. This fits for the child with the idea that it is safer not to share thoughts and feelings. For other children, the situation is just too complex to share. When Nick's social worker was asked if he could understand why he was in care, she said:

I think he's forgotten. He knew at the beginning he'd run away and said he didn't want to go home but after a few weeks he really had forgotten and had to be reminded, well, you really weren't happy at home. I tried to get it across, but his comprehension like with his reading is not good. He's forgotten a lot or doesn't understand a lot.

In some respects the need to defend against the pain translates into confused thoughts and then denial. This is sometimes compounded, as in Nick's case, by the need to keep the foster family and the birth family separate in his mind. His foster carer said:

> *If I talk to him about home life I get a blank. From the beginning he kept the two phases separate. Life here and visits at home – the two shan't cross over. And it's still there.*

Similarly, the fact that his father constantly lets him down over contact cannot be faced or talked about.

Researcher: *Do you feel he just shuts off?*

Foster carer: *Yes, he does. Sometimes it's easier not to say anything. His dad hasn't rung for ages. 'Are you worried about your dad not ringing?' 'No.' But is that really right? If you pursue it he changes the subject.*

Guardedness in terms of talking to carers is also associated with guardedness in relation to expressing emotions appropriately. Social workers and foster carers talked of these children as finding it hard to show feelings. For some children this was linked with compliant behaviour and false affect.

> *When Nick first came he was very quiet but he had a lovely smile. Everybody commented on what a lovely smile he had. He was just very nice and we thought he was the nicest one we'd ever had. I don't know why but he was the easiest – he used to get on well with David, our son.*

This positive beginning, the fact that he got on well with their own son, gradually palled as they realised that he was not able to let them get close to him.

> *It's a bit of a barrier. Here we are two years on – you can give him a pat on the shoulder but not a hug.*

The general feeling that the child does not want emotional closeness is often highlighted by specific incidents which demonstrate how different the child is from 'normal' children in their capacity to accept comfort.

Foster carer: *When he hugs me, he's just sitting there and you're holding a tree – stiff. One time he got stung by a wasp – it had got inside his pyjama bottoms. He was in pain. I knew he was worried I'd get his pyjama bottoms off and he screamed. I'm trying to hug him and he's stiff as a board. I thought, I can't even cuddle him now! He's really in pain . . . Well – he doesn't show emotion.*

Researcher: *How does that make you feel? Is that a problem for you?*

Foster carer: *It can be. I can't always find out what he really wants . . . If he's got hurt – really walloped when he fell off his bike – he's jumped straight up again, just bounced. I say, Are you all right Nick? Yes – and he goes straight off again as if nothing has happened. One time he grazed his arm and was in a terrible state – but not a tear! It's as if he's not allowed to.*

This foster mother explained it to herself in terms of Nick still feeling close to his birth mother and not needing another mother but the feeling of being redundant was still a problem for her.

Darren's carers talked about how he keeps them at a distance. He has been rejected by his birth mother, who asked for respite care when he was 10 years old having had no previous contact with social services. After a week she asked for him to be adopted. Contact was established so that he could see his younger siblings at home but his mother was often not in the same room as him and showed no warmth towards him. Unlike Nick, there were one or two occasions when Darren cried and it was then when the foster carer most wanted to help him that he pushed her away.

Foster carer: *He came home from contact and seemed down, I thought he had been crying. Then at a review his nan wanted to take Darren's brother away for the weekend but not him. At home afterwards I asked him, 'Do you mind?' Darren shrugged his shoulders but then I found him sitting on the stairs with his jacket over his head crying his eyes out . . . 'Darren what's the*

> *matter?' 'Nothing... nothing.' He stops instantly. The*
> *tears are genuine but he can't bear to show any*
> *emotion, so he cries when he thinks you can't see him.*
> *If you see him showing emotion, he clams up.*

In Darren's hostile birth family environment, shows of emotion would have brought further rejection. In this foster family, it is as if for him shows of emotion are a sign of weakness. Darren defends himself by looking for security in self-reliance. It is dangerous to allow these carers to get close. Apart from his birth family history, he has had four foster placements in less than a year. In these ways, a childhood of emotional rejection, the abrupt rejection when his birth mother effectively abandoned him, the continuing experience of rejection through contact and the insecurity caused by placement moves all reinforce a defensive strategy of shutting off from potential sources of care and concern. Only occasionally does the distress break through, so it is hard to know what to do for the best. Darren's carers said:

Foster mother: *I don't know how we can help him with his emotions.*
At the moment I feel all we are doing is putting a roof
over his head and we're there if he wants to call us –
but like when he was crying on the stairs . . .

Foster father: *You won't never get close to him. We'll always be his*
foster carers – and he'll always be Darren.

Sometimes with these children, when feelings break through they come out as anger rather than distress. This was true for a number of children but particularly children in this category. Often when asked the question, how does the child show you he or she is upset, the account that came back would be that the child did not show upset. For example, 'If he's worried he acts as if nothing is bothering him'. But in discussion of behaviour it became clear that the children were more likely to show anger than upset. Darren would often have outbursts and his behaviour at school was beginning to cause difficulties with staff and peers.

Some foster carers and social workers were able to chart a pattern where initial anger had apparently resolved itself over time. The social worker said of Liam:

Social worker: *He was withdrawn and unhappy. When I first met him he was so unhappy and angry at that time, he had been running away from home. He didn't really know what was going on. He was very angry with everybody who came to the foster home. He said I hate you, I hate you. But he doesn't say that now. Now he's softened, he looks at you and he smiles and you can see the smile in his eyes. He is more calm and the angry impression is gone but there is still some distance. I can't explain it.*

Researcher: *Reserved?*

Social worker: *Exactly – that's the correct word . . . Liam was closest to his mum compared to other children but I never saw any bonding between them, no cuddles, kisses. I never see that when he came into care and then went back home to mum. He would never give his mum a kiss.*

Liam has lost or more likely repressed his anger and in its place there is the well-behaved but distant child. In his placement there is a risk that if he behaves badly, particularly towards his foster brother, then he might leave. It seems likely that he is now stuck, emotionally frozen or on hold. Going home to his mother is not a real option, because she has frightened and assaulted him in the past. His father lets him down even over contact – and the prospect of going to another family would be fearful for him. As with other children, he remains confused. As the social worker put it:

> *He wanted to go home but doesn't give you a real reason. He said, 'I miss my mum,' and if you ask questions, he says, 'I want to go home but I don't know why, I ran away but I don't know why'.*

It is perhaps not surprising that this child is unable to recount the feelings of fear that led him to ask to be protected from his own mother or to articulate why he would nevertheless want to go home. But this quotation raises the issue of how, for these avoidant children, their natural propensity for feeling unsettled and confused about affect is reinforced by the incomprehensible position, from a child's point of view, that they find themselves in. Liam appears to be in a loving foster family, with people living ordinary lives which include him, and yet it is not clear if he genuinely has a place there – and if he does, what does this say about the other family, the birth family, that still fills his mind with memories and unresolved feelings?

Compliant

Some children kept their feelings under wraps but showed a cool, politely smiling and compliant front to carers. This seemed particularly characteristic of the girls in this group. One carer described how Dee (7) seemed not to be fully engaged in the family. She would, for example, slip away to bed without saying goodnight. Dee showed no pleasure or excitement at the prospect of a family holiday but her carer discovered that she had been quietly making lists in her bedroom of what she would take and to whom she would send postcards.

One of the useful sources of information which often raised doubts about how well the more compliant children were doing were the children's interviews. Dawn was delightful in her interview. Her degree of cooperativeness was reflected in the fact that every single part of the interview was completed properly – remarkable in a child only just turned eight. Dawn became fully involved – going to the cupboard to check on the name of a food she liked, going upstairs to bring down her favourite clothes, showing the researcher her new shoes and inviting her to see her bedroom. She spoke warmly of her foster sisters and named the foster carer first as one of her 'important people', as 'cuddly and kind'. She wanted her Mum to be placed very close to her on the poster, and had written in Mum's favourite colour which was the same as Dawn's. However, she could not find words to describe Mum (she's a Mummy Mum) and went on to talk about the 'loads of things' that Mum has bought for her.

It was Dawn's story stems that revealed her underlying anxiety and distress. She began in a fairly bland way, but each story was progressively more troubled. In the "spilt drink" story, she switched the attention from Jane to Jim, who hid himself away, first in the shed, then under the mattress in a 'little tent', where he stayed all night. In the park, the parents 'weren't watching' – both of the children were hurt and ignored. Then the Mum took Jim home but left Jane in the park. While Jane was in the park, both parents died. 'So Jim was alone and so was Jane, but she did not know it yet.' Then Jane went home and found her parents dead. In the final story, Jane herself dies. The stories were told in a matter of fact tone, which belied the distressing content, just as Dawn's own presentation conceals her loss and confusion.

Self-reliant and bossy children

The tendency to achieve some sense of security through depending on oneself rather than making demands on hostile or rejecting parents leads to attempts at self-reliance. At times the language used to describe these behaviours suggests that this self-reliance is an asset but for both social workers and carers it was generally apparent that these children were using this self-reliance to defend against distress and anxiety. As one social worker explained:

> Owen is a very self-sufficient boy, emotionally very self-sufficient. He doesn't need to talk but shows emotions in peculiar ways. He has difficulty in expressing feelings and can become very angry. He won't let people in. He is self-sufficient but there's another level where he is reaching out to you.

The foster carers also realised, even though Owen had only been with them for a few months, that the boasting was all front.

> Well, if you listen to him, he's the bee's knees. But . . . I just get the feeling that it's only surface. I thought he did believe it but when the head teacher talked about him being in tears at school – he can't be that confident.

It is hard for foster carers to know how to handle such fragile self-esteem. Do you confront the child with reality or go along with the dream? The very fragility is likely to add to the outbursts of anger and lead to attempts to manipulate situations in order to preserve this false persona. The foster carer said:

> He's a very good looking kid, says he's the best at everything, constantly telling you that but underneath . . . he doesn't show his feelings. He can be quite naughty, fights with other foster children. He can be quite spiteful, though not in adult company, so I'd call that crafty – but it just shows his insecurities. He has to be boss.

"Crafty", "spiteful" behaviour is hard to live with. Many carers, like many parents, find the idea of deceitfulness very off-putting. The mix of self-reliance and bossiness is, however, often mixed with fears which require the carers to remain sensitive.

Owen likes the door open at night – he's frightened of the dark. Maybe something's happened in his past. Perhaps he was punished by being locked in somewhere. But he doesn't crack – he wouldn't tell you anything. Likes to think he's macho.

As always, though, the foster carers will not be told what the fear is. However, one might conjecture that for Owen it may not be a specific memory which he would be able to share, even if he wanted to. It is perhaps a more wide-ranging sense of anxiety about the dark and the vulnerability of sleep, after having a series of violent step-fathers.

For several of these children, their bossiness may also have been reinforced by their family role. Mike was the oldest of a sibling group. Mike's foster carers attempt to use this as a positive part of his role in the foster family.

Foster father: *I think he's quite a confident little lad. In lots of different ways. Self-reliant in his way. He likes to be the boss. He likes to be the boss of all the children. But that's good in some respect.*

Researcher: *Are there things he likes about himself?*

Foster father: *He thinks he's good at everything. He's a real know-it-all – but that's his Achilles heel in a way because he doesn't really know it.*

Sometimes for the children, the bossiness and needing to be best was alienating other children at school. Although many children are competitive, when being best is linked with a tendency to be devious in order to achieve it, there were likely to be major problems. These behaviours interfere with the normal development of social skills in peer group relationships in a way which can have long-lasting consequences.

Dismissive of relationships

Sustaining the avoidant defence leads in adult life to a state in which relationships are talked of as if irrelevant – hence the attachment theory term, dismissing. Such characteristics could be seen in some of the older children. Roy acted as if the loss of his mother was unimportant to him and appeared to have written her off. He was very casual about contact with her and in the child interview hardly gives her a mention. His social worker said:

> Roy is now dismissive of her. Marian, his mother, allows contact with her mother every three weeks – plus his uncles, her brothers. Marian then stopped him going. Roy said, 'She can't tell me what to do. She doesn't want me so why can she tell me what to do?!'

The need to sustain a protective emotional distance from his mother was echoed in his response to other losses. Having had three foster placements prior to this placement, he would grieve at the point of the loss but would quickly put back the armour. In one placement in particular he had settled well but it was too far away, and therefore too costly in travel terms, from the area where he had lived and still went to school. So he was moved. Roy's social worker describes Roy's attitude:

> Roy dismisses that placement as a bad experience – she did this or that. When a part of his life is over, he has to demonise it and that's exactly what his mother does. He's learned that.

Even in his relationship with the social worker, it was clear that he tried to hold back and did not want to trust. Roy would never have admitted to the existence of a relationship but when the social worker, who was in the team as a student for a fixed period, left he followed him out to the car on his final visit and found it hard to let him go. He asked if he could come back. Such situations do raise questions about intensive work by students, and others on fixed contracts, and yet this worker had helped Roy through placement moves and established an excellent rapport with the current foster carers during the crucial early weeks of the placement.

For Roy, the cumulative effect of loss was clearly gathering in his mind as further evidence of his unlovability. In the placement which had worked out worst and where he had failed to get the carer's attention and upset other foster children, he had been rejected by the foster mother very abruptly. The social worker described the scene:

The foster carer said, 'I want him out now'. And when I told Roy, he cried – the only time I've seen him cry. Tears were trickling down his face. 'Can I stay here if I'm good?'

At this stage it is perhaps reassuring that Roy still has the capacity to want relationships and grieve even fleetingly at their loss.

Edward was also singled out for rejection and had been unloved by his mother from birth by her own admission; he had been a sickly child and hard to feed and she never really liked him. Edward did not react with any sense of loss to what was a major move of foster home after five years in a bridge foster family awaiting adoption placement. It could have been that he had absorbed the adoption preparation to the extent that he was sincerely waiting for his new family. But his younger brother, who had been favoured in the birth family and shows emotions more appropriately, had shown significant distress – highlighting again how different patterns can occur in sibling groups depending on family position, role in the family dynamics and parental attitudes. These patterns reflect not only different experiences but how those experiences have led to distinctively different internal working models and defensive strategies. Edward could not allow himself to think the thoughts or feel the feelings.

Retreat to objects or animals

For some of the children, the avoidant behaviour can be seen through the way in which they retreated into the use of objects rather than people when upset, as Jeremy's foster carer described:

It's not quite normal – Jeremy (9) will cuddle Toby [the dog] and he'll cuddle his cuddlies. He's got a lot of soft toys and he'll cuddle them a bit. It's a bit strained – but it's getting less slowly. But it's taken two years for him to show any anger.

One young child, Julien, aged five, had spent part of his infancy in foster care, and then been reunited with his parents, both of whom have a learning disability. He was then removed again following admitted sexual abuse of both older siblings by both parents. Having had a brief but satisfactory spell with one foster family he was reunited with his siblings in this new placement. In the early days, the social worker said, 'If upset, he wouldn't go to anybody and didn't want anybody near him'. Since that time, he has settled well and his carers spoke very warmly of him as being a 'jovial little chap' who was universally liked. However, there were still signs that when stressed he retreats.

He'll go though spells when he wants lots of love and affection and then he won't need so much and will revert to teddies. If he's upset he'll revert to teddies. It makes you wonder what happened before.

It seems likely that, although Julien has had to cope with more separations than his older siblings, he has also experienced less abuse and neglect and been exposed to more reasonable early parenting. This may have left him with a tendency to retreat, to lack trust and rely on himself but also with some capacity to use adults and to communicate feelings. It will be important to see how the balance he has achieved works out as he matures and whether he will be able to use the relationship with these carers to build a more secure internal working model.

Retreat into mental activity

It would be characteristic with avoidant children to seek refuge from feelings in ideas, thoughts, activities which draw on mental processes. As mentioned above, it is not easy for children with this level of disturbance in their backgrounds to use school as a route for comfort and even self-esteem. This is not helped by the fact that inevitably most have changed schools more than once. However, several of the children were said to like school and it seemed possible that here was an area which could be built on by carers. Laura was achieving some kind of success at school and for her it was an important part of her life. Mark too had discovered pleasure in school and was fortunate to be able to make friends, in spite of his rather cool exterior. Ability to play football was for him, and for a number of the boys, the key to easy relationships which provided intimacy and acceptance in a non-challenging way. This worked best for the children who, although closed and self-reliant in some respects, had not become bossy in a way which alienated other people, especially other children.

The other bonus of school for these children was that, although school could be demanding, it might be less demanding emotionally than life in the foster home with their siblings. Mark and Laura were both older siblings to children who were dramatically in the open book group – bubbly, demanding children who had been favoured in the birth family and dominated life in the foster families, with their raised affect and preoccupation with the birth family. These more reserved, perhaps resigned, older siblings needed space for themselves. Although Mark's foster father did his best to provide that, for example, by taking him to football matches, school also offered an environment where he could be himself and be free of the dynamics of the sibling group.

Rather different sibling dynamics would also have made school appealing to Liam, whose younger adopted brother was emotionally open and demanding. School offers in some senses a more level playing field for a child who finds it hard to compete in a home environment. Interestingly, all three of these children had parents who for very different reasons were unavailable and rejecting. Laura's mother was a drug addict who had abandoned her children on more than one occasion; Mark's parents had severe mental health problems; Liam's mother had a learning disability and had been abused in childhood. It is likely that all three children had felt some need to look after and yet be wary of their parents, denying their own emotional needs in order to stay safe. The advantage of looking at the children's behaviour using a framework of adaptive strategies, such as attachment theory offers, enables us to make such links across family histories and begin to predict what may be the developmental trajectory which flows from them.

Children's interviews

In the interviews with the children there was a sense of strain and distance but some were smiley and compliant. As researchers, it felt at times as if we were intruding by attempting to engage with them or asking even the least threatening of questions. Some curled up on the settee and gave strong signals at the beginning of the interview that they were not going to give much away. When they realised that we were happy to talk about less threatening things than birth families, they warmed up a little. Kevin was able to talk with great enthusiasm about happy times walking the foster family dog.

Researcher: *Does he come back when you call him or whistle?*

Kevin: *You only need to say 'Prince' and he comes.*

Researcher: *So he's well trained?*

Kevin: *Yeah. Prince was at one end of the woods and I was at the other and all I done was called him – not shouting – and he came straight back to me. When I'm here all I have to say is Prince [whispers] and he'd come.*

In this way Kevin was able to share his sense of the magic of the dog who was so intensely aware of Kevin that he would come to him from across the woods at a call of his name. The dog was, for him, predictably available in a way that he could not trust people to be.

Conclusion

In some ways these children were easier to live with than restless open book children. Being quieter in their behaviour and often being quite well-behaved was an asset in many situations. In the longer term, the question for these children will be whether they can warm up in response to the carers' attention and care and whether the angry outbursts will diminish or increase as they move towards adolescence. The success of placements may also depend on whether carers are able to stay with these rather cool children and still be able to find some rewards in their parenting role.

Summary

Characteristics of closed book children

- Closed and guarded;
- Compliant;
- Self-reliant and bossy;
- Dismissive of relationships;
- Retreat from people to objects or animals for comfort;
- Retreat from anxiety to mental activity.

In attachment theory terms

These children use avoidant/defensive strategies. In relationships with carers they can be initially rewarding when they are polite and compliant, but the lack of emotion and inability to accept affection and comfort from foster carers creates distance and feelings of failure.

They may cause concern

- In the foster home, because they find it so hard to trust carers with their feelings or to let carers get close.
- At school, because although some may do well enough at schoolwork, some find it hard not to be "best" and hard to allow teachers or other children to get close enough to build relationships.
- In the community, because for some there will be flashes of anger and a need to control other children and/or be defiant of authority.

8 Children on the edge

Although many children in the study showed a number of worrying and disturbed behaviours, there seemed to be a group of children who stand out for the more extreme and sometimes bizarre nature of their difficulties. These children are more likely to have experienced fear as well as a range of abuse and neglect in their families of origin. Most of the sexually abused children fall fairly obviously into this group but so also do a number of children who have experienced the more extreme forms of emotional abuse and rejection. These children can be fragile and fragmented, both frightened and frightening. They may harm themselves, be violent to others or harm family pets. Some of their behaviour problems include quite primitive, infantile expressions of distress, such as wetting and soiling.

In their relationships, they are hard to get close to – wary themselves, they make carers wary. They have the desperate survival tactics of manipulation and control, causing carers to feel uncomfortable and unsure of their capacity to love them. The children feel wholly unlovable so this is not a surprise to them. They live intense, dark, inner lives in which they struggle to make sense of the painful world in which they find themselves. The often hostile, sometimes bizarre, anti-social behaviour which emanates from their internal world may have meaning in relation to that world but it will seem meaningless in the ordinary family life of the foster home and will not be comprehensible to carers. The children themselves will find it equally impossible to explain why they do what they do and so tackling these behaviours at a conscious level will be almost impossible. They find it hard to think straight, hard to hold it together. Although there are some variations in the detail of their behaviours, this group of children seem to be on the edge – on the edge of normal relationships, on the edge of reality, on the edge of disintegration into panic and distress or destructive rage.

In attachment terms, these are children who have found it difficult if not impossible to sustain a defensive strategy against anxiety when the caregiver who should be the source of care and protection was the source of the anxiety and fear. They share some of the behaviours of the other children just described – some will be more restless and impulsive, others will tend to be more closed. They may be able to use false affect, in the form of superficial charm; they may be compulsively compliant; they may use false cognition in manipulating carers. As older children they may not any longer be trying to achieve proximity to caregivers, since this has proved dangerous in the past, but simply behave in ways that are attempts at being or feeling safe (Crittendon, 1995). For this group, the behaviours are at some level despairing and helpless, most strikingly where children self harm. Their fantasy life is more likely to be peopled by frightening images and death. Although their carers can all find something positive to say about these children, the child's internal working model is of a worthless self in a world of hostile others where survival is at a cost.

If we consider each aspect of these children's behaviour in turn, the cumulative effect of their experiences on their psychosocial functioning, at home, at school and among their peer group, will become clear. Equally clear will be the demands made on carers to cope with children whose inner worlds are so dark and chaotic and who cause tremendous concern for their future mental health and happiness.

Wary and distrustful

Because these children have experienced such adverse treatment in relationships with caregivers, it is not surprising that they treat the offer of parenting from foster carers with some suspicion. Raymond had been seriously rejected in his early years. His step-mother had singled him out for rejection in the family. She was said to have shut him in his bedroom after school, put him in cold showers when he wet the bed, hit him with a slipper and so on. As a seven-year-old coming into a permanent foster family, his foster mother noticed he was alert and wary:

> *He looked at me to see if I was approving or not. He's very sensitive to your eye contact, your face. He's always watching me and he can't bear it if I've got a down face.*

This ultra sensitivity to other people, particularly the female carer on whom his safety and care depended, was quite stressful and could feel quite intrusive; the child's eyes fixed on your face, looking for clues, trying almost to see inside your mind – what has been called frozen watchfulness or in Raymond's case, often rather agitated watch-fulness. In his mind, Raymond was always imagining and fearing the worst:

> *He used to assume that every comment we* [foster carers] *made would be negative . . . he's not so bad now but at meals when he first came, if something funny was said he'd laugh and then stop himself . . . he'd come down heavy on himself, wouldn't allow himself to laugh.*

Even simple things become a problem.

> *Everything had a negative side . . . He said funny things like if I said two biscuits are enough, he'd say, 'Oh you're never going to give me a biscuit ever again in my whole life'. Everything was exaggerated. Everything was the worst it could possibly be . . . the scenarios he worked out in his mind.*

For other children, the wariness took the form of simply not revealing feelings – either the most positive or the most negative. For Ross's social worker the fact that he was well-behaved in the foster home and appeared to be getting into some activities was seen as a very good sign – but his foster carer was less sure.

> *I have concerns that Ross really didn't want to be here and that he wasn't happy here. His social worker that has known him for a lot of years has said that Ross is the happiest he's been in his life, which if that is the case is very sad . . . He's obviously got a veneer – it's his armour and he won't let anyone in and that's his problem. It's going to take a long time before he will let anyone in.*

Even more obviously than the "closed book" children described earlier, Ross controlled all signs of feelings – even the trip to the theme park was no pleasure. As his foster carer said:

> *It's part of the veneer, you can't admit something was fun. He's the sort of character who beats himself – I'm not going to enjoy that on principle.*

But equally the carer said that he showed no signs of anger:

> *To me his response is apathetic rather than aggressive. To me he's still very much at the stage where he is only visiting.*

This was a carer who had coped with extremely difficult, antisocial teenagers before but found the flatness of her "visitor" almost too hard to cope with.

Other carers also found the lack of emotional rewards hard to deal with. Lorraine's mother had found her hard to like from a young age and was dismissive of her needs. In her interview, Lorraine appeared to see her carers as rather marginal in her life. From her carers' perspective, she was a child who was resigned to her fate and was not able to engage in anything more emotionally rewarding. When asked how she felt about moving to this foster family, Lorraine (11) said:

> *I mean I could have gone somewhere a lot worse. I could have gone to a children's home for all I know . . . and that would have been worse than coming here really.*

From Lorraine's perspective, it's as if she belongs nowhere, has no right to be anywhere, has no-one on her side who wants her. In her story stem narratives, the parents of the little girl who hurts herself in the park do not notice that she is crying and do nothing to help her – she has to approach them.

Some carers felt that the children's wariness was a direct result of their experience of sexual abuse.

> *Teresa (11) doesn't show any affection. She's not a cuddly child – if there's a means to an end perhaps – but she's not a cuddly child, she's not affectionate. She's been groomed and affection means something else.*

For a number of carers, there was a sense that children were keeping a distance but that even when they were showing affection, it was not to be trusted.

> *Tina (7) is very complex. Very manipulative. She's very pretty – and she can use it, flutters her eyelashes. Thinks about a situation – thinks about what she's going to get out of it. Very skilful – can get away with*

anything. Very good at loading the gun and giving it to someone else to shoot and watching them get told off.

This sense of children as being manipulative in a rather calculating way was bound to alienate carers as it did other children.

Frightened, helpless, sad, children

Wariness in relationships often seemed to reflect a sense of fearfulness, based on previous experiences and memories which could suddenly "pop up", intruding on daily life. Connections would not always be clear between past and present but carers often sensed in the children a web of fears and anxieties which made it hard for them to enjoy life. Sam (aged 8) needed to be carefully prepared for any new experience, such as a day out. His foster carer said:

He needs to be prepared . . to know how and why. . . He wants to go, but then his mind goes over all the negatives. It's as if he has a fear of something nasty happening to him. Then at the supper table, he came up with the memory of having his hair pulled to stop him falling asleep in the car. . . His mother used to pull his hair to wake him up.

These memories linger, having what must generally be a quite unconscious impact on attitudes and feelings. Then for no apparent reason, apart from here perhaps the link with a day out, they surface. This kind of revelation may turn up over the foster family meal table, shocking the family. What is helpful in these cases, as long as the carers can deal with their own feelings, is that these disclosures allow them access to some of the child's past experiences and present preoccupations. It also reminds carers that these memories have not really gone away – they're just put away in the back of the mind.

Although it may seem that these fears reveal themselves randomly, it is often the case that they are revealed at intimate times that provoke primitive feelings about love, intimacy and family.

If Terry's angry it usually is because something's going on and you normally need to get to the root of it. When he is going through his problems he'll normally not want to sleep in his own bed. He'll come in my bed or lay on the floor and have nightmares and things can really get out of hand.

Another example from Raymond's carer, also, was that sleeping could be a problem.

He says he can't sleep. He tells me at night – he has a picture in his mind that's upset him and he can't get it out of his mind.

Raymond's fears intrude at night, when he is less able to exclude them from consciousness, but he is also better able to talk about them to his foster carer when he is tucked up in bed and has her full attention.

Similarly, Katrina's foster carer found that two years after separation from her sexually abusive parents, she was still making new and more serious disclosures about what had happened to her. This would happen when, for example, she was having a bath. Katrina, who was seven years old, would also reveal her fears in indirect ways – such as suggesting what her carer called 'weird things', for example, that a boy in the foster home had come into her bedroom and 'wee'd all over my bed'. The bed was not wet but she was convinced that it had happened. As with Raymond, memories pop in to her head, such as of children throwing stones through the window when they lived with their parents. For a child like Katrina, the boundaries between past and present, real and feared, are likely to be confusing for her. One symptom of being lost in her past is a tendency to go off into her own thoughts for quite long spells, almost a trancelike state.

Fears of other people are accompanied by fears of rejection which seem to be linked. Joanne said that she would like to see her birth father more:

Researcher:	*Is that a possibility?*
Joanne:	*No, because he doesn't want to get in touch with me. I have asked the social workers if they would see him again and ask him. I'm afraid that if I send him a letter or something he's going to know my writing and screw it up without opening it.*

Joanne, while hoping that her father will spend some time with her, actually believes that the sight of her handwriting is so repugnant to him that he will throw it away like a piece of rubbish. This fear about her own lovability is reinforced by her mother, who finds it hard to be in the same room with her. It is perhaps not surprising that Joanne has started to self harm, a complex mix of releasing feelings through pain and attacking her unloved self. Helplessness is characteristic of adults with unresolved, disorganised attachment patterns but is also part of the picture of maltreated children in middle-childhood.

Other children who have been sexually abused but still feel distressed at the separation from family members are particularly confused. Jessica had formed a good relationship with her short-term carers and had found this second move to a permanent foster placement hard to accept. Her reaction was one of helplessness and sadness.

Foster carer: *Jessica is extremely emotional. Her confidence is very low. She'd lost all confidence. She cried at the least little thing. Very, very clingy. Very confused. She had just come out of this foster home – very sad. Cried a lot. Finds it difficult to make any adjustments. She just has really sad days.*

Researcher: *Was she feeling bereaved?*

Foster carer: *Bereaved, yes, and missing her parents. Jessica was the one who was clinging and crying, jumping up on people. She was seven but was acting like a four-year-old when she first came to us. She refused to dress herself. Acted as if she couldn't do anything. Reading – she went back to the first books. She said, 'I can't do anything'. Now she's dressing herself and is doing quite well in her books.*

Although she is more settled now, there are still some 'sad days' when it is clear that she is struggling to make sense of what has happened to her.

Although fearful of relationships, some children were constantly wanting reassurance that they are loved and good. This did in some cases become overwhelming. Susan is 11 years old, has moderate learning disabilities and has experienced neglectful care – her mother has profound learning disabilities. Striking in the interview was her inability to talk about any likes and dislikes, which was quite unusual even amongst the more damaged children in the group. It was as if she barely existed as a person. She is often on the brink of being overwhelmed by feelings of sadness and has no strategies to deal with this. She has siblings at home cared for by her mother. She overwhelms her inexperienced carer with persistent but diffuse emotional demands. Within this interaction Susan demonstrates how her internal working model of an unlovable self and unpredictable and rejecting others translates into demanding yet hopeless behaviour.

As well as fears relating to real people and situations, a number of these children show a mix of interest in, fear of and excitement about monsters and death. This may appear as a warped sense of humour on occasion. One boy (10) laughed at the advertisement which promotes road safety by showing the body of a woman thrown over a car.

Researcher: *Do you think his early environment was frightening for him?*

Foster carer: *Yes, every picture was done in black when he came here. It was all monsters and killing.*

Researcher: *Does he talk about monsters?*

Foster carer: *He used to – always monsters. That's gone. A big change. He has counselling . A psychologist. He can let off steam – and he does – she gives him playdough and he'll make hell with it, throw it. And he'll make figures, won't say who they are, but he'll chop heads off.*

Researcher: *Is he still doing that?*

Foster carer: *It had stopped but last year just before Christmas – the therapist rang me. 'I don't know what's going on', she said, 'He's throwing things, killing everything in sight'. She had said to him, 'You're doing well now, shall we start to wean you off – perhaps once a month?' And he went berserk. 'I want to come here for ever and ever.'*

For these children, threat of separation can precipitate breakdown in their fragile defences. For this child, whose contact with his parents was very destructive, the fact that he had and could use a therapeutic relationship was very necessary.

Violence without responsibility or remorse

A number of these children came from families where there is a culture of violence. Their behaviour reflected the feelings of fear, helplessness and anger which children experience when parents are violent towards each other or towards them. This can lead to children responding to stress by becoming aggressive or cruel themselves. Other children were physically aggressive in reaction to emotional abuse in early childhood. Worrying for these children and their carers is the fact that aggression is associated with a lack of conscience, a belief that it is somehow not their fault, either because it is justified or simply not within their control.

Ryan's experience was of a mother who kept him symbiotically close to her but belittled him and threatened to kill herself and him. At one contact visit, his mother seriously assaulted a social worker and Ryan joined in. On other occasions, his mother and father fought each other. Ryan was said by his carer to have the capacity to be loving but that his behaviour could degenerate to the point of hurting the foster brothers or baby foster sister, of whom he was said to be very fond. The aggression could be sparked off by small things in the foster family, but was often associated with comments from his mother at contact, that he would be going home soon and should run away. His foster carer commented:

> *Normally he treats Sabrina with kid gloves – he loves her to bits but if something upsets him, usually to do with his parents, he'll go. He goes berserk, doesn't care who he hurts or if he gets hurt. In denial after- wards. Doesn't feel bad at the time but a couple of days or weeks later when he reflects on the damage he says, I couldn't help it. I can't stop myself.*

These children are made anxious by distress in others. A crying baby, for example, might therefore provoke aggression rather than protection, since attack is how Ryan instinctively reacts to anxiety.

Although violence can sometimes be directly linked to specific current events, the force of it clearly comes from elsewhere. It is often said that the children are as confused about what has happened to them in the past and why they are violent now as the carers.

Foster carer: *David [7] lost virtually a year's schooling after being abandoned by his family – he couldn't concentrate, he couldn't get himself to go to school. He was so distressed and confused – confused is a word that comes up a lot. Staff at school kept using this word. Staff had to take it in turns to have him because he was so disruptive. He was really disruptive – he would throw things, aggressive, break things – still will kick things now . . . At first, even the little girls at school were frightened of him.*

Foster carer: *Robin [6] throws temper tantrums, draws all over things, breaks things, hurts the animals, which is unusual for him. At the moment he's been awful. Playing up at school – refusing to work. I'm not doing any work! Luckily enough his teacher's brilliant. Hitting people, doing things he shouldn't do. And he's got this noise – this waah noise and it can go on for hours. He can do it for hours and he knows it is irritating.*

This kind of breakdown in capacity to deal with feelings, defend against painful memories and current anxieties seems often to be associated with young children who struggle in the early years of school. It may seem surprising that children of six and seven are so out of control at school or are excluded from school but these behaviours are extreme. The children do not respond to the normal range of sanctions and rewards that appeal to reason. When distressed, these children are beyond reason.

Self harm

Self harm is often associated with adolescence but a number of these more troubled young children showed signs of attacking and injuring themselves. Children as young as four and five were harming their bodies – scratching legs, nipples, genitals.

Sometimes there were threats of self harm, which are concerning in young children.

Foster carer: *Jim [5] has to have routines. Like I wanted to stop off on the way home from school and pick up some bread and he just went berserk. You are expecting it and you have to cope with it.*

Researcher: *So what did he do on that occasion?*

Foster carer: *Threw his lunch box across the shop and threatened to run away. I'm sure he will when he's older. Sometimes when he's angry it's very extreme – he takes off his seat belt and threatens to kill himself. That worries me.*

The most extreme case did suggest significant suicidal ideas and confused thoughts about death and dying.

Foster carer: *On the whole Tony [10] is a lovely little boy but he is just very mixed up. Five times he's tried to kill himself. Mum's told him numerous times if he's got to be in care till he's 18 he might as well be dead. He goes to bed – he thinks of that – he jumps off the bed with a dressing cord round his neck . . . Because mum in the past has said, 'I'm going to kill myself'. A couple of times she's been rushed off to hospital – it's like – if you die you get brought back. He didn't have an understanding of death. He was saying after his granddad's funeral, 'I could hear granddad knocking on the coffin. Saying I'm getting wet.' I told him, 'When you're dead, you don't hear, you don't feel – it's very real. Not everybody can go to hospital and come back again.'*

For this child, his own distress and confusion has become linked with muddled thoughts about death and dying.

Harming animals

Always important in children's histories are the behaviours that seem out of the ordinary, particularly if associated with unusual kinds of aggression or sadism, such as towards animals.

Foster carer: *When Jim first came, he would bang his head, hit himself, do horrible things to himself but now even*

> *though he does get very angry he hurts things rather than himself. If he does even attack me it's very controlled – he'll hit me very gently, quite funny really. It's very, very rare that he does attack me.*

Researcher: *So he has some boundaries?*

Foster carer: *Yes, like when I saw him hit the dog – it could have been a lot worse. But it's funny because that dog loves him . . . but he's got to get it out somewhere.*

As this quote demonstrates, violence against other people, against the self and against animals seem to be connected. There are different levels of seriousness but the same sense of apparent meaninglessness, although for the child the meaning is likely to relate to fearful experiences in the past. Jim's social worker described another incident:

> *Jim sees himself as very bad. He just really is – you just want to cuddle him sometimes. He just tries so hard to be a toughy . . . He pulled the tail off a pet rat and his foster carer is a real animal lover. And she called me – you'll have to come round, he's really terrible. And we were just talking about something. And he was holding the rat up high. And he told me he'd pulled the tail off. And I said, 'You must have felt really sad about that,' and he said, 'No, I wasn't sad, I didn't care'. Don't let anybody think I'm really upset about anything. It's really, really sad. That he feels he's got to be really strong, really tough – nothing's going to hurt him.*

Thinking about what you have done and acknowledging feelings is simply not an option. In some cases "accidents" added to the sense of uncertainty for carers about such behaviours – how seriously should they be taken?

> *Our rabbit had to be put down – Harry (7) dropped it. It broke its back. They'd been told not to swing it round in the shopping basket, it had survived heaps. He knew he had to ask to get it out . . . we don't know if it was a naughty accident. The kids were upset about that. It's costly.*

These behaviours are "costly" for the whole family.

Infantile behaviours

Perhaps linked to self harm is the pattern of infantile behaviours, soiling and wetting, gorging food, which the children showed. The link may be to confused senses and a distorted relationship between themselves and their own bodies which, for some children, was continuing into early adolescence, as described by Kate's (11) foster carer:

Kate's got so many problems – she still wets and soils herself. Doesn't wet the bed so much now but she soils – and then she smells. Kids at school tell her. Kids here tell her. She can be five feet from the toilet at home and still wet herself. She denies it – 'I didn't know' – but it's a failure to keep herself clean ... She's stuck around three to five emotionally – when the abuse was at its worst – she's stuck there emotionally. So we're dealing with a three- to five-year-old emotionally, an 11-year-old who can't cope and sexually a 17–18-year-old. Three children in one body.

Often both soiling and wetting behaviour appear to be in the form of a message to the carer – one child left parcels of faeces in the chest of drawers or by the bed where the foster mother would find them. Even the fact that the children are smelly at home and at school was self-destructive, uncomfortable for them and damaging to their relationships.

Confused thought processes

Not surprisingly, given the distorted nature of their experiences and the emotional and psychological abuse that all these children had experienced, their thought processes were muddled. At times, carers were able to see this process and its consequences quite clearly.

Most of John's problem is that he knows what to say in his brain but can't get it out. He can't connect his brain to what he wants to say and starts to stutter – gets angry because you can't understand and then lashes out. We say, 'Stop, John. Calm down. What do you want to say?' It's knowing John, knowing what he's going to say. Stopping him before he starts – slow down. Then he gets on OK.

Part of John's problem was a very poor sense of time. Although a ten-year-old of normal intelligence, he seemed unable to grasp the time on the clock or even the normal pattern of day and night.

John wakes up really early – he might wake at two in the morning, get up and play with his toys. You go in and he says, is it time for school? We brought a big clock – we spent two hours teaching him. He knew but then he couldn't remember it. He can't tell the time and has no idea what the time relates to. Say when does Star Trek start – he doesn't know. Even with a digital watch.

Lack of grasp of current time is interesting when memories are frightening and even the recent past is hard to "remember". It is not surprising that these children found forensic or social work interviews so very difficult. Being specific as to thoughts and feelings, time and place is not possible for them. John and his siblings, all of whom had been frightened and sexually abused, used to piece together even ordinary events between them. As the foster carer put it:

Their memory's atrocious – so they can between them build up the story so it's right. Because they got through by locking away what happened yesterday, like throw yesterday away, I don't remember. When they first came, you could have given them sausages for tea every night and they wouldn't have noticed. When you asked them what they had for school lunch they say, can't remember. Then one might say, we had coleslaw and beans – and I had fish ring – that was yesterday – oh yes, chilli con carne. They build the picture up between them.

If even the recent past is hard to get your mind round, the future is even more vague.

They don't think that far ahead. They've never been allowed to think past what's happening to them today – after all, do you really want to think about what's happening tomorrow if you are being abused today? Or if today's been a good day, do you really want to spoil it and think about tomorrow. They're all going to need therapy in their own way.

Poor thinking processes linked with the range of behaviours described, being anxious and aggressive, out of control or switched off and sad, mean that these children had serious difficulties across the board at school. The younger children were being coped with in many ways but concerns were regularly expressed about what might happen for these children, educationally and socially, in adolescence.

Who am I? Problems with defining and accepting the self

For some children the general fearfulness of their past experiences and present feelings about themselves were so serious that they want not to be themselves. Angela, an eleven-year-old whose father was currently in prison for actual bodily harm and rape of herself and her mother, said, 'I don't want to be Angela'. She showed some distinctively odd behaviours which appeared to be based in a wish to actually be other children or in a poor sense of self.

Foster carer: *She does a lot of attention seeking at school. She latches on to other people's experiences and they become hers. She found some glasses and said she needed glasses to see the board. When we took the glasses off her, she said she couldn't see the board, could she sit at the front?*

Researcher: *Fantasy world around herself?*

Foster carer: *Yes – she said she was wearing a brace – she had a paper clip, bent around her teeth. She'd been telling everyone she had to wear it and it hurt her teeth. They'd just been to the dentist, her brother might need a brace in the next year. We spoke to the school psychologist – some of her stories are so elaborate they're quite dangerous. Normal children don't make a paper clip into a brace, or pick up and wear other people's glasses. Not the same as just making stories up. She picked up a Ventolin inhaler and was using it – she's a danger to herself.*

The more disturbed children had often only a rather faint grasp of reality and very poor boundaries between themselves and others. Wanting to be different, many children created imaginary worlds in which they were not just the best at everything but invincible. This could contribute to risk-taking behaviour but also kept carers and other children at a distance. In our interviews with these children, the sense of wariness was apparent but so also was a sense of fear. The children may have been anxious about the interview situation, regardless of their expressed willingness to be interviewed, but it felt more deep-rooted than that. We could sense that these were significantly abused children. In their presence, our voices dropped and we became a little tentative. One boy who had greeted the researcher initially in quite a jolly way, became quiet and anxious when his father's name was put on the ecomap and it had to be removed to the edge of the paper. He did not want his mother's name to go on the paper at all. As their stories given above indicate, these children had good reason to go to great lengths to protect themselves. It was often only with the puppets and the story stems that we were given a glimpse of some of the fears that troubled them. Even then, it was sometimes how the children were rather than what they said that was most revealing and most concerned us.

Conclusion

With these children it was hard to predict whether the placements would survive or meet the children's needs. Would ordinary good-enough parenting be enough to offer security to these children and for the children to let go of some of their more destructive and pathological symptoms? Could these carers, some of whom were exceptionally experienced and sensitive to the children, contain the children well enough and long enough to begin to repair the damage? Difficulties for the children to do with confused and negative thought processes coupled with distorted feeling patterns meant that even the slow building of a secure attachment was a challenge. There appeared to be a risk, acknowledged by all the carers, that although placements were holding, the amount of distress the children had from their abusive pasts may not be resolved significantly by the time they entered adolescence or adulthood. Some of the very damaged children were already 11 or 12 and for them, time was not on their side. On the other hand, five-year-old boys who were self-harming were equally alarming. Therapy was on offer to some but by no means all of these children. In only one case did a therapist work closely with the child and also support the carers and this seemed to be a very helpful model.

In these children we felt we could see the potential not just for disaffection in the teenage years but serious mental health problems. Their behaviours were sufficiently disturbed, bizarre and atypical to merit more attention than in most cases they were getting. Reaching their frightened internal worlds and working with the disturbance there needed to be a matter of some urgency.

Summary

Characteristics of children on the edge

- Frightened, frightening, fragile and fragmented;
- Wary and distrustful;
- Helpless and sad;
- Violent without responsibility or remorse;
- Self harming;
- Harming animals;
- Infantile behaviours e.g. wetting, soiling;
- Confused thought processes;
- Who am I? Problems with defining and accepting the self.

In attachment theory terms

These children have disorganised attachment patterns. In middle childhood they have made some form of adaptation to maltreating environments. They may use false affect and false cognition to feel safe. They may manipulate and control or be compliant and caregiving but inside they feel helpless and angry. This complex presentation can make these children hard to understand, predict or parent.

They may cause concern

- In the foster home, because their behaviour, whether this is secret soiling or aggression against family pets, is hard for carers to manage and for other children to live with.
- At school, because their bizarre behaviour, their tendency to be manipulative, aggressive or unable to think straight, makes both the

interpersonal and academic aspects of school life a problem for them.
- In the community, because they react with such helpless anger and/or distress to anxiety, that they may be unable to resist being drawn into self-destructive or anti-social behaviours.

9 Rewarding children

In spite of the fact that all children in the study had experienced some kind of adversity in their birth families and in addition had significant experiences of separation and loss, a number of the children appeared to be functioning quite well in a range of settings. These children were rewarding to their carers and seemed in many senses to be settling down as "normal" children – not apparently experiencing significant problems themselves nor causing significant problems to others. They were compliant in their behaviour, eager to please, fitting in and getting on with adults and children, at home and at school. Perhaps inevitably because of the contrast between their histories and this apparent sense of well-being, there were both implicit and explicit questions asked by some social workers and some foster carers as to whether these children were "too good to be true". The questions seemed to centre around: are these children "resilient"? Or were they simply concealing distress or anger in ways which might be storing up difficulties for the future? This needs to be carefully considered, given what attachment theory would say about the defensive strategies adopted by abused and neglected children, who may use false affect or false cognition in order to stay or at least feel safe (Crittendon, 1995).

Varied though these children were in their backgrounds and in being across the age range from four to twelve, they appeared to have some characteristics in common. They were described as more balanced in the way in which they expressed feelings – communicating feelings fairly appropriately, neither dramatically raising feelings to coerce and cajole nor shutting them down to control and avoid. They were also reportedly more likely to be showing some signs of the capacity to take a balanced view of things – to be able to think through dilemmas that faced them, if only to a limited extent given their age. In some cases, they were even said to be able to face up to and talk about what had happened to them and the reasons why they might not be with their own mum and dad. They were described as able to use carers, again at least to some extent, to help them with difficult feelings, to share happy feelings and to accept care and affection. Some were also able to use carers to help them *think* through what had happened, by discussing past and present difficulties.

A striking characteristic of the children and probably a key protective factor was that they were all doing pretty well at school – not high flyers intellectually, perhaps, but nevertheless children who did their best on the whole and were not a problem to teachers and their peers.

With these children it is particularly important to examine what appeared to be working for them. Do these factors cluster together for a reason? It will always be difficult to weigh the impact of their individual histories against the quality of their current experience in their foster families. On the whole these were less damaged children than some – none of them had been sexually abused, for example, and several had had experiences of good care with extended family members or previous carers. But they still had to deal with and resolve many of the issues/ feelings around separation and some had experienced abuse, neglect and abandonment by parent figures. These children were more difficult to classify in attachment terms. It may be that their avoidant/compliant strategies or ambivalent strategies were simply more effective or less extreme. It would be hard to think of them at this stage as having a secure pattern, although some had experienced good care from certain birth family members or previous foster carers.

Children's rewarding characteristics

Children were described as surprisingly normal. Tanya's social worker commented:

> Tanya [6] *is probably just a very normal, if I can use that word, six going on seven-year-old. She's a very attractive little girl. She always seems fairly content with life. She gets on well with peers and with adults. She gets on well in school. Never presented any problems. Quite amazing given the life experience she's had . . . She's a delightful child. I'm just so relieved that this placement is going so well and that by sheer good fortune this placement was there.*

This was one of several placements where it was felt that there had been a fortuitous match which made the social workers optimistic for the future. Similarly for foster carers, there was a sense of surprise and pleasure in the way the children were turning out.

I can't really fault Simon [11] *to be honest. Right from the beginning really – if he was in a mood in the beginning he wouldn't speak when someone came round but we don't get that now. Very polite, very considerate and always helpful, always says please and thank you.*

Unlike other children in the study, there was some sense of optimism in foster carers even about the adolescence of the children.

Researcher: *Do you think about what will happen in adolescence?*

Foster carer: *I'm not worried about that. I was lucky with my children but with Chloe I do feel if you give to her she gives it you back. I don't mean I have to give to her in order to get back but in her own self – I can see changes in her now. She needs to trust people and that's making me feel fulfilled.*

The children were described as having varying qualities which appealed to carers and formed a good platform for building relationships. One of the most significant was the ability to be balanced and flexible in the way in which emotions are handled.

Simon's got quite a good sense of humour. He can come over quite quiet and reserved until he gets to know you but he's come out of himself a lot. He's a very helpful and caring little boy.

Signs of a reasonable reserve are accompanied by warmth and humour once you get to know him and he gets to know you. Simon neither reveals himself like an open book nor shuts off from others like a closed book, but seems comfortable with his carers and makes them feel comfortable with him.

He's very appreciative actually. Unlike a lot of foster children who because they've had absolutely nothing, they come to you and they have everything and they seem to cotton onto that and expect more and more whereas Simon doesn't seem to be like that. He's very appreciative of anything you get him or do for him.

A number of the children were favourably contrasted to other previous or current foster children. The sense of Simon as being special because of these qualities adds to the value they place on him and their relationship.

Children who could share the good times and the bad achieved more of a sense of closeness with carers.

Researcher: *Will Alex tell you if he's pleased or excited?*

Foster carer: *Oh yes, definitely. He comes home from school – guess what I done today, I got a certificate today. We went to his sports day yesterday. He came third in a couple of races. He was so excited. He kept looking over! And like this morning he said, 'I feel really nervous today going up to the new school'. I said, 'You'll be all right Alex. You're going up with your friends.' But he said, 'I do feel a bit nervous – but everybody will'. I said, 'That's right – everybody will, it's a new school'. He was fine but quite excited about going.*

Alex reflects, with the carer's help, on the range of possible emotions which are associated with going to a new school.

Often it is the sense of qualities emerging in spite of adversity which appealed. Jeff had been emotionally rejected and physically abused; his mother wanted him adopted almost from birth, and he was the victim of a serious assault and head injury when he was four. He had then experienced the stress of a failed adoption placement. In spite of that, he was settling well into his foster family and they loved him.

Jeff's cheerful, resilient, he's an example to us . . . Cheeky, always got a smile. He's been to hell and back but he's always got a smile on his face . . . He was very apprehensive when he first came but he makes the most of every opportunity. He's really very willing and once he got to know us better and better he opened up. He's open about his past – hasn't shut it off.

Again the child shows an appropriate level of reserve to begin with but then relaxes, warms up and smiles at them. What is striking from these accounts also is the way in which the children apparently allow the carers to get to know them. Some carers are also aware of the children's need to get to know them. There is acknowledgement by carers that this is a *mutual* process as the relationship develops. What is pleasing for them is that the children give as well as take.

One of the most rewarding aspects of these children is the way that they have changed and improved within the foster family.

We thought if we could get through the crust we could discover a normal seven-year-old boy. He's been super. He loves helping out. He's a super boy . . . he's a lovely boy, he really is.

Those improvements were often quite dramatic, with children being very aggressive and throwing things around in the beginning but shifting towards more normal, acceptable behaviours. The moves towards emotional closeness are then seen as accompanied by behaviour that is more settled. As ever, there are major advantages if the child is able to share at least some of their feelings and this is seen as a way in which the stored anger and distress are defused.

Sometimes you can't believe – you look back and you can't believe how far you've come with him. The bad times when things were quite a struggle with him – he's nothing like that now, you forget . . . At one time there'd be major moods but now he will go quiet for a few minutes and then come out of it. There's no big thing made of it. He wouldn't necessarily tell me off his own bat but if we get a quiet moment he would then say that this or that had bothered him but I might have to give him a bit of a start: 'Is something bothering you? If you talk to me about it then I'll sort it out,' and then he'll be away and he'll say what's bothering him.

Sometimes there are real physical changes which accompany emotional change. Ashley is a diabetic and the major reason for her admission to care was that she was experiencing frequent hospital admissions because her diabetes was poorly controlled.

Ashley was a very poorly, undernourished sickly child when we met her – very insecure. She's now positive, outgoing. She's grown enormously, she's filled out and she's well.

Debbie is a severely disabled child. She is nine years old but developmentally functioning at approximately six months old. Her carers had provided respite care for her from the age of two and put a great deal of effort into stimulating her and maximising her potential. When it was no longer possible for her birth parents to care for her, long-term foster care was planned. When these carers were confirmed as long-term carers for Debbie they said, 'it felt like we had won the lottery'.

This progress is not only evidence to the carer that all is well – the children themselves can start to see how the carers are making a difference. Craig calls his carers mum and dad, something which his birth mother is said to be quite happy about.

Researcher: *What are they like ? Can you tell me a little about mum first, what is she like?*

Craig: *Kind and caring really. She helps you out with your homework if you're stuck, and stuff . . . Like if you're really worried about something she takes you in the bedroom and talks about it with you . . . She tries to cheer you up and stuff.*

Researcher: *Yes . . .*

Craig: *Really nice, really.*

Researcher: *And what about dad, what sort of person is he?*

Craig: *He's quite funny* [laughs] *. . . plays jokes on you and stuff like that. He lets you . . . he helps you with your homework . . . He's fun to be with. You'd probably say they're one of the best foster parents you'd ever get really.*

Researcher: *Really? Both of them together, would you say?*

Craig: *Put together they're great!*

Craig says that he is pleased with his social worker because she found such good foster carers for him.

School, friends and activities

Since we know from research that stability and success at school is often lacking for long-term foster children (Aldgate *et al*, 1992), it seemed important that this group of children were distinctive in making progress in this area of their lives. One aspect of the impact of school success was the fact that children who fit in at school are able to build their self-esteem.

Foster carer: *Malcolm got a lovely report. He's supposed to be at Level 2 and he is in all areas of his work. He loves school – really loves it. He won't stay off – not even if he's got a sore throat. He says he'll take a pack of Tunes.*

Foster carer: *Suzanne changed school but she's fitted in and made friends. It's a nice school and they made a big fuss of her because she was new. They treated her as special. She's such a likeable child, but then she's a child who will easily make friends. She's a child who really draws children to her. She's not bossy, or demanding or manipulative. She just seems to get on with others.*

For these children, schoolwork and friends often seem to merge together, with success in both areas. For others, school was enjoyed but was perhaps not so straightforward.

Foster carer: *He enjoys school and they've done a lot for him. I was a bit worried when he started at St James, being totally different, a huge school and there were problems at the school with bullying and because he wasn't the brightest of children. That worried him and he's a child that really . . . he's quite a perfectionist really and if he can't get things just so he'd rather not do it. But we've put a lot of work into homework, reading every night . . . He is quite behind in some things but I'm sure we'll get there eventually.*

Craig's mother has learning disabilities and he himself struggled with his school work. Now he was in an ordinary family, he and they perhaps expected that he would be at least average in his work. But he had previously missed quite a bit of school when he'd stayed off to look after younger siblings and this, combined with a more limited ability, was a source of some stress.

Where there were signs that their foster child was leading a normal active life with their friends, this gave carers a great deal of pleasure and satisfaction.

> *Neil cheerfully makes friends. You watch him at Roller King and he might know a handful of lads but he's all right. He'll be out here playing football with kids on the green – he fits in very well. I think the proof of the pudding is the number of times we get knocks on the door: Is Neil in? Is Neil coming out?*

Craig was rather similar with friends coming to call, going out to do activities, having friends round for tea.

Researcher: *What is Craig enjoying at present?*

Foster carer: *Just the fact that he can have friends round, go off to roller skating, be involved, he didn't do that before. He just enjoys things in general really.*

Their capacity to enjoy activities, which is important for their development, gives pleasure to the carers. It also provides reassurance to the children and the carers that being in care does not mean they cannot be "normal".

Too good to be true?

As should be apparent from a number of the above examples, there remain a number of questions as to whether these children are simply too good to be true. Are the qualities of co-operativeness and caring that are admired and enjoyed by carers genuine or are they a sign that the child has learned to read adults and would wish to please them, repressing their own feelings? Are they really compulsively compliant or compulsive caregivers, to use the language of attachment theory? When children make progress and give up all the angry behaviours with which they arrived, is that a sign that the angry feelings have been healthily resolved in some way or that perhaps the child has learned that staying in this family depends on quelling and controlling powerful negative emotions? And there is a challenging question, both practically and in terms of the theory – can this still mean some kind of success? Does the fact that the child is able to keep their more extreme behaviours in check create a window of opportunity for a secure attachment to develop and in the longer term create more fundamental changes in their internal working models? The fact that these children stabilise at school and with friends also builds areas of "normality" in their life and increases resilience.

It is worth reminding ourselves of the histories that some of the rewarding children bring with them and the strategies they have used to survive in the past. The social worker described the history of Peter (8) who had experienced abuse and rejection at home, in care at four and was then rejected by his adoptive family.

> Peter was so accepting of whatever happened. He was just so agreeable and that alarms me. It was like things were being done to him. However much we try to involve him in things he's just . . . well, I can't do anything about it. I just have to accept it. I question his ability to attach. If I moved him he'd only be upset for a couple of weeks and then he'd be the same as he is now. I think it makes him vulnerable. Is he really feeling or is he hiding a lot?

This anxiety was linked to the fact that such behaviour patterns appeared to go back to when he was only three years old and living with physical abuse from his mother.

> I was the social worker on standby when he was three and a neighbour reported that they'd heard Peter cry. I went out and Peter was trying to please his mum . . . I shall always have that picture. 'Tell the lady how you got the bump on your head!' 'I fell down the stairs.' It was like rehearsed – he kept looking to her for reassurance. It was like he was trying to please – which is what he's doing now.

Peter's carers are aware of the risk and are encouraged that at least he does not seem to "bottle things up".

Foster carer: *We sometimes wonder because it's early days and he's had such a lot happen in such a short lifetime that we often wonder whether we'll get repercussions later on but at the moment . . . Peter does talk – he will discuss his past.*

Julia, aged six, had suffered anxiety and separations because of her mother's serious physical illness. She had been happily settled with her older brother in a permanent foster family from aged three to aged six but for no reason that was apparent to the social worker, the foster carers had decided to 'give up fostering'. The social worker described how Julia had taken the news that she had to leave her foster family.

She froze. She absolutely froze. She didn't say anything. She didn't cry. She went quite white. She was completely immobile. Horrible experience. The foster carer was actually very distressed. And Julia showed nothing at all and continued to show nothing for about 48 hours. Shell-shocked. That's how the foster carer described it.

This blow to what must in any event have been fragile coping mechanisms was then compounded by the fact that her brother went to live with his father and she faced a future with a new and very different foster family. The social worker described how she settled immediately.

She's been there for just over two months and you'd think she'd been there all her life. She sort of settled in really quickly – too quickly in a way. I felt – oh – I felt that it shouldn't really have been like that . But it was nice to see it. Again she just seemed to fit.

Her foster carer was equally concerned at the speed with which Julia started to show affection.

Researcher: *Why do you think she's affectionate in this way?*

Foster carer: *I did wonder that . . . because she seemed to be a little too affectionate in the beginning and I thought that was because she wants to fit in, she wants to be liked, she wants to please. I did think it was all a bit false. But as times gone on . . . she is an affectionate little girl anyway, and I think it just seems more natural now than it was in the beginning.*

Researcher: *How do you think her past has affected the present?*

Foster carer: *It doesn't appear to have affected her at all but I'm sure it must have done. This shutting off when she doesn't want to speak about things, that might be part of it, which it would be better if she could talk about it.*

> *The other thing is that she appears as if she could live anywhere. If we've been anywhere, 'I'd like to live here'. Or 'I could live here' or 'I'd like to live with this friend'. And it's not something that Colin* [her own son] *would ever say. The fact that she's been used to just moving on.*

Julia has shown affection from the outset. However, perhaps there is a lapse in monitoring her own behaviour and she gives herself away by impulsively suggesting that she could live anywhere. This undermines her attempts to persuade the carer of her commitment to this family. It is not comfortable to feel that a child could on the one hand be "pretending" to be affectionate and on the other hand view with equanimity, if not some enthusiasm, the prospect of moving on from the home that you have given her.

A number of carers were conscious of the ways in which children try to please and the links this might have with their past.

> *I just felt things weren't right in her previous placement. She wasn't happy. She had lost her sparkle. But if you speak to her, she'll say she was happy because she wants to please. Like here, if I get annoyed with her she'll go out of her way to please me. Like she's got to have that approval because she feels that if she doesn't I'm going to give her away. I remember when she was at her grandmother's, her mother would make arrangements to pick her up and Jane would stand in the window and watch the clock and we, me and her grandmother would say – we'd go into her mind – I don't know if that's right, but we'd try to imagine what she must be feeling. What happened at her last foster home is like at her aunt's – it was just an existence. I am here.*

Conclusion

This group were seen as successes in the foster care system and their functioning in different areas was impressive and may well prove to be protective. Compared to other children, there did seem to be a window of opportunity in the fact of their very stability. It could be suggested that this was merely a honeymoon period, but on the whole as Peter's and

Julia's stories show, their behaviours do fit a regular pattern over time.

It is not clear whether these are signs of a secure pattern or, as seems possible, that they just have rather effective defensive strategies that work for them. The question mark for these children must always be related to the longer term. The children's patterns of behaviour would be predicted to be adaptive to the immediate sense of promoting their well-being in the short-term but might prove to be maladaptive in the long-term sense of mental health.

Summary

Characteristics of rewarding children
- Rewarding to carers;
- No problems at school;
- Can make friends;
- Too good to be true?

In attachment theory terms
These children are hard to classify. Some appear to be more like either the open or the closed book children but unlike these children they function quite successfully across a range of situations and relationships. They may have elements of secure patterns but are likely to be children who have been able to develop strategies that make them feel safe without creating problem behaviours.

They may cause concern
- In the foster home, where they are rewarding but there can be doubts about how genuine this apparently "normal" child is or whether this is the calm before the storm of adolescence, when troubled feelings may come out.
- At school, but only in minor ways, such as children choosing friends who also have problems or children who worry about succeeding and find the work too hard for them.
- In the community, in that they may be rather dependent on and trusting with strangers. On the whole these children appear less likely to turn to anti-social behaviour.

10 **Building relationships**
Providing a secure base

Meeting the children's complex needs is inevitably a very challenging task for even the most experienced, skilled and sensitive foster carers. Behaviours driven by insecure attachment patterns, as described in previous chapters, disrupt family life and present significant barriers to relationship formation. For the majority of the children, previous experiences of caregiving had led to them developing negative expectations of close relationships, as part of their insecure internal working models. Even "rewarding" children were vulnerable because of their experiences of separation, loss and, in some cases, maltreatment. If the new placement was to be successful, it was important that children's negative expectations were modified by their experiences, that the carers were able to shift internal working models in the direction of security through available, sensitive parenting. Carers needed to provide a *secure base*, to give the children a sense of *felt security* (Bowlby, 1969; Fahlberg, 1994; Howe *et al*, 1999). This would enable the children to begin to experience themselves as loved and lovable and to see adults as available and protective. Such beliefs form the cornerstone of healthy emotional development and prepare the way for positive, rewarding relationships in adult life. The raising of self-esteem and self-efficacy, the development in the child of the ability to reflect and make choices, the move towards autonomy – these come from security and are the basis of mental health. Such developmental processes contribute to resilience, a central concept in our understanding of how children cope with stress and adversity (Rutter, 1985, 1999; Gilligan, 1997, 2000).

To make sense of the information gained about caregiving among the foster carers in our study, we turned to an attachment model of caregiving. Ainsworth *et al* (1971) observed mother–baby interactions and found that caregiving could be understood along four dimensions:

- sensitivity – insensitivity;

- acceptance – rejection;
- co-operation – interference;
- accessibility – ignoring.

For secure attachments to develop in infancy, caregivers need to be sensitive to the child's needs and have the ability to respond appropriately; to accept the child and the child's dependency; to promote co-operation rather than conflict; and to be accessible to the child's signals of distress or sociability.

Foster carers who are caring for and establishing relationships with older, emotionally vulnerable children need to demonstrate the same attributes, but in ways which take into account the age, developmental stage and defensive behaviour of the child. In the research interviews, therefore, the foster carers were asked for information about how their child might express feelings of upset, anxiety, anger and pleasure. Carers were then asked to describe how they might deal with a particular behaviour, how it made them feel and what sense they made of it afterwards. They were also asked more generally about the rewards and difficulties of caring for the child. These questions elicited a wealth of material which demonstrated the complexities of the children's behaviour as well as the skilled, sensitive care which was being provided in many of the placements.

The aim of this chapter, therefore, is to apply these dimensions to caregiving in the placements. In which ways does providing a secure base for the child in middle childhood have similarities to mother–infant care? To what extent are there additional tasks and qualities which foster parenting of older children demands? For these carers, the task was not only one of emotional education but one of emotional re-education.

Sensitivity – insensitivity

Overall maternal sensitivity is defined by Ainsworth (1973) as the mother's ability and willingness to try to understand behaviours and emotions from her baby's point of view. The result sees a gradual increase in synchrony between mother and child. Within this attuned co-ordinated relationship, the baby can learn to regulate his or her own feelings and behaviours. Children whose mothers find it difficult to show such sensitivity find it harder to define and regulate their needs and feelings. (Howe *et al*, 1999, p. 19)

Attachment theory thus defines sensitivity not only as a matter of feelings but as a matter of thoughts. It is only through understanding and thinking about the child that parents can be truly sensitive. The cognitive capacity to think about one's own and other people's minds in a relatively non-defended way is referred to by Fonagy *et al* (1991) as a *reflective function* and is linked with secure parenting. In their study, mothers who appeared to have a higher reflective function could better understand their children's internal states and therefore respond more sensitively.

Many of the children in the current study were presenting their carers with a range of unusual and sometimes perplexing behaviours. Carers often worked hard to make sense of these, to link cause and effect and to impose a sense of order in their thoughts and understandings of the child and the child's view of the world. This process enabled the carers to find their bearings, to "take control" of the situation and to develop their coping and caring strategies accordingly. It was also important in facilitating the carers' attempts to help the children make sense of their behaviour. For the small number of carers who were unable to achieve these understandings, the children could appear threatening, hard to love or even to like. In these cases, morale was low and carers spoke of simply living from day to day and hoping that things would improve.

Flexible explanations of behaviour

Insights into the children's behaviour were achieved in various ways. Many carers found it helpful to consider a range of "explanations" for the child's behaviours and to move freely and flexibly amongst them. Pauline, for example, thought about Ann in the following way:

I think with Ann, there are three things which contribute to how she is and you can never tell which one is affecting her at any one time. There's heredity and I've met her Mum and I can see there are similarities in some respects. Then there is what went on at home. And then there are behaviour problems which stem from being taken away from her mother and her family. It's all part and parcel of Ann.

This ability to look at things from different viewpoints enabled the carers to try different solutions and helped them not to feel defeated if a particular approach was unsuccessful.

This reflective process was also used by all of the carers of children with severe learning disabilities, even though the disability itself could have provided a sound enough "peg" on which to hang their understandings. Janine's carers knew that many of her violent tantrums were caused by temporal lobe disturbance and therefore there was little that could be done to avoid or prevent them. Their general approach was, therefore, to simply keep her safe and wait for her to calm down. However, this did not prevent them from also perceiving elements of learned behaviour:

> When she was at home, her Mum used to feed her every time she screamed to try to stop her. This may have set up the pattern of associating food with screaming.

This insight had led them to develop strategies around mealtimes which were proving successful in avoiding distress for the child and themselves.

When carers were less able to think through alternative explanations and felt overwhelmed by seemingly chaotic and unpredictable behaviours, there was a tendency to alight on a single explanation and then to feel demoralised if the corresponding solution was ineffective. Jenny, for instance, had become convinced that the root of Sheila's problems lay in her allergy to food additives. She had controlled her diet accordingly and believed this had been helpful. However, when Sheila's underlying emotional difficulties continued to emerge, Jenny felt confused and irritated as she had no further explanations or strategies to fall back on. She was not able to think through Sheila's problems in relation to past or current emotional needs. It may also have been that Jenny, a "family builder", was frustrated by Sheila's resistance to becoming integrated into the foster family.

Making sense of the past

When mothers are trying to understand their infants, the range of explanations for joy, rage or distress is perplexing at times but fairly limited. For these carers of older children, the existence of complex and troubling past lives presented a source of significant questions. Foster carers varied greatly in the extent to which they made connections or felt it was necessary to understand the child's past experiences in order to properly understand their present behaviours. This foster mother, for example, attempts to make connections, to develop a theory which can make sense of the child's behaviour.

I know an adult who was abused as a child and she is always trying to fill up every second of her day. And I really feel that's what Sue does. She doesn't want, maybe, the memories, or when she's rushing here and there maybe she can forget that she's not with her mummy. And maybe when I try to stop her and get her to do something, perhaps then the reality comes back and that's it.

Many carers were constantly connecting to the past and describing the child in the light of previous relationships or events. Sharon described Karen as 'quite emotionless, or she has a very firm grip on her emotions'. This, she felt, was because Karen had had to care for her mother and younger brother. As a result, she became too streetwise, knew far too much about life, and yet was cut off emotionally.

She just had to function and I think that's all she was doing, just functioning day to day, with no idea of her own emotions . . . We just go at her pace. It's taken a lot of years for her to become as she is, it will take lots more to change things. If you think about it, I don't suppose anyone has ever asked her how she felt or even really cared, or worried if she is OK or not.

Sometimes, carers could see that the children were trying to replicate relationships from the past, or that they had memories or unconscious fears that could be triggered unexpectedly. Once alerted to this, carers would adjust their approaches accordingly. Joan, for instance, had found that her usual technique of sending a child upstairs for five minutes to cool off was not effective for Jordan:

. . . and we discovered later on that he had been left in his room for very long periods and that explained his reaction. Until I discovered why, we had weeks of him being really angry. Once I realised it, I used a different kind of approach and he doesn't often get angry now.

In some cases, carers accepted the importance of the past but felt that the burdens of those experiences were so great that they could only be tackled gradually and in the fullness of time. Susan thought that Bradley needed to get a grip on the present and become more emotionally stable before dealing with the past. She also felt that Bradley needed to be helped to move on a little from his past.

Whenever there's any sort of problem, he goes back into his past. 'You don't understand, you don't care, you don't know what a **** time I've had. I've been thrown from pillar to post'. Its always, always the past. And I say, 'OK Bradley. There's nothing I can do about the past. I am here today and I hope to be in your future and I can only take you from today onwards. I know we have to deal with the past, but we don't have to deal with all that, every single time.'

This strategy needed a delicate balance in order to cope with day to day living together without denying the reality of the child's first 11 years.

For a small number of carers, however, the past was seen as much less significant. This was the case for almost all of the "family builders", the couples who were seeking to establish or build on their young families through long-term fostering. They made fewer references to their children's past lives and rarely connected current functioning with early experiences. Instead, they chose to focus on the here and now, on the way that the children were fitting in with their lives and relating to siblings and wider family members. For them, perhaps, the need to see the child as part of their family was overriding during these early stages of the placements. But it reflects in subtle ways the wish to understand the child simply in terms of the current situation, where there is no other mother or father, and the attempt to create the experience of parents whose children are born to them.

For others, there was an active belief that connecting with the past was not helpful to them in managing the child on a day-to-day basis. Celia and Mike were carers who expressed this position clearly. They described the way in which Bobby (4) physically hurt himself:

Foster carer: *The psychologists say this is due to being left alone in his cot for long periods. He was trying to stimulate himself, so they say.*

Researcher:	*You sound sceptical about what the psychologists say.*
Foster carer:	*Yes, that about sums it up. Putting a label on it doesn't help. It doesn't make it any easier for him or for us to deal with. We just have to get on with it and accept that it's part of him, whatever the causes might have been.*

Carers' reluctance to think about a child's past and its meanings may make it harder for them to help a child to make sense of past-present connections as he or she gets older. It may also reflect a difficulty for some carers in facing the extent of distress contained in many children's histories. This is an understandable difficulty but needs to be addressed by support social workers. If carers find it too hard to bear the idea of the children's experiences, how are the children to be helped to bear the memories?

Standing in the shoes of the child

Ainsworth's definition of sensitivity focuses on an understanding of the child's perspective. This was a capacity demonstrated by many carers, the ability to place themselves "in the shoes" of the child, to experience the child's world through the child's eyes. Pat gave frequent examples of this throughout her interview:

> *But when I'm sitting talking like this or at the end of the day when I'm sitting reflecting on things, I think, well, how would I react? If I hadn't got a Mum and Dad who loved me, my family, all my aunts and uncles and cousins round me when I was growing up, how would I feel? And to be honest, the only thing I could do is, I would probably be hitting and kicking and scratching, saying, 'Look, this isn't what I wanted. I want to be somewhere else.'*

And, regarding contact:

> *But, if I were restricted from seeing my Mum, I think I would be very difficult . . . I try to reach inside myself all the time . . . and if it was happening to me, I would hate it and I would hate the people who were doing it to me.*

This reflective and empathic process enabled the carers to take challenging behaviours in their stride. They were seen as a reasonable and normal response, in the circumstances. As such, they could be accepted and dealt with calmly.

The process of sensitive understanding was a necessary forerunner to the business of responding sensitively to the needs of the child. Once the carers had begun to make sense of odd or challenging behaviours, they were then able to develop their strategies to cope and move things forward. The majority of the carers were managing to respond positively, using a combination of "instinct", tried and trusted techniques or imagination and innovation. A few were able to acknowledge that they were finding it hard to know how to respond or were clearly "stuck" in stressful, negative cycles.

Seeing the needs behind the behaviour

The previous chapters described how the children displayed or concealed their emotional needs, and showed a range of troubled and troubling behaviour. Some of the carers had developed the skill of being able to look straight through even the most challenging of these behaviours and respond directly to the underlying needs, rather than to the behaviours themselves. Barbara was particularly adept at this. She described how Charlotte could become extremely abusive to her when she was anxious about something. She was asked how she might deal with this:

Foster carer: *On a good day, I might suggest that she's had a difficult day, sound sympathetic, try to cuddle her if she will allow it. Just get her so she knows you love her, so that she feels that you love her and you care that she's had a bad day, then it diffuses it, but it's hard work to do that all the time.*

For the carers of children who were more emotionally "closed", however, it was harder to employ this technique. It was easy to be misled by a smiley, compliant child or to feel rejected by one who was dismissive of attempts to get close. Margaret (8) would signal anxiety by spending a little more time in her bedroom than usual. Jan would try to elicit more from her by taking an indirect approach:

She would probably go to her bedroom and if I recognised that, I might pretend I'm putting washing away on the landing, or be in her room putting her clothes away . . . not really to entice a conversation, but more to give her an opportunity, and she does seem to sense when I've got the time to listen. I mean, they get to know you as well as you get to know them.

Here sensitive responsiveness is linked to giving the message of availability – I'm here but in your own time. The carer even articulates the idea that children need to have access to carers' thoughts and feelings. Then, by encouraging the child to take the initiative, it promotes self-efficacy.

The ability to respond to the child on different levels was a valuable technique for many of the carers. Emotional, physical and cognitive development were often at different stages. Children could be functioning at different levels at different times. George (11) had the physical development and, at times, the attitude of an older teenager. However, Mary also recognised the 'vulnerable five-year-old' within him. She had 'instinctively' bought him an Action Man for Christmas, then, sensing his urgent need to play, had given it to him early. He had fallen on it with huge enthusiasm and Mary had followed it with other, equally successful toys.

Where children did not take up sensitive offers of concern, it was clearly painful for carers. The challenge, then, is how to continue to respond based on a sensitive understanding of what the child needs, even when you are being rejected.

Acceptance – rejection

Mothers who accept their babies recognise that looking after infants entails responsibilities, responding to another's needs and acknowledging that parenthood involves constraints on one's lifestyle and behaviour. They also accept their babies whether the infants are in a good or a bad mood. Rejecting mothers often resent the demands that their children make on them emotionally. Their children's dependency causes them distress. (Howe et al, 1999, p. 18)

A number of strands of this definition of accepting parenting are particularly relevant for the carers and children in this study. Foster carers of older children have to respond to needs expressed in a variety of ways, often not in age-appropriate forms and often requiring more attention than other children of their age. Carers' lives can be constrained in significant ways. Accepting children, for better for worse, may include coping with very challenging and rejecting behaviours alongside the more rewarding. The handling of issues of dependency and autonomy is particularly complex for these parents and children. There are dilemmas around whether it is safe for children to trust and depend on their carers or for carers to trust, allow dependency or give autonomy to the children. Accepting foster children also means accepting that they have complex feelings about their past and their other families.

Accepting emotional demands

Many of the carers had to accept and deal with high levels of emotional need and demand, although the children varied in the extent to which they could communicate their feelings accurately. Skills were required in interpreting the child's signals and finding ways of responding that were age-appropriate. Thus sensitivity and acceptance had to go hand in hand.

Where carers were able to interpret, accept and respond to emotional demands, the intensity of the behaviours tended to diminish in time and comfort and reassurance could be provided in more age-appropriate ways. William's foster mother, for instance, described the following scene:

> I've just taken them camping in a camper van and he loved his little snug bunk bed and he loved lying there and watching me cook in the little kitchen for breakfast. He said, 'I really love this'. He felt really safe in that camper van, really secure, because he's terribly insecure.

This account reveals not just a sensitive understanding of the child but an acceptance of his need for proximity and a secure base.

Some carers found the need for closeness overwhelming. Geoffrey's foster carers found the emotional demands too hard to deal with. At the beginning of his placement, Geoffrey used to ask for a cuddle about every quarter of an hour. His foster mother felt that this was 'not right' for a child of eleven and aimed to discourage this behaviour by 'rationing' his cuddles to a certain time each day. The demanding or needy behaviour diminished but was replaced by persistent 'winding up' behaviour such as turning the TV channel over when everyone was watching. These bids for attention were infuriating and the carers said they had to bear in mind the needs of the other foster children. Their tendency, therefore, was to try to ignore or suppress the behaviour.

Sometimes we let it go over our heads and he'd get beside himself. Literally. He's like somebody possessed. You can actually see it physically in him. Eventually, we have to say 'Geoffrey! Go and do something. You're getting on our nerves. Go and put the kettle on.'

The expression, "beside himself", sums up the high level of anxiety experienced by this child when his overtures are rejected. The carers did make some connections with his past rejection in the birth family but had come to feel that this was a difficult child who needed firmer control.

Accepting positives and negatives

Striking in a number of the interviews were accounts which reflected the high level of positive feelings which carers had for children. Mike's foster father was thrilled at how well Mike was doing and enjoyed shopping trips and trips to the sea where father and son shared fish and chips. 'He's a super boy – he's a lovely boy, he really is.' Sue's foster mother was very proud of her achievements and showed her photograph to the researcher:

Just look at her. She's got such a twinkle. She's an absolute rogue. And you would never want that squashed. It's lovely. Its just got to be channelled the right way.

As in Sue's case, the ability of the carers to accept both the positive and negative aspects of their foster children was apparent in many of the interviews. Carers were asked simply to describe their child in a few sentences and this elicited many replies which illustrated this underlying acceptance. Mira, for example, described Francis as:

Very hard work, the hardest of the lot of them, but he's a lovable child. He's got so many wonderful, good things about him, once you get under what I think are superficial, but horrendous things at times. But he's lovely. He's got the potential to be a really nice young man.

When children had exceptionally challenging behaviours, it could be hard for carers to sustain this balanced approach. It was all too easy to become bogged down by the difficulties and fail to notice progress or endearing qualities. A notable feature in several of the foster families where there were two full-time carers was the tendency for a couple to balance and counteract each other's views of the child. They could be encouraging to each other when one partner was only able to see the negatives or the lack of progress. Conversely, one of the single carers remarked that she really missed having someone else's perspective to remind her of 'the other side of the picture' when the going was tough.

Building self-esteem

If one of the major benefits of acceptance for an infant or child is to experience oneself as lovable, then most of these foster children were sorely in need of it. For these older children, self-esteem was not something that could be allowed to emerge gradually and naturally over the period from infancy to adolescence. They needed more active and urgent help to repair damaged selves. Messages of acceptance had to be linked with ways of making the children more acceptable to themselves, to the carers and to the outside world in order to facilitate their routes through school, peer groups and so on.

The majority of the carers recognised that poor self-esteem was a major issue for their child, or that it had been in the past and recovery was still fragile. Sensitivity to this underpinned much of the day-to-day care of the children and many carers were constantly alert to opportunities to 'boost the child up' or to avoid unnecessary knocks. Many carers used the small events of daily life to build their child's sense of self-worth. Wendy ensured that every one of Emily's pictures went onto the notice board. June made a point of removing all the toys and puzzles that Dean could not manage, so that he didn't have a sense of failure in his play. Many carers went to great lengths to help the children to take a pride in their appearance, to feel good about themselves and to be aware of their abilities and attributes.

Harvey's carer was aware that his fragile self-esteem could be unintentionally bruised in the day-to-day verbal exchanges of family life and he took extra care in this area:

> *You have to mind what you say to him if you're telling him off. You can't say 'you're silly'. You have to say, 'you're acting silly', or else he'll pick up on it straight away, then he'll really get a down on himself and say, 'I'm rubbish'.*

The encouragement and/or sharing of talents and interests was an important aspect of self-esteem building in many of the placements. One foster father was keen on fish ponds and was delighted that Rob (11) had also become interested, digging his own small pond beside his foster father's. This provided ongoing opportunities for praise and encouragement:

> *He loves his fish pond. Now he's in charge of his own and he's totally reliable in that department. We encourage him all we can. We say 'Rob's the top pond man' . . . He gave his talk at school on goldfish and got top marks.*

Sometimes, children who had the most severe difficulties at school or with their peers were able to find activities or interests where they really shone and received only positive feedback. Carla found it hard to make friends at school, but she could cope better in structured, task-centred groups. She was a keen and successful Guide and St John's Ambulance Cadet.

An important aspect of self-esteem building was that of creating opportunities for the children to give something to others. This was seen as a way of helping the child to feel competent as well as having the pleasure of receiving praise and thanks. Brian (6) wanted to clean his own bedroom to help his foster mother and she let him do this, feeling that it was beneficial to him. Louise sensed that it was important to William to be able to give her something.

> *When we were on holiday at half term, he said, 'I want to buy you something, Louise'. He knows I like teddy bears. He chose one with tartan paws. I didn't say, 'Don't spend your money on me'. I said 'I'd love him!'.*

Several older children were encouraged to have a special role as big brother or sister. This increased their self-esteem and attracted praise and appreciation from others.

Partiality/advocacy

As well as encouraging children to feel good about themselves in the foster home, children were being encouraged to be and feel accepted in the outside world of peers and schools. Sometimes this became a process of advocacy with the carers actively defending children or working with other people to engineer constructive experiences for them.

There was a common concern among the foster carers that, because of their difficulties, the children tended to miss out on the normal routine interactions with others that serve to affirm the individual and sustain positive self-regard. Children with disabilities were particularly susceptible to this and their carers worked hard to "normalise" behaviour and promote social inclusion. Joy spoke vividly about this issue:

You see, I know he's not normal and I know he's got learning disabilities and I want people to accept him for what he is, how he is. But there's a lot of things he's cottoned on to which he does because he needs to get people's attention. So they've grown to be his normal behaviour. So for him to be accepted, some of his behaviour has to be modified and he will get the benefits of that. I'll give you an example. We go to quite a nice hotel and he'll walk through into the breakfast room on his walker and everyone thinks he's so wonderful and it's great for him. They speak to him. They say, 'Billy, you're so clever, you're marvellous, you're such a beautiful boy'. And I just think that's part of what's building him up, not me but the response of all these other people and he'd never have got that, not how he was before.

An awareness of the children's vulnerability and disadvantage commonly resulted in the carers having a strong bias towards their children and demonstrating this in various areas of life. For some this was an unconscious process, for others, it was a conscious decision. Kim's foster carers worked hard to integrate her with other children, despite her severe learning disabilities. They felt that Kim gained a great deal from this, but that there was a two way process, in that other children and adults could learn things from Kim:

Melanie is a little girl who joined Brownies the same day as Kim. That made it quite special for Melanie. On the day they were enrolled, Melanie had every one in tears because Kim started to dribble and Melanie knew it was important to get it right and Melanie got the cuff of her Brownie uniform and wiped the dribble off her cheek. So Kim's taught other children things too. That caring is important.

In time, many children had come to trust and depend on the knowledge that their carers would 'stand up for them' and this seemed to be immensely valuable in the provision of a secure base and the building of relationships. Irene described an interaction with Naomi:

She would always tell me if she had a problem at school or if someone hit her in the playground. It's the first thing she does, as soon as she gets through the he door, it's 'Irene, someone . . .' and I say, 'Oh dear, I'll speak to your teacher. . . we'll get it sorted'.

Carers saw themselves as advocates for their foster children. Many had taken up their child's cause in meetings, in court, or in school and saw this as an essential element of the fostering role. Felicity reflected a commonly held view that the carer also had to represent the child to the social services department:

Because I do strongly believe that you are the voice for the child and you have to speak out for their good, because things do get over-looked, not through any fault, but through lack of time and resources. So sometimes you have to make a fuss.

For children with disabilities, the advocacy role was even more necessary. Joy spoke of the struggle to find leisure activities that were accessible to Billy:

He's got to learn to be with other children, to socialise, to see how other children behave. He can't do that on his own in the garden. I had a word with the Council because they've made a beautiful new play area, but there's not one thing for him. And they said they'd bring it up at the next meeting. But everything is a struggle, so much more than it needs to be. Generally, there's a lot of unacceptance.

Although some carers needed to ensure that other people were prepared to make some allowances for their children, carers of children with severe learning disabilities often found themselves working in the opposite direction. They were able to recognise aspects of their children that were developing normally and often had to remind others to treat them in an age-appropriate manner. Kim's carer found, for example, that people would often 'move in too quickly' on Kim, approaching her like a baby. This would make Kim anxious and uncomfortable, 'just like any nine-year-old'.

Working with schools

A large proportion of the children had learning difficulties and behavioural problems which manifested themselves in school, as reflected elsewhere in the literature (Aldgate *et al*, 1992). Partnerships with schools were therefore of vital importance and could be variously rewarding, time consuming or frustrating to the carers. Open communication was seen by many as the key to success. Carers made good use of "home/school books" to monitor success and difficulties and to help with consistency of approach and shared understandings. Some made a point of seeing the teacher every afternoon when they collected the child, others valued receiving or feeling free to make telephone calls whenever there was a concern. A number of carers had taken their role still further. They had become paid or voluntary lunchtime helpers or support workers in the classroom. One child had been excluded from school during lunchtime, but it was negotiated that he could stay in school, provided he was supervised by his foster father. These different forms of active participation in school life enabled the foster carers to keep a weather eye on the children in school, as well as giving messages that education was an important and shared enterprise. The message to the child was, I am here for you and you matter.

However, such positive partnerships were not always easy to sustain. Some carers felt that their children's difficulties were not fully understood or taken into account in school. Others felt pressurised by frequent telephone calls and took the view that the school ought to be able to cope. This was particularly the case where carers themselves were feeling overwhelmed by the child. These situations highlighted the need for shared understandings and behaviour management strategies to be facilitated by the social worker, in partnership with carers and schools.

Encouraging peer group friendships

This was an area of major difficulty for many of the children and one of great concern to the carers. For a few children, friendships came easily and they were comfortably integrated into the school or local community. For the majority, however, this was not the case. Many were socially isolated, some gravitated towards much older or younger children.

Several of the carers were working hard "behind the scenes" to encourage or sustain peer group friendships. Marian, for instance, had prepared the ground before Jon came to live with her. She went to the school and obtained a list of children who would be starting High School at the same time as Jon. From this she identified some that lived nearby. She approached a couple of parents and arranged that another child could walk to school with Jon for the first few days. A friendship had developed but Marian could see that Jon was finding it hard to trust and was avoiding contact. Marian then formally arranged to "childmind" this friend after school. Everyone was delighted with this arrangement and the friendship had flourished.

These moves to get the child accepted outside the home as well as inside can be experienced by the children as additional evidence that they mattered to the carer and were valued. Partiality of this kind is rarely mentioned in the attachment literature, although it is a significant tradition in family placement literature (Thoburn, 1994; Gilligan, 1997, 2000). It is an important and active part of communicating acceptance for older children and, very special for foster children, a sense of family and community membership.

Co-operation – interference

Babies enjoy having control and influencing others. Mothers who recognise, support and respect their babies' autonomy appear to co-

operate with their babies needs and accomplishments. There is a preference for shared, negotiated strategies to resolve difficulties. In contrast, interfering mothers do not recognise or respect their children's independence. (Howe *et al*, 1999, p. 19)

The movement from parental control towards co-operation develops naturally for securely attached babies as they move from total dependence to autonomy with support from the caregiver. With an infant, the caregiver is *de facto* in control and so can manage that transition comfortably. For new caregivers of older children, it is by no means clear that the caregiver is in control. Children commonly use controlling behaviour as a defence. Establishing boundaries as an "authoritative" parent (Maccoby and Martin, 1983) while respecting the child's autonomy is a necessary but not straightforward step. Where children had been out of control and had not experienced boundaries, one of the explicit tasks given to carers was to set boundaries to protect and to educate the child in how to behave. Conflict, control and boundary setting were themes in many of the interviews. This is partly because these are important issues for all parents but also because these children could present very challenging behaviours, including those that were aggressive towards foster families and dangerous to themselves.

Coping with anger and anxiety

Dealing with the children's anger and their own responses to it was part of daily life for many of the carers in the sample. Anger was often driven by anxiety and not surprisingly, carers who were trying to develop co-operative relationships had to work with children's diverse defensive strategies. One source of anxiety, of course, was the anxiety that the carers would not love them and might ask them to leave. Thus any response to difficult behaviour that was experienced as at all rejecting could heighten anxiety and increase the problems.

Carers had developed their approaches to managing behaviour through a mixture of trial and error, experience and instinct, and all were ready to admit that there were times when they became overwhelmed by their own feelings and simply "got it all wrong". In this dimension of caregiving, sensitivity and acceptance are also an integral part of encouraging autonomy and negotiation, since "getting it right" invariably had to be thought through with each child.

Emphasising the positive

The simplest and most common approach was therefore to cut through the difficult behaviour by building self-esteem and self-efficacy. It relied, in the midst of conflict, on communicating a belief that the child was basically a good thing, and on giving the child a sense of unconditional acceptance.

> *Robbie responds well to lots of positive praise. If you don't make too much of the negative things and make more of the positive he blooms. He can be helpful, very loving, very kind. A thoughtful little boy...*

Responding to the needs

Responding to underlying need was at times a useful way of resolving conflict. Cathy's carer was able to perceive her infantile needs through the 'front' of her compulsive behaviours. Cathy (7) needed repeatedly to go to the toilet before settling to sleep and would get hysterical if any attempt was made to reduce this. Co-operative strategies that relied on rational behaviour, such as star charts and rewards, were ineffective. The behaviour was so severe that the carer knew that some way had to be found to deal with the situation. Eventually, the carer 'instinctively' decided to wrap Cathy tightly in a flannelette sheet at bedtime. Cathy loved the feeling of this. When she was impelled to go to the toilet, her carer made it clear that she would only wrap her in the sheet once each night. In spite of some tempestuous scenes, Cathy eventually relinquished the behaviour, preferring to be soothed and swaddled tightly by her foster mother. Some months later, she still needs to have the sheet under her duvet. Such 'instinctive' behaviour by the caregiver is, however, based on an accurate reading of the situation and the child.

Thinking through behaviours

Sensitivity of this kind and thinking through the basis of behaviours could also be the key to staying calm and facilitating the child's own resolution of anger. Lucy's foster mother worked hard to understand what might be going on for Lucy. She talked about why it might be that Lucy had terrible rages and could bite, scratch and hit. She said:

These seem to happen out of the blue. Often it seems that she cannot accept or cope with requests like to brush her hair, if there is something else in her mind at that moment. If it doesn't fit with what's in her mind she just flips. Another thing is she's always frenetic and sometimes I think, really, she doesn't want to be here. Doesn't want to be told what to do. She has said, 'Don't tell me what to do. You're not my mummy.' Sometimes these feelings just rise to the surface and she can't help it.

The foster mother found that Lucy was persistently angry in the mornings and discovered that changing the routine was helpful. She decided to do the 'troublesome tasks', such as bathing, during the early evening – a time when Lucy was at her best. The 'nicer things', reading a story, were then saved for the morning and generally, there were improvements all round. The carer said that she knew she had to break the cycles before they got too established. Sometimes she could anticipate a violent outburst:

If I can get to her with physical affection before she explodes . . . She will never turn away from a cuddle, never turn down affection because it's too important to her.

When children did things that most parents find hard to cope with in their children, such as lying, it was particularly valuable to feel that at least the behaviour made some kind of sense. Making sense of the behaviours also enabled carers to see positive ways of handling it. As Stuart's carers put it:

Foster carer: *Because he had nothing to show for his life – so he had to pretend, to lie. He told this boy round the corner that his mum was a reporter and his dad was dead. It's sad really – because he had nothing – nothing to be proud of, that's why he needed that attention. He'd lie – and he isn't a liar – he knew it was a load of rubbish.*

Researcher: *So how have you helped him with that?*

Foster carer: *By trying to say to him – it doesn't matter that you*

207

> aren't top, haven't got the best bike – people like you
> as you are.

Avoiding and defusing conflict

Although it was generally acknowledged that there were occasions when conflict was inevitable, it was also important to avoid and defuse conflict before it got out of hand. Many carers had worked hard to develop tactics to achieve this. Barry had been assessed by an adoption agency prior to this placement as being too disturbed to cope with family life. He had learned to gain attention through a range of behaviours that his foster mother felt were specifically designed to be irritating. Her view was that Barry needed to learn to get attention in more positive ways and that she must learn not to respond. She found it helpful to have a pre-rehearsed verbal strategy that she could 'bring out' when she felt her anger rising:

> My line is: 'Barry, a lot of children have been through my home and I
> have learned over the years that these things don't worry me'.

This carer found that knowing what she was going to say enabled her to avoid becoming "drawn in" and that this particular message redressed the balance of power in their relationship without humiliating Barry in any way. But it also gave the message, 'I know you think you are exceptionally bad but you are not the only child to feel that and I can survive your anger'.

Breaking the cycle

Some carers were able to recognise a pattern in their child's moods and found that they could break the cycle by reorganising their usual routines or habits, as with Lucy, above. Cheryl's carers had developed a 'double act' to ensure that she did not experience any sense of 'waiting' for her food. Anxiety around this had caused major screaming fits in the past. They acknowledged that their strategy would seem extraordinary to an outsider, but the outcome of peaceful mealtimes was well worth it, they felt.

Anger could not always be defused and sometimes it was only in the aftermath of conflict that carers saw an opportunity to tap in to the child's vulnerabilities and offer infantile nurture and reassurance. Several foster mothers spoke of 'being there with a cuddle' once the child had calmed down. Diana used food, immensely significant to Stella, to demonstrate availability, reassure, comfort and provide a way back to the relationship.

I find that the best way is to say, 'Fine Stella, if you're not going to . . .' and I walk out of the room. So off I go into the garden or somewhere and then I hear her go into her bedroom and slam the door. When she's done that I might come back, make a sandwich and a drink and say, 'Stella, there's a drink ready for you,' and she comes out and we carry on.

Being open and direct

For many carers, use of punishment seemed too rejecting and attempts to engage with the children were seen as more important. Openness and directness from the carer seemed to facilitate the negotiation process.

I'd say, this is my rules. I'm not strict on him, because he will take notice of me. I've never been strict with him – I've never made him sit in his room. Because to me that is the worst thing you can do to a person – because I think he'd sit in there and think, oh, I hate her. It would all build up in him. The relationship I've got with Stuart, I'm straight with him. I tell him exactly what I feel, how I feel – what I want him to do at the end of the day and I don't have any confrontations with him. I might have a 'Oh! It's not fair! Can I stay out another 10 minutes?' and I might say OK because it's not a massive big issue.

The carer's strategy is to have faith in the relationship, to give the child access to her thoughts and feelings and then have the confidence to negotiate.

Showing the child another way

For some children, the carers had found that offering them their own strategy to deal with their anger had been helpful. One carer remembered her own childhood experience of biting her pillow in anger. Janice had responded to this idea and used it several times. 'Knowing what to do' in the early stages of an outburst had enabled her to regain a sense of control over herself and the situation.

For some of the most experienced carers, showing by example was used as a conscious strategy, in the belief that the effects of this would 'sink in' over time. Jean and Don felt that Don's gentle, placid manner was a daily reminder to Ricky (10) that men did not have to be angry and aggressive. Ricky had ongoing disputes with the son of a neighbour and this had become a problem at school. The foster carers decided on a proactive response. They arranged to take the two boys out for a day together in the holidays, to show them that they could relate positively to each other. The day was successful and the conflict had decreased.

Relinquish some control to the child

Many of the children could be controlling and coercive in their relationships both within and outside the foster family. Carers found themselves overwhelmed, at times, by their child's needs to be "the boss", "on top" to "manipulate" those around them.

Many recognised that a control battle with their child could never be won. Such tussles were exhausting and futile. The child would always have the last word. Some of the carers had found that a successful tactic in this arena was to actually relinquish some or all of the control over a situation to the child. Paradoxically, this frequently enabled the child to let go of the need for control and an equilibrium could be re-established.

On the morning of the foster carers' interview, for instance, Ricky had woken up in a 'controlling mood'. He had been bossy with the other foster children in the household, antagonistic towards his foster carers and taken an hour to eat a bowl of cereal. Sensing a 'blow up', Jean decided to relinquish some control to Ricky. She therefore told him that she was going to be there all day and she would walk him up to school whenever he was ready. After this, Ricky moved relatively quickly and arrived at school only a few minutes late. This can be seen as defusing the situation, respecting the child's autonomy and promoting co-operation.

Some carers were able to give and take control in this fluid way, letting go when it was of little consequence, but taking a firm hold when they felt it necessary. One foster mother described the way in which she sometimes had to "rescue" Barry from the powerful positions he could attain by being verbally hurtful to her:

Initially, Barry couldn't apologise for any of his behaviour. So I would get up and say, 'Well, I'll be the first to apologise then. I'll give you a cuddle'. And I'd get hold of him and he'd pull away and I'd say, 'Well, I'm not letting you go, because I need a cuddle back,' and eventually, the arms would come round and then he'd burst into tears and say, 'I'm sorry,' and he'd say, 'Why do I do it? Why do I do it?' He doesn't know why he does it. The trouble is, he digs himself such a big hole and he digs deeper and deeper and he can't get out of it. I have to take control then. I have to take the power off him and help him out.

The outcome of what could be described as the carer's gentle insistence was co-operation, with the child being helped to make a move towards the carer.

For some carers, however, it was hard to let go of control and there was a preoccupation with the need to assert their position and not allow the child to "rule the roost". Ruth's carers were concerned that Ruth had been "put on a pedestal" in her previous foster home where she was the favoured child. They felt that this was unhealthy, both for Ruth and her less favoured sibling. However, their attempt to redress the balance resulted in constant "battles" over rules and expectations. The negative cycles that resulted were not conducive to the building of a positive relationship in the early stages of the placement.

Some otherwise concerned and thoughtful carers were still struggling with the idea that they couldn't use occasional physical punishment as they had with their own children.

I don't know – we try to bring them up like our own children but we are very restricted in what we can do. I don't want to go round bashing children but when they get really out of order they need a quick smack. Our main worry is controlling them.

Although few carers mentioned the idea of smacking children, the issue here of 'can we bring these children up as we would our own?' and the balance of power between the children, the carers and the social services department was creating difficulties.

Accessibility – ignoring

Accessible mothers, although they might be busy on other matters, remain alert and available to their infants should the need arise. Ignoring mothers continue to be absorbed in their own pursuits. They fail to notice their children's signals . . . (Howe *et al*, 1999, p. 19).

The capacity to be alert and available to the infant is a central part of Winnicott's concept of maternal preoccupation (Winnicott, 1965). The mother keeps the infant in mind and the carer needs to do the same for the older child. This has been apparent throughout the previous dimensions of sensitivity, acceptance and co-operation but accessibility merits a special discussion since it can be quite a subtle process and was an area which some carers managed much more successfully than others.

Keeping the child in mind

It is important for school-age children to feel that their carers have them in mind even when they are at school all day. Children were reported to be delighted at receiving a special pair of trousers or a favourite food that carers had bought for them during the day. Even the active role that carers were playing in the children's school lives, including helping at school, could be said to be contributing to that sense of unbroken concern that children need to experience. The magic of being met regularly from school by a carer was greatly appreciated by some of these older children.

Whichever of us picks him up from school, his face lights up, he'll see you across the playground. And he'll run up to you and wrap his arms around you – it's lovely.

Similarly, one carer gave a moving account of how the family thought about the child during contact and looked forward to him returning.

I really miss Sam when he's not here at the week-end. Sunday about five – we're all, 'Sam'll be back in an hour' – you miss him being here, being around.

Sam enjoys contact and it is valued by his foster family, but he also clearly feels that sense of welcome and rushes to play with his foster brother as soon as he gets in the door.

Knowing that someone was thinking about you and worrying about you was an important new experience for some children.

I don't need to come down hard. To Jerry [11] it's nice to know that someone cares that much. If he's out playing, he'll go off to someone's house, and we'll be round the streets, where is he? And we say to him, never go in, if you go in anywhere come and tell us. We don't know where you are. You could have been taken away or anything. We need to know – we don't want anything to happen to you. We let him know that it's because we care about him that we need to know where he is – not just being strict for the sake of it.

Where children were taking risks and in dangerous situations, the availability of carers to rescue them was another building block for the relationship. On the occasions mentioned previously, when one child jumped into the deep end of a swimming pool and walked on broken glass, risk-taking occurred in the presence of the foster carer and became an opportunity to disconfirm the internal working model of neglectful caregiving. The foster mother responded immediately and predictably with concern and appropriate help.

In many carers' interviews, there were references to noticing signs of distress, being attuned to the signals given off by the children at times of anxiety and upset. These ranged from the overt, 'being loud, miserable, abusive' to the more subtle such as failing to say goodnight or having an indefinable aura of unhappiness. Pam could read John's mood by the way in which he put his school bag down when he came home; Carol looked for signs of picking around Paula's nails. In each of these cases, the carers were keeping the child in mind, and then quick to interpret the signals and respond to the underlying feelings when the moment was right.

Making yourself available

As in the example of Margaret's carer given earlier, who hovered near her, pretending to tidy the bedroom, in case the child felt able to speak of her worries, Sandra's carer had developed strategies for responding when she sensed something was wrong.

I kind of know now so I purposely take her out so she'll tell me [laughs] *I know now . . . if I can't get her out of it at home, I put her in the car and take her out to town or something then I know she'll tell me.*

This carer would go to the trouble of inventing the need to go shopping just to get Sandra into a situation where she might feel able to share her worries. The carer is saying not only, 'I'm here – you can trust me,' but is also actively making herself accessible in ways Sandra can use.

However, when some carers were feeling overwhelmed by the child's needs, they could be ignoring or resistant to the signals. One carer remarked that her child would not express her worries but 'hinted a lot' and expected people to enquire about what was wrong. The carer deliberately did not respond to this, seeing it as 'attention seeking' and best ignored.

It was especially important, therefore, for the carers to be alert and available to provide reassurance and nurture, when the time was right for the child. The following story illustrates a very emotionally abused child gradually beginning to trust in and then make good use of his foster mother's availability. At the beginning of his placement, Nicholas (8) was very reluctant to have any emotional contact with his foster mother. He was angry, distant and wary. She responded to this by deliberately creating situations where they could be close together but where he could take his time. She described, for example, sitting on the settee in front of children's television programmes, while Nicholas circled round the house dragging his duvet, which had become a source of comfort to him. Eventually, Nicholas would circle closer and closer and was finally able to sit next to her. Over the weeks, he took less time to come to her and would suddenly launch himself at her. In time he allowed her to put her arms around him and he eventually gave up the need for the duvet.

It almost goes without saying that in order to make the child's world feel safe, carers needed to remain as stable and as predictably available, physically and emotionally, as they could manage. Boundaries were important but so also were predictable mealtimes and bedtimes. Having tea at exactly the same time each day was all part of the child knowing what to expect and knowing that the carer had taken the trouble – this soothed the children's anxieties.

So, food and bedtimes were targeted, sometimes consciously some-times not, as good times to demonstrate availability, care and concern and to settle and sort anxieties that had cropped up in the day. Even older children wanted to be tucked in every night. In many respects such processes that were gone through were reminiscent of attachment forma-tion in infancy. They involved closeness, intimacy, both emotional and physical:

> *Jerry* [11] *always wants cuddles . . . He likes to be tucked up at night. He liked me to bath him, dry him – but I've said he's too old now, you must bath yourself. But he'd have me bath him and dry him. I do occa-sionally put his clothes on for him, to make him feel a bit special – he likes that. I put him to bed and tuck him up and right you're in. He kisses me now – whereas before it was just a cuddle but now he kisses me. But he does like being babied, he definitely likes being babied.*

These accounts underline the physical and emotional energy required in parenting these emotionally vulnerable children. Many of them were at a chronological age of increasing emotional independence and self-reliance, but their needs were those of much younger children.

Conclusion

The levels of commitment and parenting skills involved in providing secure parenting to these exceptionally needy children are clearly remarkable. Caregiving which provides a secure base for children also meets a range of other needs and promotes their welfare in all aspects of their lives. These included self-esteem building, developing talents and interests, advocacy, working with schools and encouraging peer group friendships. Such endeavours correspond closely to the key areas identi-fied by Gilligan (1997, 2000) in the promotion of resilience, the ability of children and adults to cope with stress and adversity. Parenting older children in new placements needs to simultaneously develop new relationships in the family while fortifying children with the means to cope with the demands of their everyday lives.

Summary

- Providing children with a secure base is fundamental to parenting children in long-term foster placements.
- Foster carers gave examples of a range of caregiving strategies. These can be understood using the dimensions identified by Ainsworth *et al* (1971) for understanding the development of secure attachments in infancy.

  - *Sensitivity–insensitivity*: Sensitivity required an ability in carers to think through the child's behaviours and their own responses. This allowed carers to use flexible explanations of a child's behaviour, to make sense of connections between past and present, to have empathy with the child and to see the needs behind the behaviour.

  - *Acceptance–rejection*: Acceptance required the capacity to accept the child's emotional demands, to accept both the positive and the negative aspects of the child, to build self-esteem and, essential for this age group, to help the child be accepted in schools and peer groups.

  - *Co-operation–interference*: In promoting co-operation, carers helped the child to manage their anger and distress as well as managing their own reaction to it. Carers showed how, by thinking through behaviour, they were able to defuse conflict and enable the child to begin to control their own behaviour.

  - *Accessibility–ignoring*: The need to remain accessible to the child required carers to keep the child in mind, to be emotionally and psychologically available. For older defended children, it meant having strategies to facilitate the child's approaches. The goal was to provide a secure base which the child could use to enable them to face the challenges of coping with the past, the present, and the prospect of the future.

Part III

The long-term placements: social workers, birth families and contact

11 Social work practice in the long-term placements

As can be seen from the previous chapters describing the children's behaviour and relationship difficulties and the complex parenting task facing foster carers, there is a sense that what is happening in the foster home has an intense and private life of its own, as with any family. However, social workers have not only a statutory responsibility to monitor the child's safety and welfare in the placement but also a professional obligation to support the placement and help to make it work. This combination of monitoring and supporting, the exercise of protective authority on the one hand and the provision of emotional and practical support on the other, is tricky enough in short-term placements. But it raises major dilemmas for childcare and family placement social workers when the carers have made a commitment to care for quite young children up to, and in most cases beyond, the age of 18. This tension is apparent in many of the interviews, not only with the social workers but also with the carers, when the wish to "normalise" the situation for the child as part of an ordinary family comes up against the legal and procedural requirements designed to protect and promote the welfare of the child in placement. Anxiety about the stigma of being in care added to such dilemmas. The capacity to take such tensions in their stride and get on with the job of caring for the child was evident in many foster families and some social workers also felt very comfortable with how their role was evolving. But in many cases, questions still remained as to how best this complex situation could be managed.

Although there are Children Act 1989 guidelines and Department of Health procedures relating to the reviewing of all looked after children and research has suggested effective models of practice in permanent placement (Thoburn, 1994), the absence of specific agency procedures for long-term foster care practice meant that social workers and teams developed their own patterns of working. These drew on a range of ideas about what was most likely to ensure that placements survive and meet the needs of children. Capturing the range and complexity of these ideas and the practice that results is not easy, but it makes sense to examine the roles and tasks of the social work professionals in relation to each of the three main participants: the child, the birth parents and the foster carers. The first two are almost exclusively the domain of the childcare social workers. The third is that of both childcare and family placement social workers. Each will be considered in turn, followed by an analysis of practice in terms of the levels of service provided to the placement.

Work with the children

Working with the children was the task of the child care social worker. Descriptions of the work being done with the children reflected to some extent the variety of placement circumstances (for example, new/matched or established/formerly short-term), the circumstances of the social worker (new, temporary, established or about to change) and the agency policy or practice about the priority to be given to long-term cases. The language used by social workers to describe their role covered a range from task-centred "work with" to varied accounts of "having a relationship with" the child. Their comments also reflected an acknowledgement that this was a changing situation, so that whatever the current level of visiting or support, there was always the possibility of change. There was also a view that, however fluctuating and challenging the placement might be, it was a relief to be out of the troubled waters of child protection decision making, courts and family finding and to feel that the child now had the chance of a settled family life.

Linking with the past

The child's current relationship with the social worker could benefit from the fact that in some cases the social worker had acted as a bridge through difficult transitions, a sense of having been through thick and thin together. This had value in itself in terms of continuity but was also a benefit when the child settled into a stable long-term family. One social worker for a seven-year-old said:

> Michelle's changed quite a bit since I first saw her. It started with her being removed from home – she was very different, wouldn't communicate, wouldn't ask for help. She wasn't a child really, she was just this

little person who was very self-sufficient. The work has gone from preparing her for court, on to moving placements, bridge placement, the fact that she wasn't going home, the different carers who she was having contact with – to the point where we've got a little girl in her long-term placement which she's delighted to be in, moving schools and all of those things. So she's changed dramatically.

There is a sense here that the social worker brings her knowledge of the child's history into her current visits to the settled child. This history reflects not only the facts of the birth family circumstances or previous placements but two other major histories – the history of Michelle as a four-year-old, five-year-old and six-year-old; and the history of powerful and mixed feelings associated with parting from a loved grandmother and an intense if neglectful and abusive set of family relationships. More than any life story book, this social worker holds that history for the child and looks after it. In doing so, she can make the dangerous events and feelings safe and accessible, since she has not been destroyed or driven away by such shared experiences as the tension of waiting for court decisions and Michelle's own anger and distress. The social worker's visits are an open recognition that life can carry on. It is not surprising in this case that contact only became comfortable for Michelle and her carers, and indeed the birth family, when the plan was changed so that this social worker rather than various other staff did the transport and supervision. The social worker was then able to help the child and the carer with this particular roller coaster of emotion and anxiety.

Many social workers focused their involvement on helping the child to deal with issues around the birth family. This was a piece of work which some carers were not able to manage and which in any event seemed appropriate because of the social worker's knowledge and direct contacts with the birth family. Some of this work was in the form of life story work, if that had not been done earlier, or supporting the child by transporting to contact. Other work might be more in terms of demon-strating sensitivity to the child's concerns about what was happening in the birth family. It was interesting to find two parallel cases of very thoughtful social work practice from different agencies, of which this is a good example:

His mother now lives in the town but before she lived 15 miles away and that was a great concern to Johnny, because she moved there after he left the home, to a town he didn't know. We actually took him to see where she would be living before she moved in so at least he'd have some idea, because he was very concerned. I think it has helped him a lot since she's moved back and he knows that she's only a mile down the road.

Some, but not all, of the cases reflected aspects of social work practice similar to those used in adoption placements. Life story work was a good example of this. The fact that in so many cases short-term became long-term made it less obvious for there to be a point when life story work should be done. Whether a child is comfortable with their personal history, birth family and identity issues must depend on the child's ability to understand and make sense of what has happened and that may come from a number of sources.

It was not possible to put a figure on how many children had life story work, because there were clearly so many different ways of defining it. In one case, the social worker said she had not done life story work, but she had worked intensively with the child through the moves from home and through two foster placements. She accompanied the child to contact and helped her and the carers deal with the complex situations arising in the birth family. The child (7) had a large number of family photographs, which she showed the researcher and talked through in some detail. In such cases, social workers had in fact done valuable life story work, although this had not involved the construction of a book.

In another contrasting case, the child and the carer got caught up in a mixture of poor practice and the social work debate about the nature of life story work.

Foster carer: *The social worker come down here and said she'd do a book of life – I don't know what that is. She said to me, can you go and buy an exercise book? And Alice had to find all her photos. And when the social worker went, she said, 'I'll be back sometime but if not you can get on with it'. Alice had had to cut photos up out of her album.*

Researcher:	*So she'd got them in an album already?*
Foster carer:	*Yes, but she had to cut them up to put them in the scrap book. So then when this new social worker came on Tuesday he said, about the book of life. He said – the book of life is not just about sticking photos in scrap books!*

As children were on the move and in transition, it was sometimes social workers who knew most about a child and were consistent at a difficult time. Examples given above highlight the benefits of continuity but also suggest the difficulties that can arise where social workers move on. One social worker, who had worked intensively with the child for a year, was leaving his post the following week after the interview and the case was unlikely to be allocated. He explained that he carried the child's history 'more in my head than on the files'.

Building a relationship in the long-term placement

The social workers were asked to describe a typical visit. They painted quite similar pictures of attempting to build or sustain a warm and positive relationship with the child. Visits usually involved seeing the child alone and with the foster family. The content of the one-to-one interactions varied. Many children, for example, were reluctant to engage in too much talk about that most difficult of subjects, their birth families.

Eddie, his foster carer, the foster carer's son and I sit in the sitting room. We talk about general issues. Sometimes he wants to show me something from school. Then Eddie and I will go up in his room and we go from that, and we have half an hour and we talk about contact arrangements. He answers my questions – sometimes there's not much detail. He is willing to respond but not in full. He likes to talk about all his activities at school – football, table tennis and so on. He prefers to discuss these issues rather than family matters.

Eddie is a "closed book" child who keeps his feelings well hidden from his carers as well, although it seems to be at a cost. Not surprisingly the more open children show their characteristic pattern in their relationships with the social worker.

Zoe's always pleased to see me. Always pleased to have attention. Always smiling. Honest. Always bright. Wants to do things, wants to chat, wants to talk. Wants affection, physical contact as well as talk about what she's been doing. Not more than once a month in the foster home – we might go for a walk but on her territory. It's very informal – I go in almost as a friend of the family.

This notion of a positive role in the child's life being associated with a role as 'friend of the family' is understandable in the context of shared concern for Zoe but does raise issues about the extent to which children might feel able to disclose any problems which they had in their foster family or the extent to which the social workers themselves might voice any worries of their own. This social worker was reassured by the fact that the child had felt able to phone her when in a previous placement.

Zoe's asked for contact and will be specific. In the other foster home she got home one day and said she wanted to speak to her social worker. The carer said, is it private or is it something I can help you with? She said, it's private. She was allowed to ring me and said she'd rather see me face-to-face. So I went to see her – and she said she hadn't had a contact for some time with her family. I was very pleased – it made me think if she wasn't happy with her care she would tell me.

One male social worker said that it was not so easy to be alone with a female child. Although there were issues about boundaries which had particular implications for this worker, the question of public/private, personal/professional boundaries arose for all social workers. The worker is present in the foster home by statutory rights and duties but the roles and the relationships had to be very delicately negotiated with both the children and the carers.

Responding to the child's changing needs
Social workers often spoke of the pleasure and satisfaction of watching a child become gradually more relaxed and settled in the foster home:

There was a time when things became unsettled when decisions were made about Patricia's future and some anxiety around the time – a time of regression. Then there came one thing that I couldn't put my finger on for a while – she just changed. Children in care often look anxious, there's a stressed look in school photographs, and then one day quite recently in her present placement – she'd just changed. It was the look in her eyes.

Such changes were reflected in the developing relationship with social workers.

Social worker: *Tim regards me as quite a friend. He chats away about school and the foster home and his family. He's very spontaneous, you don't have to drag conversation out of him. It's nice now . . .*

Researcher: *Has he always been responsive with you in that way?*

Social worker: *No – the relationship has definitely changed. He was a very angry child – he actually kicked a colleague trying to get him to school.*

The intensity of the involvement with the child currently was seen as appropriately reducing, although this social worker remained one of the most involved and active in the study. She attempted to define the changed role, acknowledging the possibility that the child can form new close relationships while also retaining the relationship with the person who saw them through difficult times:

Because I know Tim so well, you sometimes feel that the child transfers to the foster carers but he still has that relationship with me as well. I shall continue seeing him but my role decreases as he becomes more one of the family and I wouldn't want to interfere with his relationship with the carers, but I can't see that happening because he sees me quite differently.

For social workers who had been through the difficult times, it was clear that some children's decreased need for a relationship with them was a sign that things were going well in attachment terms in the foster family.

When I was involved with Anthony [then aged 3] when he was with his mum he was quite clingy to me. It was really disturbing. I used to go to hospital appointments and he would run to me, he would want me to go with him – he wouldn't want mum. He didn't go to mum for comfort. And since he's been with Theresa [foster carer] that's changed. When we went to hospital appointments he turned to Theresa and that was lovely.

This could lead to a more distinct cooling in the relationship between child and social worker.

Sometimes Anthony says on the phone, 'Don't want you to come round'. I think if he's feeling a bit insecure about certain things . . . The relationship has changed. He's quite happy to see me if it's a fun thing but if he's looking for comfort and for security he goes to Theresa and I think really he'd just as soon I wasn't there.

A social worker may need support and supervision to make good sense of and then live with the fact that children who have previously viewed them as source of affection and protection appear to create distance or reject them.

In other situations, children seemed to be signalling that, although pleased to see the social worker, they simply have less need for the emotional input once settled in placement, as this social worker for two brothers described:

They usually give the impression of being pleased to see me and want to show me something they've brought home from school – a new toy or to tell me what they've been doing. After that initial greeting bit – instead of that level of involvement being maintained in the way that it always has been, increasingly they are opting out of involvement with myself and just getting on with the other things that they need to do . . . Since being with their forever family their need for me – I was so involved with the planning of this and they wanted it so much that they did need to be interacting at a high level with me then, but now that that goal has been achieved and after an initial period of inter-action, that need is less and I see that as positive.

Although this shift occurred and was felt to be appropriate, it would be wrong to assume that such visits were meaningless to the children. The fact that the social worker could positively acknowledge to the carers and the boys themselves that it was now OK to have a closeness that excluded the social worker could be helpful and the sense of continuity and history would still be of value.

"Cooling off" behaviour as described above was not always easy to read and other social workers were understandably anxious that the child's reluctance to spend time with them might be more to do with negative associations with social workers, or with this social worker in particular, a fear perhaps that the social worker might move them on. Robert (8) had had several moves, including an adoption placement that failed. The social worker commented:

I've tried to keep a very low profile because at his previous placement he became quite frightened of me – frightened of change. I think he was being fed wrong information about me and the powers I had to make decisions. At the end of last year I could see fear. I'm very aware that whenever I visit, Robert thinks, is she going to move me?

Some social workers felt that the relationship was either not significant or may even be potentially harmful. Robert's social worker, however, was aware of the value of continuity, and aimed to use her relationship to reduce the child's anxiety about further moves.

I'm not seeing him very often at the moment, now that he's staying where he is. It's been suggested that I be taken off the case. I wasn't too happy with that and nor were the foster carers. I agreed with them. I've seen Robert through crises, he knows me now. He's had so many changes it would be the wrong thing to do. What messages would it give him? I've spoken to my manager – and I think I'll get my way!

Monitoring the child's welfare in the placement

This description still only gives a flavour of the wide ranging activity of social workers with children. Part of the role which should not be forgotten was the task of formally monitoring the quality of the child's welfare. As well as seeing the children individually and informally, social workers were also completing Looking after Children forms for and with these children. As one social worker for a large sibling group commented, this was quite a challenge.

It appears that there are different areas which need to be balanced as social workers decide how to work with children in long-term place-ments. First, they have to balance the need to ensure the child is safe and protected while supporting and promoting the survival of this placement. Secondly, they need to think through the balance between a role involving key social work tasks, such as offering specific practical or therapeutic help to foster children, and a role which is more that of an ongoing supportive relationship. It is most likely that the balance in these different areas will vary appropriately at different times during a placement but this needs to be a matter for professional judgement, checked in super-vision.

Working with the birth family

The role of the childcare social worker in relation to the birth family was again so varied that it was quite difficult to gauge the nature or quality of overall practice. Working with feelings about the birth family in the mind of the child seemed a particularly necessary piece of work but there were examples of direct support being offered to birth families, around reviews, around contact and generally in enabling them to remain involved with their children. This is an account by a social worker with a vulnerable birth mother.

It is so difficult to discuss things because she finds it difficult to stay on the point but she pops in to see me when she wants to. Obviously she's always consulted – she's very good at attending any meetings about him and all reviews. Contact is important for her as well as for him. She likes to get him things even on a limited budget and is very proud of being able to buy him things and comes to tell me, 'I bought him this or bought him that'. She's actually quite, almost childlike herself and likes to get one's approval. There often the role is, 'Yes, you're doing well'. Like last time I took him out I said, 'I like your trousers,' and he said, 'Mum bought me those,' and next time I saw her, she asked me if I'd seen them and I told her how nice they were.

This relationship with the birth mother is made possible by the social worker's willingness to be available to see her (which should be possible for all birth parents) but also to be available to look after her feelings. In other cases, parents used the link with the social worker perhaps as an easier way to stay in touch with the child than contacting the foster carer.

Social worker: *The birth parents normally attend reviews. I have quite good contact with the parents. I see them at other times too. It is valuable with this family. Although they've abused the children, Brenda* [birth mother] *has had quite a lot of counselling around the abuse.*

Researcher: *Do you think it helps around contact etc. if you've seen them?*

Social worker: *I do. It helps all round. We had problems around Tracey* [eldest child]. *They appreciate that day to day. They will ring me up and ask me how they're getting on.*

In such cases, social work contact with birth parents enabled placements to feel more comfortable for all parties. In other cases, work with parents could be critical to protect the placement from disruption.

There will need to be extra work with the family. As Tommy [5] *gets more settled some family members are saying they'll have him back. They could put pressure on the placement. At the time of the placement they were very constructive but as time's gone on – and if anyone had known this would happen we might have thought differently about what should happen.*

This was a case of a child who was three at placement for whom adoption had been ruled out, partly because the family was seen as both important and co-operative. This example highlights the way in which foster placements change and develop as the child gets older, but so also may the role of birth families, particularly when the child appears to have been 'made better' and memories of the difficulties in caring for him start to fade. The challenge is one of sustaining the child's sense of permanence when key players offer different views.

In several cases it was suggested that there should be a change of social worker. In this example, the mother objected to the social worker who had been involved for some years. The social worker was apparently accepting of this.

I think the work the new social worker needs to do is with mum, coming to terms with what has happened, so that mum can work with us because mum actually gets on well with Thelma [foster carer] normally and we've got to get back to that so that they can work in partnership, and mum can work with a social worker she trusts.

The importance of partnership with the birth mother was clearly articulated but in this particular case long-lasting and acrimonious court proceedings had only recently finished and more time was needed. However, it appeared that the partnership principle was taking precedence over the social worker's relationship with the child and the carer. It was not seen as possible to consider having a separate worker for the mother, which should have been an option.

Work with the foster carers

Both childcare social workers and family placement social workers were engaged in a range of tasks in relation to the foster carers. In some cases, the roles and relationships were clearly defined, in others they were confused, overlapping or uncertain. Most foster carers reported in their questionnaires that response times to contact made with social workers were good. But perhaps the more significant questions were, did social workers visit regularly enough and would carers ring for help and advice before or after the placement had got into serious difficulty?

Childcare social workers

Childcare social workers varied considerably in the levels and nature of their input to the foster carers. They could have a unique role as the person who had the most detailed knowledge of a particular child or a specific problem or disability. They could be active as advocates for carers and children, as well as developing supportive, interpersonal relationships. Alternatively, they could be new to the case (a frequent problem) or have only limited understanding of specialist requirements.

Active involvement by childcare social workers might be because the social work role was focused around a particular activity. Josie has autistic tendencies and the social worker worked closely with the foster family. She was currently doing life story work, compiling a book with the foster carer in Josie's presence. She felt that this was time well spent, as Josie may have been absorbing more than she revealed. The carer valued her support and the social worker envisaged that the monthly visiting would continue. She was from a specialist children with disabilities team and the carer appreciated her specialist knowledge. In addition, there were approximately three-weekly visits from a family placement social worker, who felt that regular, proactive support is valuable and prevents difficulties from building up.

Family placement social workers

Family placement social workers were on the whole clearly focused on their roles and tasks in relation to the foster carers. Again, there was a good deal of variation in the nature and intensity of their involvement but, as described in Chapter 4, most carers valued the support they received from their "link workers". Some further issues emerged in our interviews with the workers themselves.

Mediators

Many family placement social workers found themselves in the role of mediator between the foster carers and the childcare social workers. Family placement social workers often knew the foster family well, having done their home study or had a substantial involvement with them. There were occasions when they were able to interpret the carers' words and actions to the social worker and vice versa, helping to build understandings and partnership:

> I would like Neville [foster carer] to calm down a bit and I try to help him to understand what it's like to be a social worker. But he is not a social worker. And I try to help social workers to understand what it's like to care for these children all day every day and that it's unfair of us to put too much pressure and make too many demands on him.

A further area of mediation was in the tension between the needs of the carers to establish the child as part of their family and the continuing relationships and sense of identity with the birth family. Childcare social workers were sometimes perceived as being focused on the needs of the child in relation to the birth family to the exclusion of those of the foster family. For instance, one worker described a decision regarding contact being taken at a review, with the birth parent present. The carers did not feel able to object, but were concerned that the arrangement implied a big commitment from all the family and would have liked an opportunity to discuss and consider it. The family placement social worker was later able to mediate an arrangement that suited all parties.

Sometimes there were criticisms from family placement social workers that the childcare social workers appeared to be working as if this was a short-term placement, where there was no need to establish a sense of the child's belonging in the foster family. One had arranged contact at the same time as the child's practice for the village football team, another had arranged for the child to attend a birth family wedding, unaccompanied. On both occasions, the family placement social worker had intervened in support of the carers' views that they should have been consulted about such arrangements in view of the long-term plan for the child in their family.

Parenting

It was perhaps surprising that the very area that might be anticipated to be the focus of professional attention, parenting and the carer–child relationship, was the one where family placement workers, and indeed childcare social workers, had least confidence in offering advice and help.

There was a good deal of deference to carers and some uncertainty among the family placement social workers regarding whether or not they should advise on parenting issues. Many expressed a degree of disquiet about an aspect of parenting in the placements and yet few felt able or willing to raise the subject with the carers. Parenting was not generally an area in which the carers requested advice and the family placement social workers were reluctant to broach these sensitive matters. One worker wished that the foster mother would 'warm up' in her handling of the child and had been waiting for months for a suitable opportunity to tackle this. Another was slightly concerned about the 'horseplay' between a foster father and a child and knew he would have to find a way to mention this as tactfully as possible. Some workers had asked support foster carers to give parenting advice, feeling that a peer approach would be more acceptable to the carers. The feeling from workers appeared to be that carers were, by definition, "expert" parents and any attempt to comment would be seen as presumptuous. Perhaps carers, too, felt that they ought to be experts and found it all the more difficult to ask for help. If parenting problems are not discussed there is a risk that problems can too exclusively be laid at the door of the child – it must be him or her who is so difficult – or that "struggling" as a carer is accepted as inevitable.

A small number of family placement social workers had established themselves in an advisory capacity regarding behaviour management. This was the case in the placement of a child with disabilities, where there was no specialist service available from the childcare social workers. Initially, this had taken the form of advising on appropriate toys and activities but the role had extended over time:

Well, that sort of developed with her following my advice. Luckily, all the things I suggested seemed to work, so we got into a habit of every situation she encountered she would talk through and I would say, 'well, how about trying this,' and she is a person who will respond. Now there is no hesitation in her saying, 'Adrian is doing this. What do you think?' And together, we come up with a couple of suggestions of what she can try.

Overall, however, there was a lack of confidence surrounding this role. Many family placement social workers felt insufficiently skilled to advise on behaviour management, although they could see that the need was there. The independent fostering service provided a therapist who worked closely with the child and the carer and dealt with all behavioural matters. One local authority worker had been trying, unsuccessfully, to obtain funding for a behavioural psychologist to work with the foster carer and several mentioned behaviour management as a "gap" in the foster carer training. At the same time, many of the foster carers stated that they would like more help in this area, both parties thus highlighting a major shortfall in the support services.

Difficulties in establishing a role

In a small number of cases, the family placement social workers reported difficulties in fulfilling their supportive role to the foster carers. There were differing reasons for this. Some "family builders" were, for example, resistant to professional involvement of any kind. They wished to be autonomous as a family unit and preferred to use their own sources of support. Their workers felt that they were seen as intrusive and interfering and the tendency was to have a minimal involvement and to focus on the practicalities such as travel claims and fostering allowances.

Very occasionally, there were major differences of opinion which could not be resolved and relationships had become strained as a result. Financial matters could be an issue here and also the tendency of some families to take significant decisions (e.g. to go on holiday without the child or to take other children on emergency placements) without reference to the family placement team. In these cases, the tension between the carers' needs for autonomy and the expectations of them by the local authority had become heightened to the point where the family placement workers were feeling undermined or sidelined.

Negotiating roles and responsibilities

One of the questions that was asked was about the kinds of areas the child care or family placement social worker might feel were appropriate for them to tackle with carers and again aspects of parenting came up.

Researcher: *If the carers had problems with parenting a sexually abused child, would they talk to you or the fostering worker?*

Child care   *I would see that as a fostering issue.*
social worker:

This explicit response, whether appropriate or not, was fairly unusual. On the whole there was a lack of clarity around the boundaries between childcare social work and family placement social work. Often the roles seemed to be divided on the basis of who had been around longest, or knew the child or carer best. In a few cases, the fostering worker knew the child better than the childcare social worker because the childcare social workers kept changing. In other cases, the childcare social worker was active in supporting the carer because the family placement team had reorganised or was overwhelmed.

This role confusion needs to be resolved. The child's welfare is paramount and that is the priority of both childcare and family placement workers, as most workers clearly understood. The case can perhaps be argued along the same lines as partnership with birth parents. The goal of supporting foster carers and working in partnership with them is to ensure the well-being of the child in the context of the long-term foster care plan. This may mean, for example, prioritising the foster family's welfare in order to promote the fulfilment of this plan. This balance was being achieved in many cases. But if both workers are standing back from questions around relationships and parenting, the needs of children or carers are not likely to be met.

Levels of involvement: models of practice

Childcare and family placement social workers developed varied patterns of working which led to different intensity of involvement across the participants in the placement. This seemed to relate to their different definition of what long-term foster care was about as well as what an appropriate social work service should be.

Active and sustained involvement

In about a third of the cases, social workers saw their involvement as ongoing and proactive. They visited frequently and regularly, whether or not there were problems. There were various reasons given for using this model. In cases which were less problematic, the purpose of the visits was to sustain a trusting relationship, so that the door would be open, should a more active service be needed in the future. The following family placement social worker expressed this view clearly:

> For me, it is my way of working because I think that it is very important to build up a relationship with a carer for them to trust you so that when there are any problems, they come to you before they become major incidents. You know so they can feel safe to come and say, 'I'm having a problem. Help!' and I think that relationship is very important.

A further reason for proactive support was that it was seen to have a preventive function. There was benefit in tackling problems early, before they became larger or more entrenched. A regular visit was a means of "checking out" what was happening in the placement and catching anything that might need attention at the earliest possible stage.

This was particularly important with placements which were high risk because of the children's behaviour and difficulty in forming relationships. Will's social worker visited regularly even though Mandy, his carer, was very experienced. In some senses, regular visiting was even more important where carers were known to be generally successful, because they might be even less likely to ask for help. Visiting on request and possibly only in a crisis would not be a helpful model. Will's disturbed behaviour pattern was to constantly control, manipulate and "wind up" carers and other children in the household and it was important for the carer to have somewhere to talk this through and let off steam. In such cases, where children were particularly difficult to live with, frequent, proactive support was seen as being necessary to sustain the placement, to 'keep the carers going', as Mandy's social worker attested:

> I will sustain my support at this level for as long as it is needed because I think that Mandy needs to know that I am there for her, so I won't back out until she is quite happy for me to do so... You know, if we are going to sustain the placement, then we need to put in all the support that we can and if that means I have to go in every couple of weeks to talk to Mandy and make sure she is OK, and everything else is OK, then I will do that.

In several of the "professional" placements, regular, high level support visits were built in to the placement arrangements and the workers felt this to be a valuable service. In other placements there was also an acknowledgement that the serious difficulties of the child meant that the placement would always be a high risk venture. Active involvement would have to continue for the foreseeable future and would have to include a partnership within the professional network.

Social worker: *Melissa's therapist will work with her. I got in touch with her after Jo [foster carer] told me Melissa had had a terrible angry outburst kicking her, a cupboard,*

Researcher:

> etc. I keep in touch with the school as well so that we've got like a group around Melissa.

Researcher: Is the social worker less active in long-term placements?

Social worker: The social worker in this case is going to need to be very active.

However, if taken to the extreme, placements could become "overloaded" with support, to the point where the carers were unable to use it positively. In one placement, there were six-weekly visits from the child's social worker, six hours a week from the therapist, fortnightly visits from the family placement social worker plus the involvement of a life story worker and a reviewing officer. This created a situation in which everyone was confused about their roles and the carer still felt that she was not getting what she needed.

Taking a back seat

For some workers, there was a belief that long-term fostering should involve 'minimal intrusion' of professionals into the life of the child and the foster home generally. The placement was viewed as being 'more like an adoption' and the overall aim would be to 'normalise' family life as far as possible for all concerned. (This is interesting at a time when there is increased recognition of the need for active post-adoption support). Frequently, there had been a flurry of activity for all professionals just before and immediately after the placement had been made. Visiting had been more frequent and various practical tasks completed to assist with the child's transition into the new home and school. Once the child was deemed to be "settled", however, there was a feeling that the best, or most workable, option for the professionals was to take a back seat and allow the carers to have a sense of autonomy and the child to develop a sense of belonging to the family, rather than to the local authority.

For the family placement social workers, this meant offering support to the carers on the basis of being reactive, accessible, and 'there when needed'. Visits were made on a fairly infrequent basis (three monthly or 'the statutory minimum') and the time was spent listening, catching up, picking up on any practical matters, 'having a cup of tea and a chat'. Foster carer reviews were an annual point of contact and often the child's review was attended as a 'reference point'.

This approach was particularly prevalent for the "second families". These carers were often seen as capable, self-sufficient and able to recognise the issues which should be referred to the social worker. They were regarded as trusted 'team members' who would not hesitate to ask for help if it was needed:

> The carers are a very caring couple and a very capable couple. They are the sort of couple who haven't required constant support, they have dealt with issues. They have advised us afterwards if they need to advise us what they have done but they haven't phoned up in a panic to say, 'Oh, he's run off, what should I do?'. They have dealt with it and just let us know the next day and that's how they dealt with it.

The fostering workers were, therefore, pleased (and relieved) to let these carers 'get on with the job'. A low level contact was all that was deemed necessary to keep in touch and sustain a link with the fostering service. A higher level of input would be available if needed.

Many childcare social workers echoed this pattern of planned withdrawal or taking more of a back seat, once the placement was established. Some who had visited weekly at times of transition or therapeutic work were planning to scale that back to statutory visits or envisaged that, when the case transferred to a long-term team from a short-term team or from a disability team, this reduction would happen. In some cases this was a longer-term goal or expectation and in the case of new social workers, there was an awareness that a relationship would need to be built before the social worker could begin to withdraw but that then what was needed was, as one social worker put it, 'minimal intrusion'.

There was a sense of some social workers readily relinquishing some of the sense of responsibility to the carers.

Researcher: *Will there be a difference in your role now that the placement is long-term?*

Social worker: *That's come already like adoption. There's a changeover where you feel responsible for this little child and making sure everything's being done and then where you feel very comfortable about transferring that to the carer. This is not a verbal thing. I'll go, you've got the responsibility now. It's the fact that she is making the day-to-day decisions for this little girl and we have confidence that these are the right ones and when she needs to make bigger decisions then that's what I'm there for really.*

Clear links were made in some cases between the need to stand back and the changing nature of life in the foster family once long-term decisions were made.

Day-to-day decisions are entirely in the carer's hands ... It's an essential part of long-term fostering – if they are going to invest in these children. That won't be assisted by them having to check everything out with us.

The notion of standing back in order to encourage "investment" in the child shows a particular sense of the links between relationship building, parenting responsibility and the risk of intrusion by the care system.

For some workers, there was little doubt that more support would be needed in the future. Their "long-term" vision told them that troubles could be ahead in adolescence or that a compliant child with a troubled past might be 'a time bomb waiting to go off'. However, this did not seem to be seen as a reason for changing the model of practice in the present.

In some cases, however, both family placement and childcare social workers recognised that, although they could defend their "reactive" approach to some extent, it was generally not ideal, given the difficulties of the children. Problems could be concealed, issues left to fester and grow, carers could become overwhelmed. However, heavy workloads sometimes meant that this was all that was achievable. Equally, it was hard to impose a more active model of practice onto a placement if the carers were resistant to it. One family placement social worker was keeping a low profile because she sensed that the child did not want social services involvement and the carers were reflecting his feelings.

The worker knew that this was a situation that 'needed unravelling' and yet was rebuffed in her efforts to do so.

De-allocation

Finally, there were some family placement and child care teams that were operating a policy of children "going unallocated" or "being de-allocated" as a planned step in long-term looked after cases. This is in clear breach of the letter and spirit of the Children Act 1989 Guidance. This approach was unusual but not confined to one team. It was driven by a shortage of resources, with long-term placements being deemed "lower risk" and therefore not having a high priority for allocation. However, justification in terms of providing a more "normal" family life was offered by social workers. In these cases, the unallocated child would not be visited regularly by a social worker who knew him or her. Reviews would be undertaken by whichever social worker was deemed by the team leader to have the time. They would be chaired by an independent reviewing officer, who also might not know the child. The child would be given telephone numbers that he or she might use at any time to speak to a social worker or, in some cases, be given the name of a specific social worker who would be available to him or her. Similar arrangements were made in some of the fostering teams, with carers being told to contact the team manager if they required help or perhaps being given the name of a worker who had no active involvement but who could be called if needed. Most social workers felt these arrangements to be inadequate but inevitable in the context of their excessively heavy workloads.

There could be a benefit, according to some social workers, in allowing carers and children to 'get on with family life'. This account is from a social worker who was leaving the following week.

In some ways I see it [being unallocated] *as a healthy step. Once care is secure in the placement, the foster carer contains the situation and deals with issues and I feel that this carer has got sufficient insight into Alison's needs that she is able to do that. Whether I was here or not, the case would have gone unallocated. I believe they need to get on with it.*

It was also seen as beneficial to social workers if cases were formally unallocated.

It's about workloads. If it's actually allocated the social worker feels obliged to work on it whereas if it's unallocated they don't have that nagging question about wanting to be involved.

The social worker went on to explain that Alison would have telephone numbers which she could ring at any time and speak to a social worker. She would have a named social worker even though the case was unallocated. This was clearly unsatisfactory for any child but it should be noted that Alison was a nine-year-old with mild learning difficulties, from a background of severe neglect and possibly sexual abuse, who had already had one long-term foster home breakdown.

Conclusion

The description of aspects of practice in long-term foster placements has raised some questions about the wide-ranging definitions of what is an acceptable social work service to children, their carers and their birth families. The most conscientious social workers in childcare and family placement teams that prioritised work with long-term cases were highly valued by carers and children. However, few carers protested where there was a lack of visiting from social workers and some indeed preferred a low level of involvement. But for many social workers there was a sense that they were not able to offer the service they would like to these children or their carers. Even those in long-term childcare teams keen to provide a good service had to prioritise cases going to court or placements that were short-term, where family finding or rehabilitation was the priority. In the family placement teams, the shortage of foster carers was putting huge pressure on recruitment, training and the need to prevent carers from leaving the service. For them too, placements at immediate risk had to take priority. Perhaps this is the family placement equivalent of child protection taking priority over children in need. The children in this study and their placements were not actually in crisis and social work teams seemed to find it hard to prioritise cases on the basis that current effort in relation to regular visiting, providing therapy or educational support may pay dividends years down the line.

Summary

- The absence of prescribed models of good practice in long-term foster care meant that childcare and family placement social workers developed their own patterns of working.

- Work with the foster children by childcare social workers reflected their sense of the need to build and maintain relationships. Some had acted as a bridge for children moving between placements and had been consistent figures in the lives of the children. But in other cases, there had been frequent changes of social workers.

- Social workers had to respond to children's changing needs within the relationship as they settled in the placements, to help the children with their links to the birth families and to monitor the children's welfare in placement. Monitoring and supporting placements was not an easy balance to sustain.

- Work with the foster carers by the childcare social workers varied according to the difficulty of the child, the carer and the level of support from the family placement social workers. Family placement social workers saw their role as being supportive and as mediators and advocates for foster carers in the professional network around the placement. Neither group of workers saw themselves as having a role in discussing parenting difficulties with the carers, thus leaving a major gap in the support for the placement. This gap had not been filled in most cases by therapeutic services.

- The level of involvement by childcare and family placement social workers in the long-term placements covered the complete range, from very active to cases not being allocated.

12 Birth family perspectives on long-term foster care

When fostering was first mentioned it was a bit of a shock. We didn't know anything about it. You felt down in the dumps over it really, because you didn't know what was going to happen. It had never happened in our family before.

This comment from the grandparents of one of the children in the sample sums up the feelings of most of the birth family members interviewed (25 relatives of 20 children). Parents had lost day-to-day care of their children and grandparents had lost their informal but ongoing involvement in the children's lives. Children had moved away from the birth family and begun new relationships in a second one. Few parents interviewed had direct prior experience of long-term separation in a family. They therefore had no framework for how to manage leaving the care of their children to another family, with all plans and arrangements supervised by local authority social workers and with no prospect of the child returning to them. This chapter looks at the information obtained from the interviews with some of the birth family members about their experience of long-term fostering, of social workers and of working in partnership. It must be remembered that there was another group of birth parents who had more clearly abandoned their children and/or had more conflicted and even violent responses to the fact of their children being looked after by the local authority, whose views it was not possible to obtain.

The families were asked questions about their experience, expectations and views about fostering prior to these placements, their relationship with the current carers, their contact and relationship with the children's social workers, and their views of, and overall satisfaction with, the current arrangements in the light of the long-term foster plan.

Expectations prior to placement

As might be expected, there was considerable anxiety about the nature of foster care, what the new carers would be like, and how this would affect relationships within the family. The long-term carers with whom the children were living at the time of the research were not usually their first placement. All but two had spent time with at least one set of short-term or bridging carers before this move. The exceptions to this were the two children with disabilities, who had moved from respite to more permanent care with the same family. These children were accommodated. This model of respite and family support changing over time until eventually the child was spending most time in the foster placement had obvious advantages for the children and the birth relatives, in that it was a gradual move, and only one set of carers had been involved. However, these parents expressed the same anxieties and concerns at the start of the children being looked after as did other families.

The main group of concerns were about losing their control of the children's lives and their role as parents and grandparents.

You think "foster care", that means they are going in somebody's home, and you are not going to have a say in anything.

Whether the children were looked after on care orders under s31 or accommodated under s20 of the Children Act 1989, family members still understood that this meant a diminishing of their rights and responsibilities, and of their power and ability to influence events. Several of them specifically mentioned the concept of parental responsibility and sharing this. However, this was understood as not an equal sharing, as this parent succinctly put it:

They say that we both have parental responsibility and share it between us, but I think at the end of the day, they have a bit more of it than I do.

It was important to families that the children still retained some sense of belonging to their birth family and some kind of family identity. They did not express the idea of identity in the same language which social workers might use, and none of them emphasised the need to maintain religious, ethnic or cultural links, even the family from a traveller background where this had been mentioned as important throughout by workers planning the placement. Family members saw it more as the need for children to know who their parents, grandparents, brothers and sisters were, to understand the family they had been born into, and to keep in touch with them.

She has got to know her identity. She has got to know her mum is her mum. She has got to know that we still love her.

Adoption and long-term fostering options

The need to feel that the children still belonged in some way to the birth family also influenced their opinions on the difference between adoption and long-term fostering. Birth family members were asked if adoption had been considered as a choice for their children, and what they thought were the main differences between adoption and fostering. All of them felt that adoption was a more definite loss of the child for the family, and none of them had wanted this to happen. Some of them expressed this in strong terms.

When they told me they were thinking of asking for adoption in court I just went berserk. I couldn't possibly have agreed to that.

She just wouldn't have been my daughter, what I'd feel in my own heart. All my rights as a mother would have just gone out of the window.

Families knew that adoption of older children does not always mean a loss of contact, but they still would not have wanted the children to be placed for adoption, even if contact could have been maintained. Some of the parents had experience of other children in the family being adopted, either their own or the children of other family members. One mother had two children in separate long-term foster placements, whom she saw infrequently, and an older child placed for adoption, with whom she only had letterbox contact. She explained that the difference was that the fostered children would always know where she was and could find her when they were older. A grandparent who had a cousin adopted into the family as a baby said that her cousin had never quite fitted in with the family, and had ended up living far away from other family members having experienced several broken relationships. She attributed this to the cousin's adoption and was adamant that she did not want this for her grandchild.

It is difficult to assess the impact of these strong feelings about family rights and kinship on the planning process and on the development of the placement. The families who agreed to be interviewed were all from the group still most actively involved in the children's lives, and therefore more likely to want the children to continue to belong within the family in some way. Adoption had been suggested for a small minority of these children, perhaps because of the child's age, and not pursued for a variety of reasons. Laurie's mother reported having been put under considerable pressure to agree to an adoption placement.

He [social worker] *kept on saying it would be better if Laurie were adopted. He said he'd go into a children's home if he didn't have a family, and they would go to court if I kept saying I didn't want it. He knew I dreaded it because he wouldn't be mine, and I just wanted him to keep being part of this family, even though he couldn't live with us. Eventually he arranged for me to meet an adoption worker and then brought the papers round for me to sign. But I just couldn't. I said to him he'd just have to go to court because I couldn't do it.*

Laurie remained in a bridging placement for three years without any adopters being identified and with little contact with his family, before moving to a carer who specifically wanted to remain a long-term foster parent, and resuming more regular contact with his mother and siblings. This case, like many others, shows the complex factors which affect planning and case management. One factor must have been this mother's determination that he would remain legally a member of her family, but also significant was the difficulty in recruiting adopters for older children.

Meeting foster carers

Only five of this group of families had met the foster carers before the child was placed. This included the parents of two children with disabilities, where the foster carers had previously offered ongoing regular respite care. In the other three cases there seemed to be no real differences to explain this, other than the social worker managing to arrange a meeting in the time between the family being identified and the child moving to placement. When these meetings had taken place they had been found helpful, and had reassured the family members about the approaching placement.

The social worker took me down to the Family Centre to meet her. The children didn't know that I was going. I thought she might be going to be one of those people who are not going to shut up talking and you can't get a word in edgeways, but she wasn't, she is very, very nice. We started to talk and everything was fine.

Other families had not met the carers until the child had been in placement for some time.

I began talking to her on the phone first of all, and then she said, 'Why don't you come round for a coffee while he is at school?' So I did. And it sort of grew from there really.

Three other families knew the carers from previous short-term placements.

I really wanted them to go there. I knew from before that they would look after them and be good to them.

The considerable variation in the routes to long-term foster care and the quality of the early relationship between the foster carers and the birth families meant that families were working it out as they went along and were unsure what was expected of them. The fact that some of the foster carers were experienced was usually seen as an advantage.

They are very experienced. I don't know how an inexperienced family would be, but I mean they've got 15, 20 years of knowing how to cope.

Mothers and even grandmothers who had found children's behaviour at home difficult did not seem to resent the fact that carers could cope when they had not been able to, but to find this a relief.

I don't know how she copes with the tantrums, but she is that experienced. She knows when he is at home if he is going to be funny, she can take him out and talk to him.

And:

He has just changed while he has been there. He has got much calmer, more like he used to be.

They could see that the foster carers had skills to offer, and seemed able to accept that this met the child's needs. One mother talked about how seeing the carers cope when she could not filled her with guilt as well as gratitude.

I visit sometimes and they look absolutely knackered, and I think I have put that burden on them and feel sad. But then I just think, I couldn't do it like them and I can get on with my life again.

Another could relate this to her own lack of parenting, and the things she had missed herself.

I admire them [the foster carers]. *I just wish they could have been my parents, that I could have been fostered like that. They did try to look after me too, to begin with, buying me little presents if I was going into hospital and stuff. But I wore them out in the end, like I have everyone else.*

Several of the families mentioned the material advantages which foster carers could offer to the children, including making sure they were treated as equal with other children in the family, or given special treats and holidays abroad. Again this was expressed without resentment, and seen as good for the child. One family commented that the carer must spend all the money she received for fostering on the child, because they could see the many things he was given.

Relationships with foster carers

More than half (10) of the 17 families interviewed felt that they had made a good relationship with the current carers and spoke of them in very positive terms. They described them as 'warm', 'friendly', even 'super' and 'amazing'.

They are brilliant aren't they? They are so easy going, and I get on really well with them. We both do.

It is significant that families were able to make relationships with carers even in cases where they expressed high levels of dissatisfaction with the overall management of the case. Only two families expressed real conflict and hostility towards the carers, the remaining five being neutral, expressing neither hostility nor any warmth. These five families seemed to have very little contact with the carers directly, even though they were having contact with their children.

The two predominant characteristics of the good relationships seemed to be a mutual respect between the carers and the birth families, and a feeling they were both working for the child's good. Mutual respect was apparent in the way the birth families described the positive attributes of the carers, and also in their appreciation of the open and supportive attitude of the carers towards them.

We have become good friends over the years. I feel as if I can talk things through with them. They will listen to me. They don't just carry on as if I wasn't here.

Being taken into account, treated as an equal, made aware of information and events in the child's life, and allowed some part in making decisions were all important. It was clear that some foster carers went to considerable lengths to establish and maintain a link with the families. Julien's grandparents told how his foster mother telephoned them regularly in between contact to let them know how he was, undertook the driving necessary to facilitate contact, brought school reports and swimming certificates to show them, and even checked what presents they were buying for his birthday. This inclusive, extended family model was most evident in the two children with disabilities, and other children accommodated under s20 Children Act 1989, but also included children on care orders, where the initial circumstances of being looked after had been less positive. Contact with foster carers was maintained by telephone, and sometimes by visits to the carer when the child was not present.

I get together with her once a month, on the first Wednesday. We have a coffee and a chat, and that is good. That's nice.

Being involved in decision making and being consulted about large and small areas of the child's life were also important. Health and education were the two major areas in which problems might arise. In health difficulties parents wanted to know about referrals to specialists, including psychiatric services, and to be asked their opinion about drugs such as ritalin or other treatment. In education there had often been problems over behaviour in school, or choice of school the child attended. Alan's mother and foster mother had both wanted him to remain in mainstream, rather than special needs education. His birth mother talked of their partnership:

She [foster mother] *handles the schools, she always has, it's her area. But she comes back to me and says what do I think and shall we do this or that? And we have really fought to keep him in mainstream school, and he is. We did that together.*

Decisions and choices about appearance, including clothes and hair styles, were no less crucial in making families feel they were still involved in the child's life. Differences over these apparently small things could escalate into areas of conflict and even secrets for the child to keep from the foster family. As one mother said:

It's silly things like earrings that matter. I think she should be allowed to have her earrings in because she had her ears pierced with me. But they took them out and now she isn't allowed them. When she comes to see me I put them in, but then she has to take them out before she goes back, or it gets reported.

This mother also described how her daughter's clothes were all thrown away the first time she was looked after by carers, and how she had thought how strange she herself would feel if her whole wardrobe was thrown out in one go. (Other carers, in contrast, had kept all the previous clothes and one child showed them proudly to the researcher.)

The two cases in which birth family members were very negative about the carers, and in which the relationship between the two seemed actively hostile, had some similarities. In both cases the child had been cared for by a family member (mother or grandparent) for at least three years before beginning to be looked after, and in both there had been a protracted court case prior to the placement in long-term care. While there was some recognition that the children needed care outside the family, both of these families still wanted as much contact as possible, including overnight stays. Finally and perhaps most crucially, both of these children had been placed with foster families who clearly belonged in our "family builder" group. While it seemed it had been possible for these families to make a relationship with other temporary carers with whom the children had been placed in the past, there were high levels of tension in these particular placements. There was a lack of agreement by the birth relatives with the long-term plan for the child and the level and nature of appropriate contact. This is the grandmother of one of these children talking about her perception of the cause of the differences between herself and the foster mother.

She is just a bit too possessive. It's like she wants to be mum and I want to be Nan, but I think a Nan should have more than she does. Nannies do see their children at Christmas, they do have them in the holidays. She thinks because I want to know things like when they are going away for the weekend it's like I am trying to pry. But that isn't the case. I just like to know where she is, so I don't worry if I phone and no one is there.

The expectation of a high level of grandparental involvement was partly because she had cared for this child for part of her early childhood. The long-term foster carer of this five-year-old did want to be the child's "mum", not unreasonably since certainly the child lacked a mother in her life, and she must have felt that keeping the grandmother in touch with each move her family made was unreasonable. Such differences of expectations were clearly causing problems which could become entrenched if they were not dealt with.

The mother of another child said that while she was not sure she could manage if her daughter lived with her all the time, neither could she say to her that she never wanted her to come home again.

I suppose they want me to say to her that I want her to stay in foster care, but I am not going to. It's not fair to put the blame on me. At the end of the day they wanted her kept for an eternity, not me.

This mother had largely rejected this child during her early childhood but found it difficult to admit any difficulties or to let her go. Here the anger is at the social services department but such levels of confusion and hostility are likely to affect how the children settle in their foster homes. As shown by research into how children manage relationships with birth parents separated by divorce, co-operation and lack of conflict between the two sets of carers is one of the main factors in helping children manage the separation (Hetherington and Stanley-Hagan, 1999). This is so much harder to achieve where parents and looked after children have unresolved feelings from conflicted but entangled previous relationships and carers are coping with the child being torn between birth family loyalties and relationships that are on offer in the foster family.

Relationships with social workers

The relationships between the birth families, social workers and the social services department were more complicated than those of the birth families and the foster carers. Families rated their overall relationship with social services less positively than their relationship with carers. Only two of the families were very positive in their rating of general satisfaction, four families were very negative, and the rest gave more mixed responses. One difficulty was that they had not had consistency in their relationships with social workers. Once the child had been placed long-term, they knew that the carers were not expected to change but change is a common feature of social work, and in all of these cases there had been changes in the social worker allocated for the child, and often in the team responsible for the case, the managers, and the office as well. The lowest number of social workers recalled in the interviews was two; the highest was 'more than ten'. One mother could not remember how many workers she had had in the seven years she had been involved with social services.

I have lost count of how many social workers I have had. I can remember at least half a dozen, and there is probably another half dozen that I have forgotten, because some of them might have been on the case for two or three months but I only met them once.

In three of the cases there had been no allocated worker for a period, in one instance for over a year.

She [the carer] *rang me up again last week and said we hadn't got a social worker again. And I said I just hope they give us another one more quickly this time.*

There was no doubt that having a known person to relate to over time, who knew them, the child and the past history was important to families. Many recalled their first social worker with great clarity, and their departure with regret.

She worked with him from day one, and with us. She was marvellous. She used to come and see me every two or three weeks and have a cup of tea. I had a Christmas card from her after she left, too, just wishing us well. When she was the one on the case we always knew what was happening.

When social workers changed, the families had to work at re-establishing a relationship, and it seemed as if there was a diminishing amount of energy available for this with each change.

You confide in them, and then they leave, and then he goes weeks or months before he has another worker. They introduce themselves and you talk to them and then they leave. It's constant, ongoing, all the time, and the foster carers too, they don't have anyone to talk to, about things that might worry them.

When it had been possible to make relationships with workers, the qualities families valued were similar to those they valued in foster carers; a willingness to share information, a recognition of the families' right to participate in decisions about the children and a mutual sharing of respect. They seemed to value both the relationship and the activities of the social workers, what June Thoburn calls the words and deeds of practice (Thoburn, 1994). The presence of one without the other was not seen as helpful. One mother contrasted two of her social workers. One was 'too much by the book, it's like she has read how to do it, so she does' and the other was 'very friendly, but just hopeless at the paperwork'. What she would have preferred was a mixture of the two. Workers who were approachable, responsive and efficient were valued.

In one case, parents with learning disabilities, who had had all four children removed following allegations and then their admission of sexual abuse, were accepting of the situation and spoke warmly of the social workers:

Researcher: *How do you feel about the social workers now?*
Father: *They've done well. Pete's done well.*
Researcher: *And you mentioned that other social worker, Sue?*
Mother: *She's another one – she's nice and all. She used to help us a hell of a lot.*
Father: *I like Pete. There's nothing wrong with Pete.*
Researcher: *So even though you've had to go to court you still feel social services have been OK?*
Mother: *Oh yeah – they've been really good.*

In this case, the social worker visited the parents at intervals and they felt comfortable ringing him to ask about the children. In another case, the birth parent commented:

> *One we had she was only a student, but she was so easy to talk to. She spent a lot of time with us and with Ruth, and she really helped make things easier.*

Parents also appreciated practical offers of support such as transport to see the children, or help in sorting out their own financial problems.

The fact that parents and workers might have been through difficult times and had disagreements, or even been through contested court proceedings, was not always seen in a negative light. As other researchers have pointed out (Thoburn *et al*, 1995; Cleaver and Freeman, 1995), it is still possible to make relationships with parents and grandparents in spite of disagreement. What seems to matter most is an ability to communicate and to enable parents to retain self-esteem. The actual or perceived loss of this was what families found hardest to tolerate.

> *They made me feel as though I was being punished for nothing that I have done, do you know what I mean? I can't explain easily. They made me feel so belittled, really put down by how they talked to me.*

Several families mentioned the stigma they felt was attached to having children looked after, and the consequent difficulties in talking about this to anyone outside the family. They needed to have an explanation, a story to give to others, in much the same way that their fostered children did.

There's too many people around here looking for a reason to put you down. I don't talk about it much. I say I've got two children at home and one away with special needs. I wouldn't want any of us to be picked out as different. That's enough to tell people.

One mother commented thoughtfully on the different attitudes to mothers and fathers who are not with their children.

I bet the dads don't go through what I go through daily not being with them. Me not being with them is seen as so much different. Mothers not being with their children is seen as one of the most unnatural things in the world. I suppose even I think that really.

Parents wanted to feel that social workers offered them support in coping with these feelings. Many of these parents were struggling with their own difficulties and needed support in their own right. It is hard for child care social workers to meet the needs of the children and the needs of the parents, and sometimes impossible to provide what parents would like for themselves. Several of those interviewed understood that the social worker had primary responsibility for the children's welfare, and said that they would have liked there to be a worker for them as well as for the children. Two mothers wondered if they could meet and talk to other parents who had children in care.

I thought there was just me, and then my boyfriend said we did know of at least one other person who had lost their children into care. There ought to be a coffee morning or a group or something. They have them for almost everything else, why not for us?

Working in partnership

The principle of working in partnership with families and with other professionals to promote children's welfare is one of the most important in the Children Act 1989, and has become an accepted goal of practice. The parents who agreed to be interviewed were a self-selected sub-group of the main research. They all still had contact with their children, and therefore with carers and with social workers. They had expressed a wish to remain involved in their children's lives and were attempting to continue to work with foster carers and with social workers. They had a willingness to put partnership into practice.

Partnership in long-term foster care has additional dimensions to those of family support or child protection because of the triangular relationship of the social worker, the foster carers and the birth families. There are three members of the partnership, with the child the focus in the middle, and there can be alliances between any members and also tensions. The birth families, like the foster families, indicated an awareness of this, and it was possible to pick out different models.

Families tended to choose between the foster carer or the social worker, depending on who was easier to talk to. As we have seen, most of the families interviewed were able to make and maintain a relationship with carers, and in some of these families the carers had taken over many of the traditional social work tasks but also made other more informal and friendly gestures. One carer reported giving the mother a lift to the school parents' evening and also letting her have a packet of cigarettes whenever she saw her. For a minority, the social worker was the main point of contact, and there was little direct contact with the carers. In two cases the mothers could not form a working relationship with either, and these parents were extremely isolated. Obviously from the study as a whole, it can be seen that such distance could be a result of foster carer or social work practice but could also be a result of parental hostility. Angry, resentful parents are less likely to attend reviews or be prepared to engage in discussions with social workers or carers. In one case parental violence had meant that an injunction had to be taken out to prevent birth parents from approaching the estate where the foster family lived.

One example of working together and the way in which alliances can arise is at decision making meetings. The most regular meeting is the six-monthly looked after children review. All of the families interviewed knew that there were regular review meetings for the children. A small number did not attend, but most did. Many of them found these intimidating, as one mother said.

There is a review meeting later this week. They are terrifying, but I will go. I haven't missed one in two and a half years, because it is important to me and to Juliet that I am there.

Parents felt that it was hard for them to express their point of view, and said that they often felt overwhelmed by the professionals. As one mother said, 'They have already decided what they want'. Parents who found the meetings most comfortable were either the ones with the closest working relationships with the carers, or with a particularly supportive social worker. The parents of one of the children with disabilities said that she knew the meetings would be alright, because she and the carer had decided what they wanted to do beforehand, and used the meeting to tell the social worker! Another parent said that the social worker always visited her before the review, and usually arranged for a family centre worker to be there to offer her personal support.

A second example of working together is contact arrangements. Findings and issues around contact for the whole research group are explored in the next chapter. This group of family members were the only ones able to speak about it directly. As for the group as a whole, contact arrangements for those interviewed varied widely. With the exception of one family whose contact had been temporarily suspended on the advice of a child psychotherapist (for over six months at the time of interview) all of them had some contact with their children. The level varied from once a year in a Family Centre to several times a week in the family home, on a completely informal basis. Contact was by agreement with one exception, where a court order had been made and an independent mediator asked to work with the birth family and the carers, because agreement could not be reached.

Contact is bound to be a point at which emotions emerge more strongly, and there is potential for disagreement. It is commendable that in the majority of these cases it was being managed satisfactorily. There were no major safety concerns for any of these particular children in seeing their birth families and this was an important factor although there must always be some concerns when children have previously been sexually abused. The history of sexual abuse in several cases meant that the contact was supervised by two social services staff. Problems that parents did mention were both practical and emotional. There were financial difficulties in paying travel expenses or taking children out from foster homes on a regular basis, and also difficulties in maintaining a more ordinary relationship with children in rather artificial surroundings.

You tend to slip into a routine. It gets a bit monotonous. We get to the park, I sit on the bench, they go to the swings, then on to the beach, and if it's raining we have to try to find a shelter somewhere, buy a drink or something. Then a little walk and it's back to the foster home.

There were also difficulties in maintaining an appropriate emotional level. Several of the parents mentioned that it was still hard for them to see and then leave the children, even when they had been in placement for some time.

I don't get as upset as I used to. I try hard not to cry when I am with her. The social worker has said maybe I can see her more often than three times a year, but I don't know if I can cope with that.

One mother anxiously asked the researcher whether she thought it was better for children to see their parents or not, when you knew they wouldn't come home again. These anxieties about showing distress mirrored those of carers, social workers and probably the children.

In terms of partnership and working together, those families with strong relationships with foster carers were able to manage the contact much better. In two cases, the foster carer had played an important part in re-establishing links between the children and their families which had broken down in previous placements. In several others, the carers took a lead role in making the arrangements directly with the family. In one case, the carer liaised with grandparents who then supervised some contact with the child's mother in their family home when the whole family visited on a Sunday. Another mother described going out in the school holidays with the foster mother, her own son, and another fostered child.

Given the many difficulties social workers will face in providing consistency over time to families, they could give some thought as to how best to strengthen and utilise the relationship between carers and parents to fill the gaps. Again the different models of fostering arrangement are important, and some carers will find this harder than others. However, an investment in training and support at the beginning of placements for carers might pay dividends later.

Although there were a number of cases where tensions were arising of various kinds, the fact that it was possible at least in some cases to have constructive, mutually respectful relationships for the good of the children in what is an inherently difficult situation was encouraging. In those cases where carers, social workers and birth family members are able to make and maintain a comfortable three-cornered relationship, there were obvious benefits for everyone, especially the children. As one grandfather said:

> The contact between the foster mother, the social services and the parents – or the grandparents – it's like one big family. It is not a segregation of one from the other, you are not looking on it as authority over you. You are all on a par, and it's a great feeling when it can be like that.

Summary

- Birth family members gave their views of how long-term foster care was working for them. Most of those interviewed had been able to establish a working relationship with foster carers and in several cases spoke of them in warm and appreciative terms. They valued carers who gave them information about the children and included them, where possible, in the child's life.

- The process of coming to terms with being a parent or grandparent of a child in care was ongoing. Knowing that the children were doing well in the care of foster carers with whom relatives themselves felt comfortable could help this process.

- Where conflicts with carers did arise, they usually stemmed, not surprisingly, from disagreements about the respective roles of birth and foster family members in the child's life. Some birth relatives were able to appreciate the importance of the child developing good relationships with carers and feeling a sense of belonging to the foster family as well as the birth family. Others wanted to assert their prior claim and to insist on the child's primary allegiance being to the birth family. Review meetings and contact could then become the focus for this tension.

- Feelings about social workers and social services departments generally were more mixed. Continuity of social worker was a major issue. Where there was a relationship with the social worker, even where cases had gone to court, there was a basis for future work. Where social workers had changed frequently or where temporary social workers dipped briefly into their lives, families had found this more difficult.

13 Contact

Contact with birth relatives is a key issue for children permanently separated from their families. It has concerned practitioners and divided researchers for many years (Fratter *et al*, 1991; Mullender, 1991; Ryburn, 1994, 1997; Thoburn, 1996; Fratter, 1996; Quinton *et al*, 1997; Thoburn *et al*, 2000; Neil, in press). Although recent controversy has centred primarily on contact after adoption rather than in long-term foster care, contact in foster care has still attracted some research attention (Cleaver, 2000; Triseliotis, 2000). The Children Act 1989 (s.34) states that children should have 'reasonable contact' with their birth families. But the definition of 'reasonable' contact will vary from case to case, most obviously where some children are on a programme for returning home and others are in long-term placements. As part of the general local authority obligation under the Children Act (s.22:3) to safeguard and promote the welfare of looked after children, contact should be for the benefit of the child. But the nature of that benefit and how it is to be achieved needs to be determined in individual cases. Contact is one of those areas of practice where legal principles and research findings are important, but assessment of each case, particularly assessment of the psychological impact on the child, is crucial. As Rowe *et al* (1984, p. 116) concluded, 'Inflexible policies and practices are entirely out of place in this particular aspect of foster care'.

In the long-term foster placements in this study, children had divided loyalties between foster carers, who were their current source of care, and birth families, for whom they had strong but often complex and ambivalent feelings of love and anxiety. This creates a potential pressure point when the two family lives overlap for the child, the focus of contact. Close examination of the variety of contact arrangements and the quality of the children's experience of contact in this sample raised significant questions and concerns, which this chapter will explore.

Contact arrangements

Where parents, grandparents and siblings were known and available, face-to-face contact was likely to be happening. (Although these are relatively early days, this presumption of contact gives a very different picture from the Rowe *et al*'s (1984) study where a minority (43 per cent) had contact beyond the first year in placement.) The majority, 47 (81 per cent), were having face-to-face contact with their birth mothers. In other cases, mothers had died, had left the area or did not want to have contact. In contrast, only 22 (38 per cent) children were having contact with their birth fathers, reflecting the lack of involvement of fathers generally. It was not possible to tell from the information available the extent to which this was by the fathers' choice, by the mothers' choice, because social workers had not been able to locate them or for other reasons. Only one father, who was imprisoned for the rape and assault of his wife and daughter, was not having contact with his children by a decision of the local authority, supported by the court.

Contact with other adult family members, such as grandparents, aunts and uncles, occurred for 22 children (38 per cent), grandparents who had been primary caregivers playing a significant role in some cases. Contact with siblings was a major challenge for agencies, given the complex sibling relationships which existed. Here contact was often being facilitated, even in difficult circumstances. For example, contact was being arranged with siblings at home, even where a birth mother did not really want much contact with this child. Contact was also set up with siblings in adoptive families geographically remote from the child's placement. Where children had siblings at home or in other placements, contact arrangements were often with combinations of parents, grandparents and siblings. In several cases where there were large extended families, the child had contact with everyone at once. Some of the barriers to contact needed financial and practical solutions, such as transport, but others required careful negotiation by social workers with all parties.

Only four children had no contact with any birth relative and they were among the most potentially troubled in the sample having been bereaved, entirely rejected or abandoned, in each case following abusive care. The absence of contact simplified the carers' role with such difficult children and may have simplified the child's focus on this new relationship. But this did not mean that birth family members did not continue to preoccupy children, particularly if children did not know the whereabouts of their parents or even whether they were alive or dead, an issue for one eight-year-old who was otherwise doing very well in his foster family. Several children were very aware of brothers and sisters. One rejected child, for example, had a much loved older sister in his family who had not been allowed by the family to keep in touch with him.

In several cases, children were continuing to have contact with previous carers, which was handled informally by the carers themselves. In one case, previous carers still cared for older siblings, so this became a part of sibling contact. Where this had been a successful previous placement and the move to the current family was planned and smooth there were no problems. But in one case, the previous long-term placement had ended by the decision of the carers and the new foster carers felt uncomfortable about managing an informal contact arrangement with them.

Frequency

Perhaps the trickiest decision to make about contact is the frequency. Most cases already had established patterns of contact prior to the long-term foster care plan. Some were at quite a low level of frequency, equivalent to adoption, because adoption had been the previous plan. However, few cases appeared to be having or moving towards contact levels which were significantly less than that experienced while in short-term care.

Table 13.1
Frequency of contact with birth mothers N = 58

	N = 53	%
None	11	19
Weekly	9	16
Monthly	24	41
6–8 weeks	6	10
3–4 months	6	10
Yearly	2	3
Total	58	100

The majority, 33 (70 per cent), of the 47 who had contact with birth mothers had contact at least once a month (Table 13.1). Research on contact has not enabled workers to say that certain levels of frequency are suitable for certain circumstances or have a specific impact on the child and his or her relationships. Our interviews with social workers certainly confirmed the uncertainty in this area, if only because the same frequency would be seen by one social worker as limited but by another as generous.

To get a flavour of the factors involved in determining frequency, it is helpful to consider examples across the spectrum.

Gerry [8] had staying contact every weekend with his father and his brother, who was in another foster placement. The father worked long hours and could not care for the boys full time. This arrangement, which was liked by the children and acceptable to the foster families, also allowed the brothers to spend time together without having to leave the separate placements where they had become well-settled. All arrangements were made between foster carer and father. Some flexibility was built in, with the boys occasionally having more or less time depending on the foster families' plans for outings or the father's work patterns.

Matt [11] had contact three-weekly for an hour, supervised, at home. This enabled him to see his brother, who was in another placement, and his younger siblings, who were still at home. The mother had been very reluctant to have contact with Matt but had agreed to this limited amount of time. Matt also had more frequent unsupervised contact with his grandmother.

Dale [11] had supervised contact every 3–4 months with her mother and siblings. Like Matt, this was a chance to see her younger siblings who were at home. Her mother sometimes cancelled contact but would often say that she was going to get the children back.

Derek [10] and Shaun [7] had waited some years for an adoption placement. In the long-term foster placement they had supervised contact annually with their mother and other relatives.

Factors such as the child's relationship with the birth parent, whether the parent was a risk to the child, the need for supervision, the relationship between foster family and birth parent, and the care plan might affect the frequency. However, there appeared to be no direct relationship between key factors across cases. Some contact that needed to be heavily supervised was fortnightly, other contact which was unsupervised and at home might be three to four monthly. Although this might superficially suggest a lack of consistency, different patterns could be appropriate for each case. Alternatively, it may have been that once certain patterns were set it was difficult to think about changing them. In some cases where placements were getting settled, it might be seen as risky to upset the birth family by changing arrangements or reducing contact, particularly in cases where birth relatives might go back to court or where children were accommodated.

Contact venue

The place where contact takes place is also very important for children and families. A significant minority, 16 (34 per cent), of those who had contact with birth mothers saw them in the birth family home. Most of these were children who had siblings at home. A smaller proportion, six (13 per cent), had contact in the foster home. One child had unsatisfactory contact at school, apparently when the mother turned up. The rest, just over half of the children, 25 (53 per cent), were having contact in neutral or social services department venues. This could mean going on outings with parents, helpful for a sibling group meeting with their mother, or meeting in a family centre, which had a child-friendly atmosphere.

Social work supervision

The purpose of "supervision" or the social work presence could vary from protecting children from sexual, physical or emotional abuse through to facilitating contact, as in one case with weekly contact where the mother's multiple sclerosis was so advanced that she was confined to bed and was almost unable to speak. In total, for 29 (63 per cent) of the children who had contact with their mothers, there was a social services member of staff present, sometimes in the birth family home.

Practical and emotional support for contact

Practice varied enormously here. At best, the social worker known to the child prepared the child, took the child to and from contact, talked the contact through with the child and then let the foster carer know how the contact had gone. At the other end of the spectrum were situations where unfamiliar and various social work assistants or volunteers accompanied children or drove children to contact and then afterwards dropped the child at the door of the foster home without further comment to the foster carer. One carer summed up the difference for her and the child (7).

Contact was not going that well but we've just changed it. It was taxis plus different escorts but now the social worker is doing it. Contact is now fine. So it wasn't the contact, it was the arrangements that were the problem. So we know who's picking her up and I get feedback after each contact so I know what to expect. I'm happier and Andrea's happier.

It should be the case that where social work assistants or contact workers are being used, they should know the child, be consistent, be trained and supported to take on a more active and complete role in terms of facilitating the contact experience.

Practice varied also in terms of the financing of transport. There were teams in the same local authority where taxis would collect parents and teams where even the bus fares had been refused. This latter occurred in more than one agency. In one case, a child's birth mother had ceased contact and he valued his contact with his birth father very much. Transport costs were refused and although money may not have been the main factor, the father's contact became much less predictable. In another case, parents with learning disabilities, both on benefits, were refused the bus fare to travel once a month to see their looked after children in a town some miles away. The social worker commented that it was important for him to visit the parents in advance of the contact to encourage them to attend. This was good social work practice in any event but the relative cost of social work time and mileage expenses for this visit compared to the modest bus fares to meet the contact needs of a sibling group was striking. The parents themselves did not complain about this cost in their interview and seemed quite accepting of it, but nevertheless it did seem to be a surprising decision.

In another case, the foster carer was expected to drive the child to relatives' homes when they rang the foster home and showed an interest in seeing the child, which was infrequent. When she queried this, she was apparently told it was her job as a foster carer to do transport arrangements for contact.

The social worker said some foster carers have to go to and fro all the time. He said it's not like it's every week. I said you're making me feel terrible. Leah's the most important thing here but at the end of the day we can't do everything to suit the grandparent and the aunt. In the end he made out it was my fault because of the way I feel.

In this particular case, the carers had come forward specifically for this child whom they knew. They were an older couple who lived on disability benefits apart from the fostering allowance. The expectation appeared to be that, as the foster carer knew some birth family members, she should take on contact as an informal arrangement, but she was also treated as a departmental employee, expected to do her "job".

Getting the right support in every sense for contact was given priority in some cases but too often there was a sense that, given the stable pattern in a long-term placement, contact was no longer a controversial and difficult issue. From the cases in the study, it would be impossible to overstate the emotionally charged nature of contact for most children, carers and birth families.

Quality of contact

The most difficult area to address, yet the most important, is the quality of the contact experience for the child. This is, of course, going to be affected by the practical arrangements of the kind described above, but it will also be significantly affected by the nature of the relationship between the child and the birth relatives with whom they are having contact. Where the children have come from situations of abuse and neglect, contact exposes them to birth relatives who, as documented in earlier chapters, have emotional and behavioural problems of their own. These problems do not go away because the child is in foster care. On the contrary, in some cases anger and a sense of loss makes it possible that they will be intensified. The child's experience of contact will also be affected by the relationships in the foster family, the foster carer's expectations of their role vis-a-vis the child and the birth family.

These emotional and psychological factors may seem entirely obvious. Yet in many cases it was not at all clear that they were key factors in driving the *practice* around contact – neither the plans and practical arrangements, nor the work needed with children, carers and birth relatives before, during and after contact to ensure that contact was a comfortable and beneficial experience for the child. If birth relatives or foster carers or the child are not happy or not co-operating fully with arrangements then this will have an impact on the child's experience of contact. Such difficulties are not an argument for limiting contact, but they are an important reminder of the need for skilled social work practice to maximise the benefit and minimise the risk to the child and the placement.

The contact experience of each child was rated on the basis of the various interviews. Contact was not observed but the information from interviews was enough to highlight areas of concern, although the figures must be seen as approximate. The categories overlap to an extent and some children had contact of different quality with different relatives. The picture of actual and potential concerns reflected in Table 13.2 should not be surprising when one takes into account the children's experiences of abuse and neglect, their age, their behaviour problems, the difficulties of their parents and the natural anxiety of carers about the security of these placements.

Table 13.2
Quality of contact in the interview sample

	N	%
No contact with adult relatives	6	11
Comfortable contact	3	6
Satisfactory contact but some risk factors	17	32
Problem contact: arrangements	9	17
Problem contact: relationships	18	34
Total	53	100

Comfortable contact

Contact worked best when children could move comfortably between the two families. Not surprisingly this was easiest in situations where there was no anxiety about the parent or relative that was having the contact, either in terms of harm to the child or in terms of undermining the placement. The cases where contact was least complicated and was working well were the two children with severe disabilities where the respite carers had become long-term carers and continued to closely involve birth parents. These birth parents still had some complicated feelings of sadness and loss but the contact went well as part of a shared parenting arrangement.

In the third case where contact was clearly working well and with no risks attached, Gerry was having weekly, weekend staying contact with his father. The fact that his father was the non-abusing parent, came into the foster family home and discussed the contact with the carers was important. The fact that the carers saw the benefit of the contact and, what was striking in this case, were able to show honest mixed feelings i.e. 'we are pleased he loves to see his dad but we do miss him when he's not here,' also helped. For the child, this frees up the experience because it allows him to have mixed feelings himself sometimes. So also does the story he can tell himself about his father: 'my dad can't look after us because of his work commitments'. All parties in this case can tell stories about the arrangement that do not include too much anxiety or blame. Gerry can therefore rush in both directions with pleasure, as the carer described, to see his father and to come home again.

Satisfactory arrangements but some risk factors

There were cases where contact worked fairly smoothly and without evidence of major upset to the child. But in each case there were risks that had to be managed and therefore some anxieties for carers, social workers and children. This is rather a diverse group but fell into a number of sub-categories.

In the first group, there were the sibling groups of sexually abused children who had supervised contact with parents. The second group were children where there had been sexual abuse allegations concerning older siblings or where children had been neglected. These children also had supervised contact in neutral venues. In this second group the parents, several of whom had learning disabilities, were giving strong and explicit messages to the children that they missed them and wanted them back. Thirdly, there were children who experienced more mixed messages, such as a birth mother who had frequent contact but was rather cool towards her son. This mother's caregiving style prior to care had been described as unpredictable, out of control and frightening.

In these cases there were no significant concerns about the current contact arrangements, so they could be said to be working satisfactorily, given the difficult histories of the children in their birth families, with the risk of further sexual and physical abuse minimised. Yet these were children with complex memories and feelings both of closeness to and being unsafe in birth families. It did appear that aspects of the arrangements for contact could help even these children to feel safe. In one case, the foster carer, one of the "professional" group of carers, took charge of contact, did the transporting and supervision. This offered security and continuity to the children and made it less likely than in other cases for children to become out of control. As mentioned above, consistent figures to transport and liaise between the parties and to help children feel safe were important.

It was also necessary to help the child manage the situation. One child seemed able to use the official care plan, reinforced by the social worker and the carer, to cope with her parents' talk of her return home. She'd say, 'I can't go home because I've got to stay here until I'm 16'. Although these contact situations had some risk factors, thoughtful arrangements appeared to make the contact feel safe. But listening to foster carers and birth families and monitoring the children's experience of and reactions to contact would continue to be essential. Although risk of abuse was minimised, the emotional experience for maltreated children in the presence of their parents was still potentially stressful.

Problems with contact arrangements

The most obvious problem with contact was where there was no plan and children and carers felt unsettled. One very preoccupied, anxious child had not had a social worker for the first six months of the placement and there had been no plan for contact agreed. In another case, a carer was expected to manage contact with a birth mother and a birth father, who might ring out of the blue. This led to gaps of up to a year, at the end of which she might be expected to take the child to the home of parents, both of whom were known to be drug users, or other relatives.

In this group were cases where there was no planned contact because it was seen as preferable to allow carers to work directly with birth parents. There were some examples of what looked like very good practice here, where parents would not sustain regular contact on set days but would respond to a phone call from the carers to see the child at a mutually convenient time.

However, the interviews with birth relatives and foster carers did raise concerns about some informal arrangements. Birth relatives who gave mixed messages which confused children (see below) could also give mixed messages which confused carers and made them feel awkward, uncertain, even guilty for depriving the birth families of the children. Social work practice needed to be more active in helping carers to disentangle complex emotional and psychological communications and patterns of behaviour around contact. Contact should never be unplanned in the sense that it is left entirely to foster carers without careful attention being paid to the detail of the informal arrangements and the feelings that birth relatives and carers have about each other and the child.

In other cases it was a particular aspect of the plan, for example, the length of stay or the safety of the children during contact, that was an issue. One five-year-old had weekend staying contact once a month with a grandmother who had some objections to the foster carers and wanted to maintain a more significant role in the child's life than felt comfortable to these "family builder" foster carers. The carers' anxiety was compounded by the fact that the child's mother, who was a drug addict, might sometimes be present in the household. As new parents of a very young child, handing a child over for the weekend provoked reasonable parental anxieties. Other cases also involved foster families who were concerned about the well-being of children during contact. Carers in one case were concerned that the children were visiting parents in a secure psychiatric unit.

For some carers, there were seen to be discrepancies between the plan and the level of contact and they felt that they had not been properly consulted. Birth parents saw things differently. One case highlighted several of these issues. The carers saw the frequent contact as complicated and intrusive, and made the placement feel less like a long-term one. It left them less time to be a family, especially when contact used to happen at weekends and the foster mother had been expected to supervise some of it. The carers also felt that the children would not settle unless the birth mother made it clear that she would not be having them back, and that at the moment frequent contact just raised hopes that they would go home. They said, 'it is called a permanent placement, but it doesn't feel as if it is'.

The birth mother saw herself as still her children's mother, with a large stake in their future, and wanted as much contact as possible. This was a case where there had been several attempts at rehabilitation and she was still hopeful. Although still seeing the children fortnightly, she feared her contact was being cut away bit by bit, and thought social services would like it to be 'more like an adoption'.

Where contact is unpredictable or where foster carers and birth families are unhappy about arrangements, the children undoubtedly experience some anxiety themselves. Their divided loyalties are intensified and they may see themselves as a source of upset for the people that they care about and depend on, often foster carers and birth parents. These are cases that reinforce the need for ongoing work around contact.

Problems with relationships

At least a third of the children appeared to be experiencing sources of stress and potential harm in their relationships with parents and grandparents during and around contact. It is logical to consider these difficulties around contact using the same dimensions as were used to define caregiving in the birth family in Chapter 2, since caregiving patterns that have their unconscious origins in the parents' and grandparents' own histories are likely to persist in many respects.

Unpredictable, preoccupied and entangled relationships

It was very difficult for children whose primary birth family caregivers, parents or grandparents, continued to give distressing and confusing messages to the children through reviews but mainly through direct and, significantly in this group, indirect contact. Children in this group had often been either the favourite or the scapegoat for their emotionally preoccupied mother or grandmother, but in both cases the children continued to hope for and strive for proximity and acceptance from caregivers who talked of loving them forever but then disappointed and rejected them.

Social workers' accounts gave some indication of how these psychological distortions operated but the interviews with the birth relatives gave the most powerful insight into what the children were experiencing. As researchers it was possible to feel drawn into this double bind in a way which enabled us to see why the children alternately became distressed or out of control. As researchers knowing the history of rejection of the child, it was still possible to be saddened by relatives' accounts of grief at their loss. This may be entirely appropriate but if it was complex for adult researchers to understand and manage, how much harder it must be for an emotionally dependent and entangled child to disentangle.

Detail of cases can best demonstrate this process. Adam's grandmother had looked after him from birth. Having asked for him to be looked after, she then left the area, raising his anxieties and making face-to-face contact difficult. In letters and telephone calls she told him how much she loved him and wanted to see him. She made promises of holidays together which she failed to keep. She blamed social workers for keeping them apart. The social worker responded to this situation thus:

> Grandma would pick him up for two weeks and then after four days say I can't cope with him any more – so what I did was to set up regular contact three times a year. Adam [11] appeared quite happy about it and was doing relatively well at school. Then his grandmother was saying that she didn't think it was enough and she was making quite a fuss in the background and then he started blaming me and everyone else in the whole world.

From the interview with the grandmother, it seemed likely that, as soon as Adam arrived at his grandmother's, he was exposed to a mixture of sentiment, demand, resentment and conflicting expectations that overwhelmed him, made him anxious and led to his "berserk" behaviour. In her interview, she said, 'I spoilt him really. I think that's why the bond is so deep between us. It's something nobody can change and I miss him terribly.' Later she said, 'His heart is at home with me,' and 'All I can do is give him love,' and 'He was my number one idol'. Adam has no strategies to deal with these messages, when he knows she rejects him and lets him down. It must therefore be his fault when contact ends, since his grandmother is so obviously devoted to him and all he can understand is his own bad behaviour. Between visits, the letters and calls, some of which he has initiated himself from public telephones, flood him with misleading information about their relationship and her feelings. He then longs to see her face-to-face to fulfil these hopes and promises, but is rebuffed and told that it is because he is naughty.

Unfortunately, although the carer attempts to help Adam with these feelings and says she knows grandmother is 'pulling the strings', she reiterated, 'his gran really loves him' several times in the interview. One suspects that she too finds it difficult to disentangle the messages. The only hope here is that Adam can benefit from consistent care with the foster mother, who is very fond of and committed to him and has managed to remain on good terms with the grandmother. He still asks the question, though, 'Why does Gran say she misses me when she doesn't want me?' The social worker was risking the grandmother's reaction by appropriately trying to set realistic contact plans. However, given the unconscious emotional needs that drive the grandmother's behaviour, she is unlikely to respond well to the rational drawing up of contact agreements.

In another rather similar case, the mother again uses telephone calls to maintain the mutually preoccupied relationship with her daughter (9). In this case, though, the mother is more clearly seeing the daughter as someone who will look after her and so tells her about her health problems, her problems with men and so on. She phones her daughter to say how much she misses her and cannot sleep because she is so upset about losing her. Such calls leave the child with unresolvable feelings of responsibility and anxiety. This is one of the cases where the insecure attachment was described as a "strong" attachment.

Finally, there are several cases where, rather like Adam, the child during contact revisits the experience of being confused and scapegoated at home by a birth mother who says she loves her but that she is a bad child. In one case, the child was reverting to behaviour that she had given up in the foster home. She was reportedly running round the streets and had hit her grandmother. With these children, through contact, the "information" they get and even the memories they have about themselves, their birth families and the reasons they are not at home, become even more confused, so that children become preoccupied with trying to make sense of their situation. This often leads to requests for more contact from the children themselves, still hopeful that they can break through to a loving mum. It is very possible that these placements will become unstable in adolescence when children are able to act on these impulses.

In this atmosphere of raised emotion, it is not surprising that these children generally fall into the "open book" category; they do not trust reason and use displays of emotion, accompanied for some by anxious, restless and risk-taking behaviour. They need help to think through what is going on so that they can begin to develop strategies to deal with relationships with the birth family.

Rejecting, hostile
For another group of children, the rejection they experienced at home, amounting to emotional abuse in some cases, was continuing through contact. In most cases, children were being compared unfavourably with other siblings, either siblings at home or siblings in care. Rachel's mother was explicit in her interview that she had never bonded with her and thought now that it was a mistake that the adoption plan had been changed when Rachel was an infant. Stefan and Ben's mother was initially keen not to see them at all. Although she tolerated contact at home, when the boys see their siblings she insists the children play in the hallway or in the garden while she is elsewhere, physically and/or psychologically. Interestingly they have different reactions, as their social worker observed.

Ben's feelings for his mum are totally different to Stefan. He loves his Mum. He has little teddies in his room in the foster home – that's mummy, that's Charlene, that's John, that's Ronny. And he'll be there with them. He plays games with them. He gets very distressed when leaving contact. Like the ones I've supervised, when he gets back in the car he'll say, 'I didn't kiss Charlene'. And I'll say you did and he'll say, 'Stop the car, stop the car!' and it's as if he can't leave. It's distressing for me to be around during this. He cuddles his Mum while she pats his head, whereas Stefan doesn't go near her.

Both boys use their usual strategies for feeling safe and achieving proximity to the mother; Ben shows his feelings, Stefan conceals his. Ben in his interview said that he wanted more contact. Stefan said he did not care about contact and did not put his mother on his ecomap, although he has cried secretly after contact on occasions.

Parental behaviours in this group during contact ranged from indifference to active rejection, including parents finding it almost impossible to be in the same room as the child who was visiting. Some carers knew how stressful contact was for the child and wanted them to talk about their feelings, which a child like Stefan found hard to do. For him, the avoidant strategy for surviving in the birth family home where there had been violence as well as rejection was still working for him during contact. For such children, contact could be very important, and yet managing it emotionally and making sense of it cognitively was tough. The challenge for carers was to enable them to use other strategies more appropriate to the foster home, such as seeking comfort, to help deal with this stress.

Frightening

Finally, there were two children who were exposed to violence and fear during contact. Because they are so serious it is worth paying some attention to these cases. Greg's contact with his parents was characterised by unpredictability, violence and emotional abuse. His mother had said to him, 'if you are in care you might as well be dead' and Greg has made attempts on his life. His foster carer describes Greg's parents' manipulation.

His parents did manipulate him around contact. They said they wouldn't let him have his toys because he didn't run away from his carers, didn't give him Christmas presents because he didn't run away

– things like that. So in January they said, you have to run away and meet us at a certain pub and if he didn't they would tear up his birth certificate, send back all his toys and forget he ever lived.

Violence had occurred at contact between his parents and between his mother and social workers. On one occasion, Greg had joined in on an assault on a social worker. As the current social worker described:

The parents have a history of assaulting social workers, my two predecessors, one was in hospital with broken ribs. Mother's unpredictable during contact – she's very affectionate towards him but she's not always like that – she is quite manipulative ... She scares professionals – I imagine if I was a child I'd be pretty scared as well. I know she has told him to run away and been manipulative that way, saying if he doesn't do certain things 'he's not a child of mine', 'I'll tear up your birth certificate' and making those type of threats ... We're all on our guard all the time – you can't really relax. The parents seem to be quite unpredictable. There is a level of anxiety – they are unpredictable and irrational – especially mother.

From the social worker's point of view, contact is a very tense encounter but, at the time of the research, the fortnightly supervised contact was being looked at by this social worker with a view to increasing it in response to requests from the parents and from Greg.

Social worker: *There was a point when stopping contact was considered but there is such a strong attachment ... Greg does really want to see his parents and they are adamant they want to see him.*

Researcher: *And his best interests?*

Social worker: *Greg wants contact and the Children Act says it should be encouraged. Even the foster carers, despite the difficulties, think Greg needs to have contact. At the moment it's fortnightly at about an hour and a half. We are going to see ... if we can increase it or keep it the same or whatever.*

Consideration was being given to increasing contact, even though the quality of contact seemed so damaging on almost every count. The links between the idea of a "strong" attachment, the child's wishes, the parents' wishes and the Children Act seemed to have bypassed any detailed assessment of the links between contact and the child's emotional well-being. This social worker was a temporary social worker on a short-term contract and the approach was not typical in the study but nevertheless such actions were causing concern to the carers and the child's therapist on Greg's behalf.

Another case from a different local authority showed equally worrying issues for a child around contact. Fraser (10) had been seriously frightened and physically abused by his father during his early childhood and witnessed violence against his step-mother, of whom he was fond. During contact at his father's home, Fraser was exposed to the risk of violence against himself and his step-mother, who "supervised" contact. On occasions the step-mother was not present. One argument offered for not changing arrangements, in spite of concerns about Fraser's distress, shown in 'trancelike states' after contact, was that since Fraser was accommodated there was little the local authority could do. In these cases, frightening parents can frighten and intimidate social workers and foster carers, as is recorded in a number of child death enquires (e.g. Rikki Neave, Bridge Child Care Development Service, 1997), just as entangled parents and grandparents can entangle them. Social work supervision, rigorous reviewing, and perhaps consultation with child mental health experts are the ways in which such complexities can be acknowledged and resolved. But listening to foster carers and paying attention to children's psychological well-being are central.

Managing two families

From the children's perspective it was clear that they had to find ways of managing their feelings about their two families. Fahlberg (1994) describes resolving the loss of birth families for foster children in terms of reaching a point where the child can accept the membership of two families. Contact brought this issue to a head. Children often showed their particular attachment pattern in dealing with this source of anxiety. Some "open book" children had rosy ideas of birth families and foster families having meals together, living together in 'gynormous' palaces and being like one family. Closed, avoidant children tended to keep the two families entirely separate and refused to talk about the birth family to the foster carers or researchers. "On the edge" children were sometimes still frightened of birth parents, but in some cases hoped for reunions, with even very emotionally rejected children hanging on to the idea of return to the birth family. Several "rewarding" children appeared to be giving messages to carers that they no longer cared about their birth family and loved the carers, calling them mum and dad, instead. Other "rewarding" children appeared to be managing two families by keeping both happy, calling them both mum and dad or saying one thing when with the birth family and another when with the foster carers.

This example of Kerry (7), by her foster carer, demonstrates the emotional work children have to do.

Kerry's protective – is mum going to be all right? Mum's now having another baby. Is mum going to be all right? Will she lose the baby? She's a bit embarrassed about her. She was not really enjoying the contact. She just gets lugged around the shops and they don't do anything fun. So Kerry's actually asked her to have contact on her territory [in the foster home]. She does hide mum away if there are other people in the house who don't know mum. She's affectionate towards mum when they are on their own. When Kerry was in care before and we were doing the assessment and mum, Kerry and I were together, Kerry would smile at me but keep her distance and be affectionate to mum.

Kerry tries to look after her mother and even her mother's new baby. The sense of a growing difference that contact highlights between the new life and relationships in the foster home and the old life is likely to become starker as time goes on. A number of children were described as protective of birth parents, a role they played at home, and of course through the contrast with their new life, they have to protect parents and themselves from any embarrassment. In the meantime, just as Kerry starts to get settled, her mother has a new baby, providing fresh challenges.

Conclusion

Contact for children in long-term foster placements is a particularly difficult and painful issue but it can also offer the possibility of retaining family links and resolving sad feelings while receiving good care in the foster home. Almost all children wanted to see their families and almost all carers understood this and saw the potential benefit of contact, even when many were concerned about its current impact. Contact for these children had all the difficulties of any contact situation in which children have to keep two families in mind and have to find a sense of themselves in the two different roles and images held by the two families. In addition, in long-term foster care there is the complicating factor of the passage of time which, for some of the youngest children, will mean that the foster placement and contact established at four may last fourteen plus years and continue to be complicated in adult life when there are grandchildren to share. As these children grow older and change, foster and birth families change, social workers change and attitudes to contact change: these contact arrangements will constantly need to be reviewed. The question that emerged from this study is, reviewed on what basis? Sometimes a lack of clarity about the *why* (the potential benefit of contact for this child) and the *what* (the nature of this child's current experience of contact) can lead to problems about the *how* of contact (frequency, venue, supervision, practical arrangements).

Is the test of contact whether it fits the Children Act? Whether it meets the needs of this child? This should be the same test, in that the welfare of the individual child is the goal of all planning and practice. Within that goal, contact plans need to be consistent with the long-term care plan for security into adult life in this placement, since that has been deemed to be the most likely to meet the needs of the child. Where foster carers were excluded from discussions about contact arrangements, they often felt an appropriate level of parental anxiety. This anxiety might be about relatively small things, such as whether the children would be able to have a proper lunch on the journey to contact, but it is this kind of concern and commitment, 'keeping the child in mind', that should be valued and encouraged in long-term carers taking on a full parenting role. Contact worked best when foster carers felt consulted and more in control, so that contact felt safe for the child and could be fitted into their family life. On this basis, all sorts of levels of frequency and risk could be handled comfortably. The most unsatisfactory were those cases where contact was almost entirely out of the foster carers' hands and was an arrangement between social worker and birth family of which the foster carers were informed. Fundamentally, what is required is a fresh approach to contact practice in long-term foster care.

Summary

- Contact was at high levels for children in the study, with 81 per cent having contact with their birth mothers. Contact with birth mothers was also frequent, with 70 per cent of these children having contact at least monthly. Contact was also regular with grandparents and siblings. Levels of contact were not dissimilar in many cases from contact in short-term foster care.
- The quality of contact arrangements varied between teams and between authorities. Some contact was actively facilitated with all parties, including birth families, in ways that helped the children to benefit. Continuity of social work support and arrangements that felt safe to carers were important in cases that worked well. In other cases, contact was unplanned and unsupported.
- The quality of contact was affected where behaviours by birth relatives that had caused children emotional difficulties at home continued to affect them through contact.
- Foster carers felt high anxiety for their foster children when they were not involved or consulted about arrangements for contact. Practice in relation to contact needs to address the needs of children and carers in the light of the long-term plan, where carers are acting as fully committed parents.

14 Different meanings, shared concerns: The challenges of growing up in foster care

We have told the stories and taken note of each perspective in the long-term foster care system: child, foster carer, childcare social worker, family placement social worker and birth family. Along the way we have moved inevitably between tracing differences and observing similarities, seeing each case as unique to an extent and yet, as researchers, looking for connections that can help to make sense of a complex phenomenon.

We need to acknowledge that there are different meanings attached to growing up in foster care but some areas of shared concern. In order to make sense of both, we must simultaneously address two very different discourses, as we have tried to do throughout the research project. One is the discourse of systems, legislative and procedural, which surround decision making, planning and practice. The other is the discourse of relationships and the psychological dimension: the intrapersonal, the experiences of individuals across time, and the interpersonal, the relationships between children and their foster carers and birth parents, but also between social workers and children, family placement social workers and carers, social workers and birth families. This interpersonal network is inescapable and any attempt to tackle systems head on without thinking carefully about the role of personal history, emotion, anxiety, defences against anxiety, hopes and fears is likely to fail. However, it would be equally foolish to ignore the role played by the legislation, the courts, the Looking After Children materials, the financing of foster care, the pressures in local authority social work teams and so on – the potential pressures and flashpoints which affect all parties when we try to describe the building of secure attachments in foster families. In this final chapter, we attempt to stand back from the detail of the separate aspects that make up the rest of this study, in order to generate some overarching themes which may help to explain some of the current challenges facing long-term foster care.

Different meanings

The meanings of "long-term foster care", the definitions, the vocabulary used to describe this phenomenon were an important part of the study since, as we stated at the outset, there are no official or legal definitions. "Long-term" and "permanent" appeared to be used interchangeably in most cases, with few interviewees trying to distinguish between these two expressions. "Foster carer" was the term most commonly used, although "foster parent" was used occasionally by participants and by us as researchers, partly but not wholly because "female foster carer" seemed so much less comfortable than "foster mother". The choice of "foster home" or "foster placement", "my family" or "my foster family", "mum and dad" or "Sue and Pete", "my sister" or "my real sister", even "looked after" or "in care", varied across all interviews. Such words are potentially full of significance but have different meanings for different individuals. "Mum and Dad" may mean anxiety while "Sue and Pete" might mean love and security – or vice versa.

As we saw in earlier chapters, *social workers* were preoccupied with the boundaries both between long-term foster care and adoption as permanence options and between long-term and short-term fostering. At the permanence boundary, long-term foster care was sometimes described in terms of length of time e.g. until she's 16/17 or grown up, unlike the "forever" of adoption; sometimes in terms of function e.g. 'permanent foster care means they will be the ones who do the 18th birthday party, put her through college, meet her boyfriend, pay for her wedding'; sometimes in terms of relationship e.g. they really love her and are committed to her; and sometimes, rather fatalistically, in terms of the child's choice, e.g. she can stay with them permanently but will probably choose to go home in her teens.

Boundaries between short-term and long-term foster care were even less clear. This was not surprising in some ways, given that the majority of placements were with carers who had also fostered short-term, but surprising in other ways, in that although significant work went on around the transition to a long-term plan, there was uncertainty as to whether long-term foster care was different. Did long-term carers have more autonomy, for example, or should contact arrangements reflect the changed plan? The boundary was more likely to be marked by some idea of "normalising" foster family life, perhaps by a planned withdrawal by some social workers, described in terms of not "intruding". However, other workers could see the potential for stress in a long-term placement of a difficult child and said that these were cases one could never stand back from. For these more active social workers and teams, the role might be different once the long-term plan was agreed and attempts at reunification were not on the agenda, but the situation for the child and carers in terms of troubled behaviour and the continuing role of the birth family would have to be carefully managed throughout childhood, as it had been to date.

For *foster carers*, different kinds of motivation affected the meaning they attached to long-term fostering and the "sense of permanence". Although all carers were very clear about children's need for security of family life and therefore expressed the intention of sustaining this placement, to some extent they shared the range of ideas that social workers expressed. At the permanency end, their commitment was towards being available to care for/parent the child into adult life as they would any child of their family. Variations here were in the flexibility of their expectations. Where they were "family builders", the expectation was that, like "own children", long-term foster children would pass seamlessly through childhood into adulthood as a child of the family. More experienced "second families" allowed for the possibility that things might change, children might even go home in their teens, but foster carers said they would always be there for them. Several children were in placements where they could see how that had worked for other fostered children, now adults.

The role of the child's choice in determining the length of long-term was also significant for some carers. Some families saw it as a very positive commitment when they gave the message to the child that they were available as long as the child wanted to stay there. This is, of course, very different from what would be said in birth or adoptive families, whatever the reality of children's choices in adolescence. This children's rights approach, supported some might say by the Children Act, seemed at risk of giving the child too much responsibility, especially as all of these children were under 12. It also appeared to be at risk of reducing a child's sense of permanence. Most children get the message from parents as they grow up that, whatever happens, they are always a child of the family.

Related to this, for a small minority of carers was some indication that, if the child's behaviour got much worse or birth/adopted children in the family were adversely affected, then foster children might have to leave. Here, in effect, foster children might be seen as having been given the choice to behave, but if they chose to misbehave, they would have chosen to leave. This view of the optional and therefore impermanent nature of a long-term foster care plan is far from the message of unconditional acceptance that the children were seeking. But at this stage in the placement it was all rather theoretical and in the future – whether carers act on such statements will only emerge over time.

From the *birth families'* point of view, it was very clear that long-term foster care was seen by some as temporary and as leaving them either in the driving seat or at the very least in a position where the child could come home at any time. Other birth relatives were much more resigned to the situation, accepting that they could not care for the child when he or she was at home and that the foster carers were doing a better job than they could. However, it seems likely that only in a handful of cases could one say that birth parents fully accepted the situation. Whatever the strength of messages given by courts, permanency panels, reviews and individual social workers, the situation was far from over for most birth relatives and feelings were far from resolved. This, of course, should not be surprising given the personal trauma and public stigma of having a child in foster care, but it reinforces the difficulty in achieving shared meanings around the nature of the placement.

But what did the *children* themselves make of long-term foster care? They were sometimes able to articulate their sense that their placements were forever or through childhood or perhaps to a specific age. One carer explained how the penny dropped over the washing up.

Sean said to us, 'You're different, you have people forever'.

There were variations. Beth (10) said what everyone else around her appeared to be saying was that she had to stay in care until she was 16 but she might want to go home then. Nevertheless, she had anxieties about the idea of going home and had already checked if the foster mother would have her back again if home did not work out. Being able to state the official position in this way perhaps protected Beth, as it did others, from too much pressure from her family but she still had fantasies about living in a palace with both families. Regardless of the sense which almost all children had of their official position and the long-term foster care plan, for them too the situation was largely unresolved with feelings of yearning for the real or fantasy family that had been left behind, mixed in many cases with remembered fears and more than a suspicion that they were not really wanted at home.

Shared concerns

Of all the varied issues in these cases, three came out as being particularly significant shared concerns:

- What does it mean to spend your childhood "in care" or "looked after" by the local authority?
- Do long-term foster carers "care for" or "parent" children?
- Is long-term foster care a positive option or a last resort? Are security and living with uncertainty compatible?

Being in care

The status of "being in care" was viewed uncomfortably in different ways by children, foster carers, birth families and social workers, a situation which the move to calling them "looked after" children is unlikely to change. This common ground, the shared negative meanings around "care", arise at least in part because "normal" family life in which parents look after their children is a central part of our shared positive cultural meanings about childhood. The breech of cultural expectation that care by strangers involves has been reinforced by the stigma which is now attached to children in local authority care, a stigma which has been increased by media "concern" about how many children leave care to become criminals, homeless or mentally ill.

Those closest to the system and with an overview of a range of cases, the social workers, had more reason to be optimistic than most. They saw children removed from abusive or neglectful homes and thriving in foster care, as almost all the children in this study were described as doing; becoming healthier, attending school more regularly and losing some significantly disturbed behaviours. They also knew that other options, such as adoption, were often not available for these children because of their age, their behaviours or because they were in sibling groups. For a few, adoption as an option had been tried and failed, adoption placements being unavailable or breaking down. But social workers were also only too well aware of how fragile the foster care solution can be. If this placement that is just coping breaks down, will the child have to go to an out of county placement or into residential care or even back to an unchanged birth family home because of a lack of foster placements? Most of these children had experienced some kind of move since being in care. Any placement move, but especially from a placement that promised permanence, can precipitate a downward spiral. If children feel betrayed, let down and unlovable, they are even more disadvantaged in starting the next placement. A placement move which is experienced as a rejection or an exile contributes to those feelings. A move after a significant period of being looked after and going back to the birth family, if nothing has changed, may increase the damage and speed up the downward spiral when the child inevitably returns to care.

Not all children reported problems with their care status; some even said living with foster carers made a good story to tell that provoked interest and led to friendships. Others kept it a secret. However, the taunt in the playground, 'Well, at least I've got a mum and dad,' or 'At least my mum and dad didn't get rid of me,' and several similar comments which the children told us about, were undeniably painful. The dilemma for some children, though, was that previously they had also been stigmatised when they were poorly dressed or smelly or got into trouble and had no friends. Children "in care" in our study had to weigh the cost of loss and stigma against the benefit of having friends call round and stay for tea, playing football at the weekend with your team, dressing in nice clothes to go to the school disco, and so on. Of course, receiving good care and being free from the fear of physical, sexual and emotional abuse was no small consideration. Children in this age group were not able to articulate this cost/benefit analysis, but they were simultaneously demonstrating the sense of loss *and* the pleasure in their new achievements. Resolving this tension was clearly one of the tasks involved for the children in being in long-term foster care.

For the children, the presence of a social worker in their lives was very much a part of being "looked after". Children who had had long-term relationships with social workers were pleased to see them. Several named them as important people in their lives and some would have liked to see them more. In other cases, in this very mixed group, factors such as the newness of the social worker or the established nature of the foster family relationships, meant that social workers were more marginal in their lives. But none said they did not like their social worker or did not want to see them.

For birth families, having a child in care was not a desirable situation. And yet if there was one point that all relatives interviewed agreed on, it was that having a child adopted would have been so very much worse. The fact that, in significant ways they had not entirely lost the child and could see the child grow up, with the possibility of some kind of family relationship in adult life as a far prospect, was something to hang on to and build on.

For foster carers, there were also significant and conflicting factors to weigh in the balance. On the one hand, they felt keenly at times any stigma that the child might experience at school and a few worried about the pressure they thought was put on children sometimes by reviews and meetings, which were not part of a "normal" childhood. In their empathy with the child's experience, they talked of how hard it must be to have this experience of losing your birth family and having to start again with strangers. They also feared the inherent uncertainty of the situation, for themselves and the child.

On the other hand, however much they wanted to secure the child's future with their family, they were often not in a position where they would have or could have adopted the children. Their own family circumstances would not always have fitted with adoption. Some said they thought it would be wrong to break the ties between the child and the birth family so finally. The continuing role of the birth family was a major factor in most cases but the sheer difficulty of the behaviours presented by the child made them anxious about not having the right to call for help, even if they rarely needed it currently. Most families were not in a financial position to adopt, either, where they could give up even the often inadequate allowances they received. Although theoretically a number of these issues could be resolved with post-adoption support, contact and allowances, these were not generally on offer and at least one carer who had lost the social work support after a previous adoption of a child with a disability was not going to take the chance again. Similar factors seem likely to make a residence order unattractive, particularly when it means sharing parental responsibility with some very troubled birth parents.

More positively, whatever their concerns about children growing up in care, foster carers could often see, either in their own families or in other foster families, that although there was movement and difficulty there could also be stability and progress. Foster carers in the study were still in touch with children first placed more than 20 years ago, seeing them as "family" and becoming grandparents to their children.

Foster caring or foster parenting?

Connected to the nature of local authority care as a context for childhood was the key issue of what role the foster carers were expected to play – were they carers or parents? As parenting and the nature of relationships was a focus in the study, this was an important issue. Here the two different discourses mentioned above come into obvious conflict. On the one hand, parenting as defined by who has parental responsibility legally is the role of the local authority and the birth parents or, for accommodated children, the birth parents alone. On the other hand, parenting as defined by who meets the child's physical and extensive psychological needs, providing clean clothes, breakfast and a cuddle before the child goes to school each day, is clearly the foster carer. From the practical point of view of care and decision making, day-to-day responsibility for the child was generally accepted as the foster carer's. Where major decisions had to be made, such as which school a child should go to, carers could be, and in one case quite significantly were, overruled. Similarly, in situations where the decisions affected the birth family, such as around contact, there was often a sense that foster carers' views were not being adequately taken into account. Finally, the extent to which social workers or foster carers actively opted to share parenting responsibilities and roles with birth relatives, such as around school events, varied considerably. This sharing could be quite extensive, with foster carers offering to collect and take a birth mother to a parent's evening or a school performance or both sets of parents being at the hospital if the child was ill. But it might be quite minimal where birth parents had severe mental illness, could be aggressive or actually did not want to be involved in reviews or decision making.

Since the terminology was changed from "foster parents" to "foster carers" as part of developing a task force of short-term foster carers, the naming of long-term carers has been potentially problematic. What seems likely to be more important for the child's comfort and well-being, as well as the adults', was that there be some measure of agreement around the parenting/caring role that foster carers played. For example, in two of the most comfortable cases, there was a high level of agreement that the foster carers would parent the children. In these cases, in fact, the emotional permission from the birth parents was accompanied by the fact that the birth parents continued to parent the children, having quite significant staying contact with them, a model that was in many respects shared parenting. Completely different were situations where parents were off the scene entirely and so the foster carers and child had a clear sense that this was a parent–child relationship.

In some cases, there was extreme disagreement about roles. This could happen where carers clearly expected to be parenting the child, in both decision making and psychological terms, which is why they chose to foster long-term. They then found themselves in conflict with birth relatives, sometimes supported by the court or by social workers, who envisaged a much more active role for themselves in the care of the child. Some birth relatives were still feeling very angry and refused to accept that the foster carer had any significant role in the child's life. It was in these situations that contact, in particular, became the focus of anxiety for carers and often children. This could be because of the messages birth relatives might be giving children about return home or because foster carers worried, for example, about relinquishing the care of a young child to a grandparent for the weekend.

In some cases, the different meanings identified above contributed to uncertainty about the carers' role. One foster family wanted to make a long-term emotional commitment and saw the child as a daughter, and yet the basis for the long-term fostering rather than adoption choice was that the child's most significant emotional tie would be to the birth mother.

One less obvious but significant concern was about situations where it seemed that, however many adults were *potentially* in the role of parent and whatever level of agreement there was, the child was not experiencing emotional parenting. One child had frequent contact with a birth mother who had been emotionally and physically abusive. He was in a foster home where he was the less favoured child and there was a rather cool relationship with the foster carer. Another child was in a placement where the birth parents and the carers had developed quite a close relationship around the idea that it was the child who was very difficult. Indeed these were troubled, difficult children. In both cases, there was agreement that the child should be parented by the carers. There was no conflict, but somehow the children were not in a loving relationship with either parent.

Perhaps the necessary agreement is not so much about what role the carers should have but that it should be more *child focused* – how is the child going to be parented, in both decision making and psychological terms, and who is going to do it? If the parenting is genuinely shared, which was appropriate only in a small minority of our cases, then this can be acknowledged. If birth parents are not able to contribute to the physical and emotional well-being of the child, except in limited ways through contact, then long-term foster carers must be in that parenting role and be supported in it. Perhaps we need to worry less about labels, such as mum/dad, parents, carers, and more about the quality of the parenting and relationships each child experiences.

Long-term foster care as positive option or last resort. Are security and living with uncertainty compatible?

Closely related to issues around being in care and parenting is the concern as to whether long-term foster care represents a positive option for children. Does it offer the best of both worlds, care with the foster carers and continuity with birth families, or is it so uncertain, so inherently stigmatised and impermanent, as to be an option of last resort? We will need to await outcomes before answering that question properly but even at this stage there were some very contrasting experiences.

Some carers, for example, felt a definite difference in their caring/ parenting of the child when the long-term plan was made, regardless of its insecurity in legal terms.

We've got a lot closer relationship, especially since we've known she's staying here permanently. Because I always held something back because I thought she was going. And I also didn't want Roxanne to get too close to me so that she had to go away to someone else because that would have been another break in her life. Not just for my own sake but for Roxanne's sake. I kept a little bit of distance with her. Now I know she's staying permanently we don't need to do that anymore because there's not going to be a move.

There is a feeling of control in the situation and a new confidence which that gives her to invest in the child's future. In Roxanne's case, the birth family had contact each school holiday and wanted her to return home, but somehow the social worker's commitment to the long-term plan allows the foster mother to feel protected and settled.

At the other extreme would be a very different case where conflict and uncertainty seemed rife. The care plan for Lena was permanent fostering in this placement. However, this did not fully mesh with the reality of the situation. Mother wanted Lena home and was constantly giving her messages that this could happen. Lena wanted to be at home and was confused about why this could not happen. Lena could not commit herself to the foster home and the foster mother was uncertain in her relationship with her and resentful of her strong feelings for her birth mother. The contact arrangements seemed to reinforce these barriers, rather than reduce them. There was an 'uneasy truce' which did not feel like a firm enough foundation for permanence. In this case, the confusion was primarily at the level of feelings. The plan is clear and yet the participants are caught up in strong feelings of every kind and contact leads to upset, in spite of supervision. Lena is a chatty, compliant child and yet in the story stem exercise she revealed anxieties about parents who ignore hurt children and then die.

Living with uncertainty of this kind, both legal and emotional, is handled differently in different placements. Some carers ignore it. Others accept that this is part of fostering and do not let it get in the way of parenting the child. Some hold back from the child and are preoccupied by it. The range is from uncertainty as an irrelevance to uncertainty as the major concern of the placement. Important here inevitably may be the carers' motivation to long-term foster. Lena's carers are new carers, "family builders" who have young children of their own and would like this child to be a close part of their family. But the same could be said of Roxanne's carers. The differences appear to lie somewhere in the combination of the child's relationship patterns, the foster carer's expectations, the past and current role of the birth family, the arrangements for contact, and the sense of permanence generated by the social work system.

When outcomes for these placements are tracked at a later stage, it will be important to look back to these factors and see if there are connections between the role of uncertainty and whether placements lasted. With existing legislation, long-term foster care placements will mean living with uncertainty. This can be managed in permanent placements, as previous research has shown (Thoburn, 1991a; Thoburn et al, 2000). In this sample too, long-term foster care was seen by many social workers, carers and birth families as a positive choice. But the challenges are significant.

Risks, protective factors, attachment and resilience

The multiple factors linking uncertainty and placement security highlight the complex interplay of risk and protective factors. As part of the longitudinal design, we drew up for each case a list of these risk and protective factors, which we have hypothesised will affect the future development of each placement. These factors fell into groups around the child, the carers, the birth family and the social work service – and the relationships between them. We were interested in what factors seemed likely to promote both the stability of the placement and the well-being of the child. In particular, we were interested in how such factors contributed to raised self-esteem and self-efficacy in the child, the hallmark of the securely attached child and key factors in resilience (Rutter, 1985, 1999; Gilligan, 1997, 2000).

It was here that we could begin to see potential upward and downward spirals most clearly, what Rutter (1999) has called 'chain reactions'.

There could be a chain of protective factors in some cases. Children's success at school could make them more rewarding in relationships with carers, leading to raised self-esteem, which enabled them to be appropriately assertive in peer groups, which in turn gave them a greater sense of self-efficacy. Alternatively there could be a chain of risk factors. A child's rejection by her birth family added to significant emotional and behavioural problems, which created tensions in the foster family, increased her anxiety and sense of powerlessness, in turn lowering self-esteem and reducing her sense of self-efficacy. We could also see ways in which one key risk factor in the birth family, such as violent birth parents, could exacerbate one key risk factor in the social work network, such as temporary agency social workers, and mean that cases were felt to be out of control. In one such case, the protective factor of an actively involved therapist, who supported the determined, committed foster carer, appeared to be likely to hold the risks in check and sustain the placement.

It may be that the Looking After Children review system needs to take a "risks and protective factors" approach in considering how to evaluate the placement and anticipate/prevent breakdown. However, no checklist approach can be a substitute for professional judgement when it comes to weighting different factors: ten protective factors in the foster family may be outweighed by one risk factor, such as extreme aggression or sexualised behaviour in the child. Similarly, masses of risk in the child might be outweighed by an exceptionally sensitive carer. Such protective factors can act as 'buffers' (Rutter, 1999) enabling the child to be cared for safely. One of the most interesting aspects of the study was that it was not necessarily the most disturbed "on the edge" children who were in the least secure placements. Some very demanding children were with highly committed carers, selected because of their parenting capacity and motivation to rise to the challenge of difficult, distressed children. In contrast, young children with few apparent difficulties, "rewarding children", were in placements with "family builder" carers who had high expectations of this "normal" child and the role the child might play in their family.

This brings us to the question of the *fit between child and placement*, which has cropped up in various guises throughout the book, whether under matching, caregiving behaviours or contact arrangements, and appears to be a major feature of how placements are experienced. The nature of the fit or match can be seen along a number of dimensions: the cultural, class or racial match; the child's feelings for the birth family matching the carer's capacity to be inclusive; the likelihood of the child committing emotionally to the foster family at an early stage with the carer's need that they should do so; the child and the carer's shared liking for fishponds or football on the telly; the child's "open book" or "closed book" presentation matched with what the carers find appealing or can cope with in a child. This foster carer describes how her rewarding but in some ways rather closed child, Kay, fits in with her husband's pattern.

John's a very calm person – and so is Kay really. John loves to read and so does Kay – she loves reading. There's books galore at night . . . So she'll cut off. She'll sit there and everything will be going on around her and she'll read. And John does the same.

In one of our families where dramatic bubbly children were enjoyed and valued, Kay's behaviour would be experienced very differently.

The sense of the exactness of fit was often a source of delight to carers. There's a touch of magic, rather like falling in love.

Mick can look at me and I can look at him and we both know – we've got that link.

Ray asked to come back to us and he just slotted back in again. We just sort of clicked right away really.

Attachment theory has proved particularly helpful in thinking through such relationships and in understanding what risk and protective factors children bring from their early childhoods to the new placement. We anticipated that this would be so, but have found, as the research progressed, that it was able, like any good theory, to make sense both of what we knew and what otherwise did not make sense (Howe *et al*, 1999). We would argue that a significant protective factor in placements is likely to be the quality of the relationship between the carer and the child. This need not be a "perfect" relationship but it needs to be "good enough". The persistent absence of even the tentative beginnings of a warm and mutually rewarding relationship between parent and child, however smooth other circumstances are, is likely over time to lead to disappointment, the child's needs not being fully met, and possible breakdown.

Closely linked to this relationship will be the resilience characteristics of the child: those they bring to the placement, those they build on within it, and those promoted by the foster carers. The majority of the children had problems with self-esteem and self-efficacy. Their internal working models were generally negative about self and others. Their behaviour patterns were predominantly heavily defended and based on their need to survive. They found it hard to reflect on and make sense of themselves or other people. But there were glimmers of hope for many of the children, sometimes from positive experiences with a birth relative, a previous foster carer, a social worker, friends or at school. Sensitive carers were able to build on these, either in terms of their own emotional availability, their capacity to be and to help children become reflective or in terms of actively developing areas of competence in the outside world of school and peer groups. Although these placements are in the relatively early stages, caregiving that promotes resilience in the context of a secure base relationship and provides a sense of permanence, core ideas from a range of research literature but reinforced in this study, seems to be a valuable model for long-term foster care.

The future of long-term foster care?

Our starting point was that long-term foster care exists and needs to be recognised and understood. Having examined the histories and current circumstances of these 58 children, their foster carers, birth families, and social workers, that need appears to be urgent. This is never going to be an easy area of practice for policy makers to guide or social workers to operate in. It has all the potential for being upsetting, untidy, messy and hard to control. It does not respond well to simple categories and regulation. It means living with a paradox around security as defined legally, bureaucratically and emotionally. This, however, is not an argument for seeing long-term foster care as a last resort, a position that can lead to children remaining at home in maltreating families, waiting too long for adoption or drifting in unplanned short-term care. It is an argument for demanding the highest possible professional standards, interpersonal skills, creative ideas, theoretical knowledge and active commitment from social workers, supported by their managers and agencies. It is an argument for supporting and resourcing this sector of the child care service properly. The carers and the children not only need access to expert social work support, they also urgently need access to therapeutic and educational support. These children may be few in number relative to the general population of children but most are at serious risk of emotional and behavioural problems as they move through the teenage years into adult life and parenthood. In the longer term, they may prove to be very expensive indeed, in terms of individual distress as well as in terms of resources. If we want to ensure that when these children leave care it is to find social stability and successful relationships in adult life, the skills, ideas and resources need to be put in place now.

Bibliography

Ainsworth M D S (1973) 'The development of infant-mother attachment', in Caldwell, B M and Ricciuti H N (eds) *Review of Child Development Research*, Chicago: University of Chicago Press, 3, pp. 1–94.

Ainsworth M D S, Bell S and Stayton D (1971) 'Individual differences in strange situation behaviour of one year olds', in Schaffer H (ed) *The Origins of Human Social Relations*, New York: Academic Press, pp. 17–52.

Ainsworth M D S, Blehar M, Waters E and Wall S (1978) *Patterns of Attachment: A psychological study of the strange situation*, Hillsdale, NJ: Lawrence Erlbaum.

Aldgate J (1980) 'Identification of factors which influence length of stay in care' in Triseliotis J, *New Developments in Foster Care and Adoption*, London: Routledge and Kegan Paul.

Aldgate J (1990) 'Foster children at school: Success or failure?' *Adoption and Fostering*, 14:4, pp. 38–49.

Aldgate J, Heath A and Colton M (1992) 'Educational attainment and stability in long-term foster care', *Children and Society*, 6:2, pp. 91–103.

Barth R P and Berry M (1988) *Adoption and Disruption: Rates, risks and responses*, New York: Aldine de Gruyter.

Berridge D and Cleaver H (1987) *Foster Home Breakdown*, Oxford: Blackwell.

Berridge D (1997) *Foster Care: A Research Review*, London: HMSO.

Borland M, O'Hara G and Triseliotis J (1991) 'Placement outcomes for children with special needs', *Adoption and Fostering*, 15:2, pp. 18–28.

Bowlby J (1969) *Attachment and Loss*, Vol. 1, *Attachment*, London: Hogarth Press and Institute of Psycho-Analysis.

Bradshaw J, Stimson C, Skinner C and Williams J (1999) *Absent Fathers?* London: Routledge.

Bretherton I, Ridgeway D and Cassidy J (1990) 'Assesssing internal working models of the attachment relationship: an attachment story completion task for three year olds', in Greenberg M T, Cicchetti D and Cummings E M (eds) *Attachment in the Preschool Years: Theory, research and intervention*, Chicago: University of Chicago Press, pp. 273–308.

Bridge Child Care Development Service on behalf of Cambridgeshire County Council (1997) *Report on Professional Judgements and Accountability in Relation to Work with the Neave Family*, Cambridgeshire County Council.

Bullock R, Little M and Millham S (1993) *Going Home: The return of children separated from their families*, Aldershot: Gower.

Cleaver H and Freeman P (1995) *Parental Perspectives in Cases of Suspected Child Abuse*, London: HMSO.

Cleaver H (2000) *Fostering Family Contact*, London: The Stationery Office.

Crittendon P (1992) 'Quality of attachment in the preschool years', *Development and Psychopathology*, 4, pp. 209–41.

Crittendon P (1995) 'Attachment and psychopathology', in Goldberg S, Muir R and Kerr J (eds) *Attachment Theory: Social developmental and clinical perspectives*, Hillsdale, NJ: The Analytical Press, pp. 367–406.

Department of Health (1999a) *The Government's Objectives for Children's Social Services*, London: Stationery Office.

Department of Health, Home Office, Department for Education and Employment (1999b) *Working Together to Safeguard Children: A guide to interagency working to safeguard and promote the welfare of children*, London: The Stationery Office.

Dockar-Drysdale B (1968) *Therapy in Child Care*, London: Longmans.

Erickson M, Egeland B and Pianta R (1989) 'The effects of maltreatment on the development of young children', in Ciccettti D and Carlson V, *Child Maltreatmemt: Theory and research on the causes and consequences of child abuse and neglect*, New York: Cambridge University Press.

Fahlberg V (1994) *A Child's Journey Through Placement*, London: BAAF.

Fanshel D and Shinn E (1978) *Children in Foster Care*, New York:Columbia University Press.

Festinger T (1986) *Necessary Risk: A study of adoptions and disrupted adoptive placements*, New York: Child Welfare League of America.

Fonagy P, Steele H, Moran G, Steele M and Higgit A (1991) 'The capacity for understanding mental states; the reflective self in parent and child and its significance for security of attachment', *Infant Mental Health Journal*, 13, pp. 200–17.

Fratter J (1996) *Adoption with Contact*, London: BAAF.

Fratter J, Rowe J, Sapsford D and Thoburn J (1991) *Permanent Family Placement: A Decade of Experience*, London: BAAF.

Freeman P and Hunt J (1998) *Parental Perspectives on Care Proceedings*, London: The Stationery Office.

George C (1996) 'A representational perspective of child abuse and prevention: internal working models of attachment and caregiving', *Child Abuse and Neglect*, 20:5, pp. 411–24.

George V (1970) *Foster Care, Theory and Practic*, London: Routledge and Kegan Paul.

Gibbons J with Thorpe S and Wilkinson P (1990) *Family Support and Prevention: Studies in local areas*, London: HMSO.

Gibbons J, Gallagher B, Bell C and Gordon D (1995) *Development after Physical Abuse in Early Childhood*, London: HMSO.

Gilligan R (1997) 'Beyond permanence? The importance of resilience in child placement practice and planning', *Adoption and Fostering*, 21:1, pp. 12–20.

Gilligan R (2000) *Resilience*, London: BAAF.

Goldstein J, Freud A and Solnit A (1973) *Beyond the Best Interests of the Child*, New York: Free Press.

Goodman R (1997) 'The Strengths and Difficulties Questionnaire: a research note', *Journal of Child Psychology and Psychiatry*, 38:5, pp. 581–586.

Hetherington E M and Stanley-Hagan M (1999) 'The adjustments of children with divorced parents: a risk and resiliency perspective', *Journal of Child Psychology and Psychiatry*, 40:1, pp. 00–00.

Holman B (1988) *Putting Families First: Prevention and child care*, Basingstoke: Macmillan.

Howe D, Brandon M, Hinings D and Schofield G (1999) *Attachment Theory, Child Maltreatment and Family Support: A practice and assesment model*, Basingstoke: Macmillan.

Kelly G (1995) 'Foster parents and long-term placements: key findings from a Northern Ireland Study', *Children and Society*, 9:2 pp. 19–29.

Kelly G (2000) 'The survival of long-term foster care', in Kelly G and Gilligan R (eds) *Issues in Foster Care: Policy, practice and research*, London: Jessica Kingsley.

McAuley C (1996) *Children in Long-term Foster Care*, Aldershot: Avebury.

Maccoby E E and Martin J A (1983) 'Socialisation in the context of the family: parent–child interaction', in Hetherington E M (ed.) *Handbook of child psychology: Vol 4. Socialisation, personality and social development*, pp. 1–102, New York: Wiley.

Main M and Goldwyn R (1984) *Adult Attachment Scoring and Classification System*, University of California, Unpublished Manual.

Main M and Solomon J (1986) 'Discovery of an insecure-disorganized/disoriented attachment pattern', in Brazelton T and Yogman M (eds) *Affective Development in Infancy*. Norwood, NJ: Ablex.

Masson J, Harrison C and Pavlovic C (1997) *Working with Children and 'Lost' Parents*, York: York Publishing Services Ltd.

Mullender A (ed) (1991) *Open Adoption: The philosophy and the practice*, London: BAAF.

Neil E (2000) 'The reasons why young children are placed for adoption: Findings from a recently placed sample and implications for future identity issues', *Child and Family Social Work*, 5.4.

National Foster Care Association (1997) *Foster Care in Crisis*, London, NFCA.

Packman J and Hall C (1998) *From Care to Accommodation*, London: The Stationery Office.

Quine L and Pahl J (1985) 'Examining the causes of stress in families with severely mentally handicapped children', *British Journal of Social Work*, 15, pp. 501–517.

Quinton D, Rushton A, Dance C and Mayes D (1997) 'Contact between children placed away from home and their birth parents: research issues and evidence', *Clinical Child Psychology and Psychiatry*. 2:3, pp. 393–413.

Quinton D, Rushton A, Dance C and Mayes D (1998) *Joining New Families*, Chichester: Wiley.

Rowe J and Lambert L (1973) *Children Who Wait*, London: ABAA.

Rowe J, Cain H, Hundelby M and Keane A (1984) *Long-Term Foster Care*, London: Batsford.

Rowe J, Hundelby M and Garnett L (1989) *Child Care Now – A survey of placement patterns*, London: BAAF.

Roy P, Rutter M and Pickles A (2000) 'Institutional care: risk from family background or pattern of rearing?', *Journal of Child Psychiatry and Psychiatry*, 41: 2, pp. 139–149.

Rutter M (1985) 'Resilience in the face of adversity: protective factors and resistance to psychiatric disorder', *British Journal of Psychiatry*, 147, pp. 23–51.

Rutter M (1999) 'Resilience concepts and findings: implications for family therapy', *Journal of Family Therapy*, 21, pp. 119–144.

Ryburn M (1994) *Open Adoption: Research, theory and practice*, Aldershot: Avebury.

Ryburn M (1997) 'In whose best interests? – post-adoption contact with the birth family', *Child and Family Law Quarterly*, 53.

Schofield G L (in preparation) *Adult Reflections on Experiences of Long-term Foster Care* (UEA Research Project).

Sellick C and Thoburn J (1996) *What Works in Family Placement?* London: Barnardo's.

Sinclair I, Gibbs I and Wilson K (2000) *Supporting Foster Placements: Research Report*, SWRDU, Department of Social Policy and Social Work, University of York.

Smith T (1998) *Family Centres: Bringing up young children*, London: HMSO.

Steele M, Hodges J, Kaniuk J, Henderson K, Hillman S and Bennett P (1999) 'The use of story stem narratives in assessing the inner world of the child: implications for adoptive placements', in *Assessment, preparation and support: implications from research*, London: BAAF.

Stein M and Carey K (1986) *Leaving Care*, Oxford: Basil Blackwell.

Thoburn J (1991a) 'Survey findings and conclusions' in Fratter J, Rowe J, Sapsford D and Thoburn J, *Permanent Family Placement: A decade of experience*, London: BAAF.

Thoburn J (1991b) 'Permanent family placement and the Children Act 1989: implications for foster carers and social workers', *Adoption and Fostering*, 15:3, pp. 15–20.

Thoburn J (1994) *Child Placement: Principles and practice* 2nd edition, Aldershot: Arena.

Thoburn J (1999) 'Trends in Foster Care and Adoption', in Stevenson O (ed.) *Child Welfare in the UK*, Blackwell Science.

Thoburn J, Lewis A and Shemmings D (1995) *Paternalism or Partnership? Family Involvement in the Child Protection Process*, London: HMSO.

Thoburn J, Norford L and Rashid S P (2000) *Permanent Family Placement for Children of Minority Ethnic Origin*, London: Jessica Kingsley.

Thoburn J (1996) 'Psychological parenting and child placement', in Howe D (ed) *Attachment and Loss in Child and Family Social work*, Aldershot: Avebury.

Triseliotis J (1980) *New Developments in Foster Care and Adoption*, London: Routledge and Kegan Paul.

Triseliotis J (1983) 'Identity and security', *Adoption and Fostering*, 7:1.

Triseliotis J, Borland M and Hill M (2000) *Delivering Foster Care*, London: BAAF.

Waterhouse S (1997) *The Organisation of Fostering Services*, London: NFCA.

Winnicott C (1960) *Child Care and Social Work*, London: Bookstall Publications.

Winnicott D (1965) *The Maturational Processes and the Facilitative Environment*, New York: International Universities Press.